The Accidental Administrator®:
Cisco Router Step-by-Step Configuration Guide

FIRST EDITION

Version 1.2

Don R. Crawley
Linux+ and CCNA Security

soundtraining.net
accelerated i.t. training

Seattle, Washington
www.soundtraining.net

Telephone: (206) 988-5858

Email: info@soundtraining.net

Website: www.soundtraining.net

Cover design by Jason Sprenger, Overland Park, Kansas, *www.fourthcup.org*
Back cover photograph: JMC Photography
Interior photographs: Paul R. Senness
Editorial consultant: Claudette Moore
Technical consultant: Tom Davis

Reasonable attempts have been made to ensure the accuracy of the information contained in this publication as of the date on which it was written. This publication is distributed in the hope that it will be helpful, but with no guarantees. There are no guarantees made as to the accuracy, reliability, or applicability of this information for any task or purpose whatsoever.

The author recommends that these procedures be used only as a guide to configuration of computers and/or devices in a test environment prior to usage in a production environment. Under no circumstances should these procedures be used in a live, production environment without first being tested in a laboratory environment to determine their suitability, their accuracy, and any security implications.

ISBN-10: 0-9836-6072-7
ISBN-13: 978-0-9836607-2-9

PO Box 48094
Seattle, Washington 98148-0094
United States of America
On the web: www.soundtraining.net
On the phone: (206) 988-5858
Email: info@soundtraining.net

The Accidental Administrator®:
Cisco Router Step-by-Step Configuration Guide

FIRST EDITION

Version 1.2

About soundtraining.net

soundtraining.net is a Seattle-based company that provides advanced technical training in an accelerated one- and two-day format to I.T. professionals. soundtraining.net's students include network administrators, network engineers, support desk personnel, and anyone involved in computer network design, installation, operation, and maintenance. soundtraining.net specializes in Cisco and Linux product training, plus workplace skills training for I.T. professionals.

Among the training topics offered by soundtraining.net are:

- Cisco ASA Security Appliance Training: Installing, Configuring, Optimizing, and Troubleshooting
- Cisco Router Fundamentals 2-Day Hands On Workshop
- Networking Fundamentals
- Linux Server Training: Installing, Configuring, Optimizing, and Troubleshooting
- Mastering End-User Desktop Support
- Project Management for I.T. Professionals Two Day Seminar
- Secrets of Successful Time and Task Management Using Outlook
- Managing and Supervising People for Positive Results

Subscribe to our newsletter for the latest information about new classes, blog posts, and special offers: www.soundtraining.net/newsletter

soundtraining.net can present training onsite, at your location, at your convenience. Call **206.988.5858** or email **onsite@soundtraining.net**.

Acknowledgements

Any book, small or large, is a large undertaking, of which the author is only one part. There are never enough pages to thank all the people who deserve the author's gratitude. Here are some: Denise Barnes, Randy Rash, Jeff Martin, Robin Lockwood, Rob Duvall, Steve Edmiston, Claudia Mayorga, Cleo Crawley, and Philip Wiest.

Thanks to everyone who bought one of my previous books, especially those of you who posted reviews. I pay attention to the reviews and this book reflects some of the things you taught me through your reviews. (Some of those lessons were a bit painful!)

Thanks to Jason Sprenger for making my books look so much better.

Thanks to Paul Senness for helping with the interior photography and my general sanity.

Special thanks to Tom Davis for his insights from the field on all aspects of Cisco routers, and especially IPv6.

I feel like I hit the big leagues when Claudette Moore agreed to give me some comments on the manuscript. Claudette, you're an amazing human being. I'm honored and humbled to know you.

In 1992, I met Janet Slaughter, who is now my wife. Marriage is amazing when you're with the right person. Thank you, Jannie. That's all I need to say about that.

For Janet

Contents

CHAPTER 2:
Understanding the OSI Reference Model

CHAPTER 3:
Fundamentals of TCP/IP

CHAPTER 9:
Troubleshooting

CHAPTER 10:
Remote Router Control

CHAPTER 13:
Managing Cisco IOS Passwords

CHAPTER 14:
Understanding and Configuring Internet Protocol Version 6 (IPv6)

CHAPTER 15:
Cisco Router Security Fundamentals

Preface

My first exposure to a Cisco router was with a Cisco 1601. I walked in to a training room and there was this strangely shaped gray box sitting on the table. Little did I reckon how profoundly it would affect my life for the next 15 years. I've always been a geeky, nerdy kind of guy. I used to get teased about it in school. I have always loved playing with technology. At the age of 12, I re-wired a tape recorder and accidentally set my bedroom on fire. When I plugged it in and powered it up, flames shot out. So, learning and loving Cisco routers was just a natural step in the progression of this geek's life.

The way I like to learn is to build a working system, in this case a router. Once it's working, then I try to decipher the theory behind it. That's what this book is all about. It's not designed to give you much theory on how things work. My goal in writing it is to help you build a working config. I figure you're smart enough to do your own research on how it works, so I don't include that in the book. Besides, that would make this just another one of those 1200 page books on routers. There are already plenty of them and most of them are pretty good. Why do more of the same, right?

As I started to write this book, I bought new routers for the screen captures and demonstration videos (check out www.soundtraining.net/videos/cisco-router-training-videos). As I was writing it, however, I realized that you might be working with older gear, perhaps even a 2500-series or a 1600-series. Based on that realization, I decided to include screen captures from a variety of routers. You'll find screen captures from 2501s, 2611s, 1721s, 1841s, 2821s, 871s, and a brand new 1941. It's interesting to compare things like file sizes from then and now. (Check out the difference in file size for the IOS on a 2501 compared to the IOS on a 1941.)

People often ask me if my books will help them pass the CCNA or some other certification. The answer is that my books and classes are not designed for that purpose. My stuff is designed to help working IT pros get up to speed in a hurry on particular aspects of information systems and technology. Will this book be helpful as you prepare for the exam? Of course it will, but that's not what it's designed to do and it will not give you all the information you need to pass the rigorous Cisco certification exams. What this book will do is help you build a working router configuration in a minimal amount of time.

The most important thing you can do is to enjoy the process of learning. Take your time, experiment, and have fun learning how to manage the most popular routers in the world!

Enjoy the process of learning and living!

Don R. Crawley, CCNA Security, Linux+
President/Chief Technologist
soundtraining.net
Seattle, Washington USA
www.soundtraining.net

How to Use this Book

This book began life as a series of lab exercises for a Cisco router class I taught. Obviously, it's been modified considerably. It still follows the order of a two-day Cisco router workshop. You can begin at the beginning, work through all the interactive exercises, and at the end you'll have a functioning router. Of course, you'll need to modify various aspects of the configuration such as the IP addresses and routing protocol configurations to match your network, but at a very basic level you'll have a functioning router.

Preparing Your Management Workstation

For the purpose of this book, your management workstation refers to the computer you use to manage the router. Although you can use a computer running Mac OS, Linux, or Unix, this book is written from the perspective of someone using the Windows 7 operating system.

Here's what you need in order to complete the exercises in this book:

PuTTY terminal emulation software. It's available for free from www.putty.org. Many people prefer other terminal emulation software packages such as SecureCRT (http://www.vandyke.com/products/securecrt/), TeraTerm (http://en.sourceforge.jp/projects/ttssh2/), or other packages. You're welcome to use whichever package you prefer, but I recommend PuTTY and the exercises in this book are based on PuTTY.

What Routers Do You Need?

This book is written primarily using a Cisco 1941 router for the screen captures and exercise procedures. You can, with slight modifications, use any Cisco IOS-based router for the exercises. The only consideration is that, for some of the security-oriented chapters, your IOS image must support encryption.

I also used Cisco model 871 and 2821 routers, plus the GNS3 router emulator (www.gns3.net) with software images from 2600-series and 1700-series routers. There are even a few screen captures from a legacy 2501 router, just for comparison to newer routers.

What About Cables?

Console Cables

If you're using a 1900, 2900, or 3900 series router, you'll need a USB console cable (USB Type A to 5-pin mini Type-B cable).

If you're using an older router, you'll need a DB-9 to RJ45 console cable and a serial port on your management workstation. If your management workstation doesn't have a serial port, you'll also need a USB-to-Serial adapter.

Network Cables

The specific network cables you'll need for the exercises will vary based on the routers you use and the installed interfaces. For many routers, Ethernet cables (Cat 5 or 6) will work. For some older routers with serial WAN interface cards, you might need serial cables.

Chapter Diagrams

There's a diagram at the beginning of many chapters to help you configure your devices. I tried to make the diagrams as generic as possible to make them as relevant as possible, regardless of which router you use.

What about Errors and Updates?

I wish I could tell you that this book has no errors in it. My colleagues and I have gone over it many times to correct errors, clarify points, and add things I inadvertently omitted. As I'm writing this, I know from experience that I'll discover something as soon as the printed book arrives on my doorstep. That's why I maintain an errata page. It's located at http://www.soundtraining.net/bookstore/errata. I publish notifications about updates and corrections on Facebook (www.soundtraining.net/facebook), Twitter (www.soundtraining.net/twitter), LinkedIn (www.soundtraining.net/linkedin), and on my blog (www.soundtraining.net/blog).

With any technical book, when you first receive it, visit the publisher's errata page and go step-by-step through the book making corrections as needed.

If you find anything I've missed that's not on the errata page, please send me an email and let me know: don@soundtraining.net.

Support Resources

Online Resources

I have created several online resources specific to this book, plus the usual social networking sites that everyone expects. Use Facebook, Twitter, LinkedIn, or my blog to get notifications about updates and corrections.

Web Page: There is a supporting web page with live links and other resources for this book at www.soundtraining.net/cisco-router-book

Videos: Watch the companion videos for this chapter. They're available at www.soundtraining.net/videos/cisco-router-training-videos

Errata: www.soundtraining.net/bookstore/errata

Facebook: www.soundtraining.net/facebook

LinkedIn: www.soundtraining.net/linkedin

Twitter: www.soundtraining.net/twitter

Blog: www.soundtraining.net/blog

Tech Support

I'm not able to provide individual technical support via email or on the phone. If you need tech support, please post your questions in public forums such as Facebook or LinkedIn. I may see your question and answer it myself or one of the other people visiting such sites might answer it. Either way, your question and the answer will be posted in a public forum where others with similar problems might benefit from seeing it.

If you really want individual technical support via phone or email, Cisco's SMARTNet offers 24/7 support with Cisco-trained engineers at reasonable prices, based on the type of equipment you own and the level of support your require. Search on Cisco SMARTNet or here's the URL: http://www.cisco.com/web/services/portfolio/product-technical-support/smartnet/index.html

Introduction

Author Stephen King says the most important thing an aspiring author can do is write. My wife, Janet, is a ceramic artist and she says the same thing about making pottery. Although there are big differences between writing a book, making ceramic art, and managing a router, one concept is the same. That's the importance of doing. As with writing and art, you can read and read about configuring a router, but there's no substitute for actually configuring one. Build a test lab with three or four routers (or use GNS3, as I mentioned earlier) so you can play and experiment without worrying about downing the network.

Once you build your test network (some people call it a sandbox), start doing the exercises in the book. The exercises are designed to deliver a working configuration. As with most things in IT, there are many different ways to configure a router. So, after you build the working configurations according to the material in this book, go back and change things and see how it works. For example, instead of using MD5, try using AES and see what happens. You get the idea. Just experiment, play, and have fun!

(If you get excited about what you're doing and your spouse rolls his or her eyes at your excitement, you'll know you're on the right track.)

One of the wonderful things about working in IT is the ever-expanding body of knowledge. You can never know it all. That was intimidating to me when I first became a technical trainer. Today, it's exciting for me because I know there's always something new to learn. I hope you enjoy the process of learning new things about router configuration through this book!

Now, let's go configure!

"Technology, like art, is a soaring exercise of the human imagination."

—Daniel Bell, The Winding Passage, 1980

CHAPTER 1:
Understanding the Fundamentals of the Cisco Router

Chapter Introduction

This is the "rip open the box" chapter. When I get some new device, whether it's a router, a firewall, a switch, a server, or even a coffee maker, I can't wait to rip open the box, power it up, and see what it does. (You should have seen me when Janet, my wife, gave me a telescope for my birthday!)

I recently got a new audio deck for my car. I got it installed and started listening to music right away. If I would have taken 15 minutes to review the quick start guide, I would have gotten a lot more enjoyment out of the deck right away. Instead, I just started messing around with it, but I missed a few key operational items that would have been very helpful to know. That's what this chapter is. We'll get the router set up so you can manage it and, along the way, I'll share a few key operational items that will add greatly to your enjoyment of the process. Of course, your router won't play Pandora from your phone, but it will most certainly route packets better than my new audio deck.

So, let's rip open the box, foam peanuts be damned, and let's see what this thing can do.

Chapter Objectives

- Learn how to prepare your management workstation, including hardware and software

- Connect a console cable to the router

- Understand the boot sequence and different types of memory on a router

- Understand the different login modes

- Familiarize yourself with Cisco IOS commands

- Get help when working the command-line interface

- Build a configuration in the Cisco Configuration Professional Express

- Build a configuration using the startup script

- Configure banners and see the effect of the gentle overlay

Conventions used in the interactive exercises:

Commands are displayed in ***bold italics***. Enter commands in ***bold italics*** as written.

Options and keyboard input are shown in **<arrows>**. For example, **<1-99>** indicates that you must choose a number between one and 99. **<In/out>** means that you would specify "in" or "out" (without the quotation marks). **<Enter>** means that you should press the Enter key on your keyboard. Click **<Next>** means you should click the button labeled Next. Comments are displayed in (parentheses).

Remember to check the prompt shown in the exercise instructions to see the proper mode for the execution of a command. Also, check the prompt on the router to ensure that you're operating in the proper mode to execute the required command.

Online Companion Resources

Videos: Watch the companion videos for this chapter. They're available at
www.soundtraining.net/videos/cisco-router-training-videos

Web Page: There is a supporting web page with live links and other resources for this book at www.soundtraining.net/cisco-router-book

Facebook: www.soundtraining.net/facebook

Twitter: www.soundtraining.net/twitter

Blog: www.soundtraining.net/blog

Use the following diagram to connect your router and management workstation for this chapter.

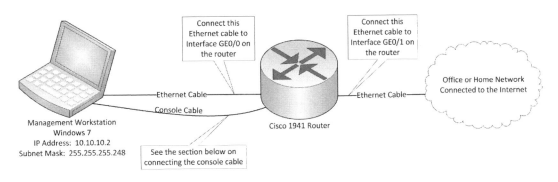

Diagram 1: Connecting a console cable

Connecting to the Console Port on a Cisco Router

Beginning with Windows Vista, Microsoft no longer includes terminal emulation software. As mentioned above, I recommend the use of PuTTY, a freely available package from www.putty.org. The exercises in this book incorporate the use of PuTTY.

Connecting via the Traditional Serial Console Cable

Your management workstation is connected to the router for monitoring and control purposes through its console port, using a flat, eight-wire rollover (console) cable. This allows you to use your computer as a "dumb" terminal for the router. It does not allow network functionality. Traditionally, HyperTerminal was used to execute the software commands and to view the console messages (you can use any terminal emulator VT100 or higher). The settings are 9600/n/8/1 with no flow control.

Figure 1: An official Cisco serial console cable, photo by Paul R. Senness

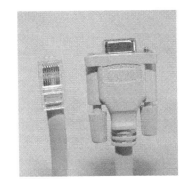

Connect the DB9 to the serial port on your management workstation and the RJ45 connector goes into the port marked Console on the back of your router. Be careful, it's easy to get confused and plug the console cable into an Ethernet port. Don't do that!

Figure 2: The RJ45 console port on the back of a Cisco 1941 router,
photo by Paul R. Senness

If your management workstation does not have a DB9 serial connector, you must use a USB-to-Serial adapter.

You'll probably need to manually install the drivers that come with it. Once you install it and plug it in, you'll also need to know which comm port it is using. The easiest way to do that is to check under Devices and Printers where you should see it, along with an indication of which comm port it was assigned. You may need to scroll to the bottom of the window to see it.

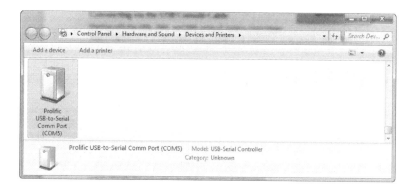

Figure 4: Viewing devices connected to a computer running Windows 7

Notice in the screen capture that my computer assigned the adapter to comm port 5 (COM5). Beginning with the 1900/2900/3900 series of routers, there's a much better alternative. Read on!

Soundthinking Point: The USB-to-Serial Adapter

I have used USB-to-Serial adapters from two separate manufacturers. In both cases, my experience has been painful. In my experience, they're necessary evils that frequently cause my laptop to bluescreen. I've had students and colleagues, however, who've never had a problem with them. I hope your experience is better than mine. Regardless, you must sometimes use such an adapter.

Figure 3: A USB-to-Serial adapter dongle, photo by Paul R. Senness

Connecting via the USB Console Cable

Starting with the 1900, 2900, and 3900 series of routers, Cisco began supporting the use of a USB console cable instead of the traditional serial console cable. The advantage of using the USB console cable is that you no longer have to use a management workstation with a DB9 serial connector or a USB-to-Serial adapter.

Figure 5: A USB console cable,
photo by Paul R. Senness

In order to use the USB console cable, you must install the USB Console Driver by performing the following steps:

1. Download the file *cisco_usbconsole.zip* from www.cisco.com. (This requires a Cisco username and password, but, as of this writing, it does not require a support contract.)

2. Unzip the file you downloaded and double-click the file setup.exe.

3. The InstallShield Wizard begins. Click **<Next>**.

4. When the Ready to *Install the Program* window appears, Click Install.

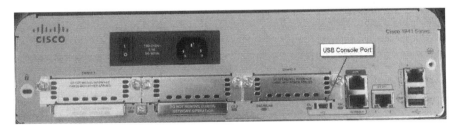

Figure 6: The USB console port
on the back of a Cisco 1941 router,
photo by Paul R. Senness

Additionally, in order to use the USB Console Cable, as with the USB-to-Serial adapter mentioned previously, you'll need to know which comm port it is using. The easiest way to identify the comm port is to check in Devices and Printers:

1. Click on Start

2. Click on Devices and Printers

3. Scroll through the display until you see the icons for Cisco Serial and Cisco USB Console. Note how the comm port is indicated below the Cisco Serial icon.

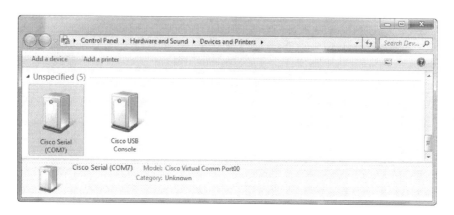

Figure 7: Windows 7 Devices and Printers after adding the Cisco USB console driver

In this example, the Cisco Serial port is assigned to comm port 7 (COM7).

Cisco Internetwork Operating System (CIOS)

- Like computer operating systems, there are a variety of releases available. The version you have depends on when the router was purchased and the specific features needed such as protocols, interfaces, and other features.

- This book is based primarily on version 15.1(4)M1, although other versions of the IOS are used occasionally.

The Boot Sequence of a Router

Different Cisco products have different components and mechanisms for booting. For many routers, the boot sequence is similar to this. The IOS can be loaded from several locations (listed in order):

- ROM: Read-only memory, normally used for repairs and diagnostics.

- Flash Memory: The router's storage memory, somewhat comparable to a computer's hard drive.

- TFTP Server: A trivial file transfer protocol server, typically running on a Windows or Linux/Unix computer. A TFTP server is used to backup configurations and software images. It can also be used as the loading source for the router's software image, although in my experience, I don't see that done very often.

The Router's Memory and Startup Sequence

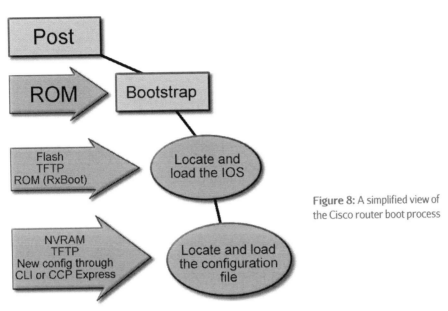

Figure 8: A simplified view of the Cisco router boot process

Router Memory

ROM (Read Only Memory)

The router's ROM is the source for permanent programs and routines. These programs and routines are used to boot the router and for repairs and diagnostics.

Two programs are in the boot ROM:

- ROM monitor (ROMmon)
    - A diagnostic image with a limited command subset
    - Used for recovery procedures
        - CIOS software image replacement from a TFTP server
        - Password recovery
- Bootstrap (RxBoot)
    - Finds and loads the CIOS software, per the configuration register
    - Can be located in FlashRAM or on a TFTP server

On some routers, the boot ROM chips can be upgraded with chips from Cisco.

DRAM: Dynamic Random Access Memory

The DRAM is used by the router while it's running. It loads the software image (the operating system) and the configurations into DRAM during the boot process.

- The DRAM is the router's operating memory.

- The configuration stored in DRAM is referred to as the running-configuration (running-config).

- View the contents of DRAM with the command "show running-config" which can be abbreviated to "show run."

NVRAM: Non-Volatile Random Access Memory

The NVRAM is a small bit of memory that stores the startup-config. The startup-config is the router's saved configuration. When you're modifying the router's configuration, the changes are made in the router's running-config (DRAM). When you're satisfied with the effects of such changes, you normally copy the changes into the startup-config (NVRAM). Copying from running-config to startup-config makes the changes persistent across boots. You may be familiar with the command *write memory* which copies the running-config into the startup-config.

- The NVRAM contains the configuration stored after default parameter questions are answered during initial configuration using the setup script.

- Upon subsequent boots, the router will read its configuration from NVRAM until it is erased.

- The configuration in NVRAM is referred to as the "startup-configuration" or "startup-config."

- You can view the contents of NVRAM with the command "show startup-config" which can be abbreviated to "show start."

Flash Memory

Think of flash memory as the router's hard drive. The flash memory is where the software image is stored, along with Cisco Configuration Professional Express, security software, and other files used by the router.

- Flash memory holds the operating system. The Cisco IOS is normally loaded from flash memory.

- You can partition flash memory and use the router as a TFTP server to hold configuration files.

- You can view the contents of flash memory with the command "show flash."

IOS Software Commands

Working in the Cisco IOS Command Line Interface

There are several different modes of access to the router. It's important to ensure that you're using the correct mode for the tasks you wish to accomplish.

Several of the modes are explained below the graphic. Notice, in the graphic, how the prompt changes depending upon the mode in which you're working.

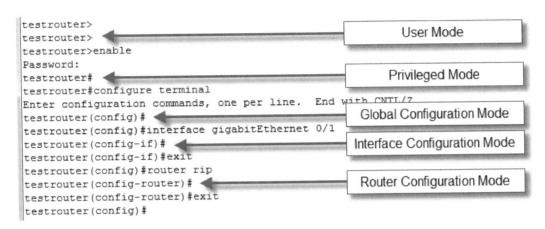

Figure 9: Some of the administrative modes on a Cisco router

User EXEC mode (>)

This mode is really not very useful. It is read-only mode and pretty limited as to what you can read. You can't make any changes here and all you can read are non-security-sensitive configuration parameters. You can't even execute the command *show running-config.*

- The prompt is a greater-than symbol (>).

- User EXEC grants access at privilege level one, which is discussed in chapter 15.

- The command set is much smaller than for privileged mode. Enter a question mark (?) while in user EXEC mode to see the limited number of commands available. Notice that none of the commands available in user EXEC mode allow you to modify the configuration.

- User EXEC supports a limited set of commands.

- User EXEC is mainly useful for very basic monitoring.

- Think of this mode as read-only.

Privileged EXEC mode (#)

This mode is where you do a lot of your monitoring and debugging. You can make only a handful of changes here, but when you want to use *show* and *debug* commands, this is the place.

- The command prompt for privileged EXEC is a pound sign (#).

- Privileged EXEC grants access at privilege level 15, which is discussed in chapter 15.

- In privileged EXEC, you have all access to all commands.

- Working in Privileged EXEC mode is similar to admin, administrator, or root.

- While in privileged mode, you can access all other modes including global configuration mode, router, interface, and subinterface modes, as well as all other modes.

- Access privileged mode by typing "enable" at the user mode ">" prompt (abbreviate with "en")

Global Configuration Mode ((config)#)

This mode is where you make changes to the router's configuration that are not specific to, say, an interface, a routing protocol, an access-control list, a serial line, or any of the myriad other configuration sub-modes.

- Global configuration mode is accessible only from within privileged EXEC mode.

- This mode is used for configuration commands that are universal to the router (not specific to an interface or protocol, for example).

- Think of global configuration mode as a portal through which you can access all other configuration modes.

- Enter global configuration mode from privileged EXEC mode by typing "configure terminal." (Most people abbreviate it "conf t.")

- From "global configuration mode, you can enter specific configuration modes including:
    - Interface
    - Router
    - Access-List
    - Bridge
    - Frame Relay
    - Others

Interface Configuration Mode ((config-if)#)

This is just one of the many configuration sub-modes. I decided to include a couple just as examples of such modes.

- Interface configuration mode is one of the sub-modes under global configuration mode.

- It allows configuration of interface parameters such as IP address, speed, and duplex.

- Interface configuration mode can be used with both physical (fast Ethernet) and virtual (vlan) interfaces.

- Unfortunately, the prompt does NOT indicate which interface is being configured. You must either refer to an earlier point in the configuration process or simply re-enter the interface command.

- Enter interface configuration mode from within global configuration mode by typing "interface [interface name]." For example, to configure interface Fast Ethernet 0/1, you would type the command "interface fast Ethernet 0/1", but most people shorten it to "int f0/1."

Line Configuration Mode ((config-line)#)

The router has several lines which can be used to connect to it for management. The two most commonly seen lines are "line console" and "line vty." Numbers, starting with 0 are used to identify which line is being configured. For example, to configure the serial console line (the one connected to the blue console cable), you would type "line console 0" from within global configuration mode. (Most people would shorten it to "line con 0.")

Virtual terminal lines are used when connecting remotely through Telnet or SSH. Typically, a Cisco router is configured with five virtual terminal lines identified as "line vty 0 4" which indicates virtual terminals lines zero through four. To configure a virtual terminal line for remote access, you would type the command "line vty 0 4" from within global configuration mode.

Some routers also have an auxiliary line which is used when you want to connect a modem to the router. You must specify which line number (even if there's only one line).

Other Configuration Modes

There are many configuration modes on a router, including router, access-list, dhcp, aaa, frame-relay, just to name a few. You can check out the different modes available on your router by entering a question mark (?) while in global configuration mode.

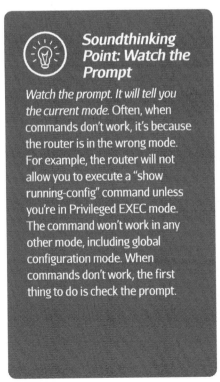

Soundthinking Point: Watch the Prompt

Watch the prompt. It will tell you the current mode. Often, when commands don't work, it's because the router is in the wrong mode. For example, the router will not allow you to execute a "show running-config" command unless you're in Privileged EXEC mode. The command won't work in any other mode, including global configuration mode. When commands don't work, the first thing to do is check the prompt.

Executing Higher-Level Commands While in a Sub-Mode

There is a way to execute higher-level commands while still in a sub-mode. Precede the higher-level command with the modifier "do" (similar to "sudo" in Linux or Unix systems). For example, suppose you wish to show the running config while you're operating in interface configuration mode. Enter the command as shown in the screen capture:

```
testrouter(config-if)#
testrouter(config-if)#do show running-config
Building configuration...

Current configuration : 1742 bytes
!
! Last configuration change at 00:22:32 UTC Wed May 30 2012
! NVRAM config last updated at 21:06:58 UTC Tue May 29 2012
! NVRAM config last updated at 21:06:58 UTC Tue May 29 2012
version 15.1
service timestamps debug datetime msec
service timestamps log datetime msec
no service password-encryption
!
hostname testrouter
!
```

Figure 10: Using "do" to execute higher-level commands while in a sub-mode

Context Sensitive Help

If you spell a command incorrectly or make a typo, the router will display a caret (^) just below the point where the error occurred. To obtain the correct syntax, argument, or keyword, re-enter the command to the point where the error occurred, then enter a question mark for a list of all possible options to complete the command. In the screen capture, I intentionally misspelled running-config. Notice how the router places a caret directly below the spot where the error occurred. In essence, the router is saying, "I understood everything up until the first "n", but then the command didn't make sense to me." Notice how, by entering a question mark at the point in the command where the error occurred, the router will display all the possible ways of completing the command.

```
testrouter#
testrouter#show rnning-config
                   ^
% Invalid input detected at '^' marker.

testrouter#show r?
radius          region       registry     reload
resource        rhosts       rib          rif
rmon            rom-monitor  route-map    rudpv1
running-config

testrouter#show r
```

Figure 11: Context-sensitive help on a router

Help is always available with the "?" You can enter a question mark at various points and the router will display command options.

Helpful Editing Features

As with many operating systems, use the "up-arrow" key to repeat the last command. You can use the "up-arrow" and "down-arrow" keys to cycle through recently entered commands

Shorthand

The CIOS allows the use of abbreviated commands to expedite configuration. For example:

copy startup-config running-config can be shortened to *cop s ru.*

show running-config can be abbreviated to *sh ru* (the actual abbreviated commands will vary based on the version of the CIOS, the feature sets installed, and the router model).

Some people will explore just how short they can make commonly used commands. On the surface, that may seem like a fairly "geeky" thing to do. In the real world, however, saving keystrokes not only can save time, but may also help avoid repetitive stress disorders.

As with many computer operating systems, you can also press the Tab key to complete a partially entered command.

Figure 12: Using the tab key to complete a command

Building an Initial Configuration on the Cisco Router

You can build a base configuration on a Cisco router in any one of four ways:

1. Enter the commands manually in the command-line interface.

2. Apply a saved configuration from a text file. This is probably the method you'll use most frequently after you become comfortable with managing a router.

3. Answer questions in the router's question-driven setup script.

4. Configure the router through the Cisco Configuration Professional (CCP), the router's web interface that provides a graphical user interface for configuration and management. The Cisco Configuration Professional includes a program called CCP Express which helps you perform an initial configuration on the router. This is probably the most commonly-used method by admins who are new to the Cisco platform. Older router platforms use a similar program called Cisco Security and Device Manager (SDM). I've included an appendix at the rear of the book showing how to use SDM.

Interactive Exercise 1.1:
Building an Initial Configuration using CCP Express

Note: In order for the following procedures to work properly, your computer must be configured with a static IP address. If you're not familiar with how to change your computer's IP address settings, please refer to Appendix A.

Note: The following steps will only work on a router with its factory-default configuration. If the router has been modified since the box was opened, the following steps will probably not work. It is possible to reset a router to factory-default configuration. The steps are explained in Appendix D.

As mentioned above, CCP Express is a browser-based application that allows you to perform initial configuration steps on your router. In order to use CCP Express, you must connect your management workstation to your router via an Ethernet cable.

The following steps are performed on a Cisco 1941 router. The steps will be similar on other routers, although the interfaces may be different from one router to another. The following steps will not work on older routers such as 1600s, 1700s, 2500s, or 2600s. If you're working with a router that doesn't support CCP Express (or, alternatively, SDM Express), you can use the steps in Interactive Exercise 1.3, later in this chapter.

Supported browser: The only browser officially supported for use with CCP is Microsoft Internet Explorer (6.X or later). I have used CCP successfully, however, with Firefox 12.0.

1. Connect one end of an Ethernet cable to your management workstation and the other end to Interface GE0/0 (Gigabit 0/0) on your router. (Refer to the diagram at the beginning of the chapter if you have any questions about how to connect your management workstation to the router.)

2. Configure your management workstation with an IP address of 10.10.10.2 and a subnet mask of 255.255.255.248. (If you're not familiar with how to modify your computer's IP address settings, see Appendix A.) It is not necessary to modify any other IP settings on your management workstation at this time.

3. Open an Internet Explorer browser window (other browsers may also work) and enter the URL https://10.10.10.1. Press the Enter key to connect.
   (Note: You must allow pop-ups from 10.10.10.1 in order to use the Cisco CP Express to configure your router.)

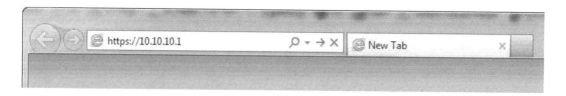

Figure 13: Initial connection to Cisco CP Express through a browser

4. Click through the security warnings.

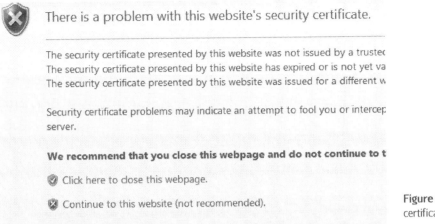

Figure 14: The usual security certificate warning

5. You will be asked to authenticate several times. Each time, enter the username *cisco* and the password *cisco*. You will change the username and password later.

6. You will also receive a Security Certificate Alert. Click yes to accept the certificate. (Obviously, in the real world, you should verify the identity of the site(s) to which you're connecting before accepting such a certificate.)

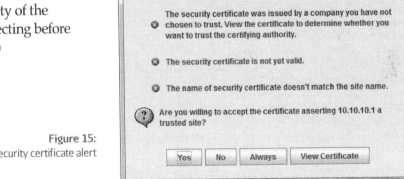

Figure 15:
The usual security certificate alert

7. CCP Express will open, followed immediately by the Cisco CP Express Wizard. Click the button labeled *Next* in order to begin the process of configuring your router.

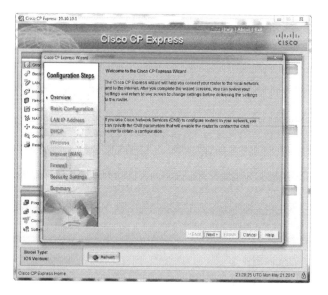

Figure 16: The Cisco CP Express
Wizard splash page

8. In the Basic Configuration window, enter the following values (you're welcome to use your own name and password, of course, but these values will be used throughout the book):

    – Hostname: cisco1941

    – Domain name: soundtraining.net

    – New username: yourfirstname (I used "Don")

    – New password: p@ss1234

    – Enable Secret Password: p@ss5678

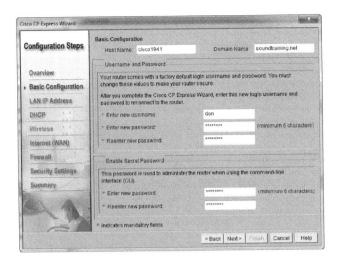

Figure 17: Cisco CP Express
basic configuration

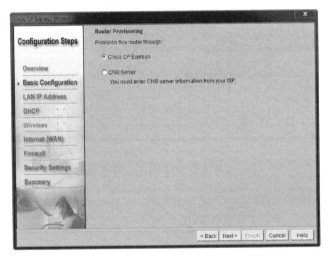

9. Click **<Next>**.

10. The Router Provisioning window appears. Confirm that Cisco CP Express is selected. Click **<Next>**.

Figure 18: Choosing how
to provision the router

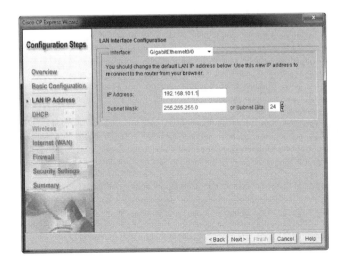

11. The LAN Interface Configuration window appears. Configure the following values:

   – Interface: GigabitEhternet0/0

   – IP Address: 192.168.101.1

   – Subnet Mask: 255.255.255.0
   (or Subnet Bits: 24)

Figure 19: Assigning
a LAN IP address

12. Click **<Next>**

13. The DHCP server configuration window appears. Configure the following values:

    – Check the box labeled Enable DHCP server on the LAN interface

    – Starting IP Address: 192.168.101.11

    – Ending IP Address: 192.168.101.254

    – Primary DNS: 208.67.222.222

    – Secondary DNS: 208.67.220.220 (In case you're wondering, these are the addresses of the OpenDNS servers. If you want to know more about OpenDNS, their website is at www.opendns.com.)

    – Check the box labeled Use these DNS values for DHCP clients

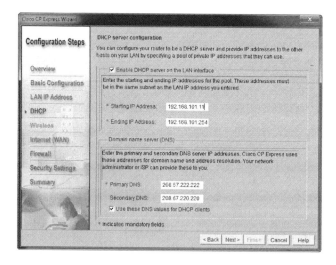

Figure 20: Configuring DHCP through Cisco CP Express

14. Click **<Next>**

15. In the WAN Configuration windows, ensure that the GigabitEthernet0/1 interface is selected and click the button labeled *Add Connection*

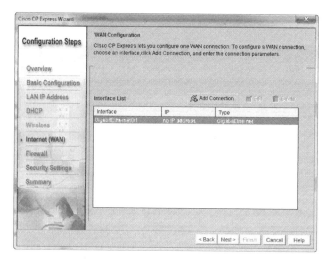

Figure 21: Cisco CP Express WAN configuration

16. In the Add GigabitEthernet0/1 Connection window, change the address type to **Dynamic IP Address** and click **OK** (You can also choose to configure a static IP address, but for the purpose of this exercise, select Dynamic IP Address.)

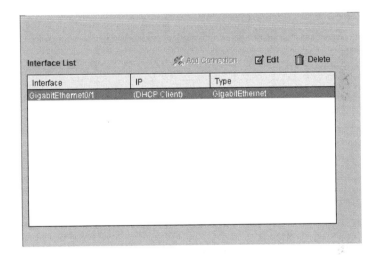

Figure 22: Configuring the WAN interface for DHCP

17. The Interface List should now show the modified WAN interface.

Figure 23: Displaying the just-configured WAN interface

18. Click **<Next>**

19. The Internet (WAN) – Private IP Address window appears. Confirm that the box labeled Enable NAT is checked and Click **<Next>**

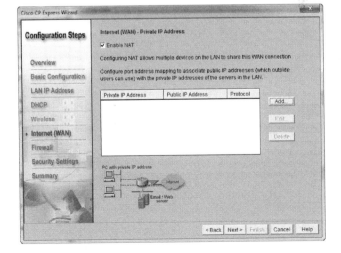

Figure 24: Enabling Network Address Translation

45

20. The Security Configuration window appears. For the purpose of this exercise, it is not necessary to make any changes. Take a moment, however, to review the services that are disabled and the other aspects of the security configuration. In a real-world scenario, you might want to modify some of these settings based on your particular network and your needs as an administrator. The settings are, however, good for starting the process of securing your router. Click **<Next>**.

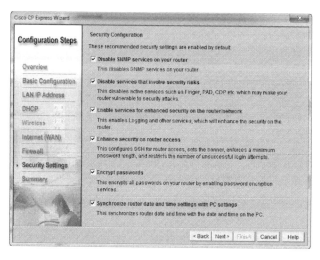

Figure 25: Cisco CP Express security settings configuration

21. The Cisco CP Express Summary page appears. You are given an opportunity to review the settings you've just configure and, if necessary, go back and make necessary changes. Review the settings, comparing them to the previous steps in the book. When you're satisfied that the settings are correct, click the button labeled **Finish**

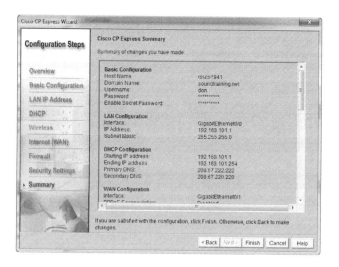

Figure 26: Cisco CP Express Summary

22. The Cisco CP Express – Reconnection Instructions window appears. (Note that, as of this writing, there is a typo in the instructions. Where it says FE0/1 and FE0/2, it should say GE0/1 and GE0/0. It's not a huge deal, but it could be confusing if you're a beginner.) Note that, by default, it will save the instructions to a file on your desktop. Since that's not a bad idea at this stage, go ahead and accept the default and click **OK**.

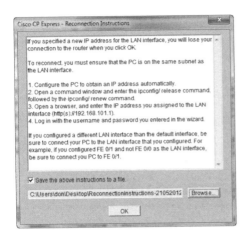

Figure 27: Cisco CP Express reconnection instructions

23. After you click **OK**, a warning dialog will appear advising you that you will lose connectivity after the new configuration is delivered to the router. After about a minute, the button labeled OK will become available for you to click. Go ahead and click **OK**.

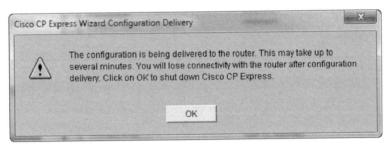

Figure 28: Delivering the new configuration to the router

24. Cisco CP Express will close. You will now have to connect using the IP address 192.168.101.1. You will also need to configure your management workstation to obtain an IP address automatically.

25. Test your configuration by attempting to connect to Cisco CP Express at 192.168.101.1. If you have your router's WAN interface connected to the public Internet, you can also test your configuration by attempting to connect to www.soundtraining.net in a Web browser. (Do not test your configuration by pinging public Internet servers such as public websites. Many of them are configured to deny pings for security reasons.)

Managing the Router: Graphical Tools

Cisco Configuration Professional (CCP)

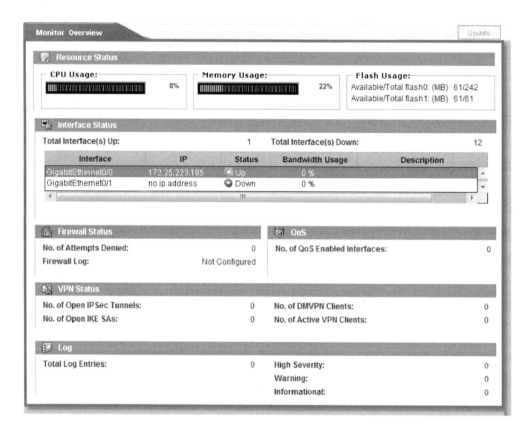

Figure 29: Cisco Configuration Professional monitoring page

Cisco Configuration Professional (CCP) is a Flash and Java-based GUI administration tool. Designed to simplify deployment and management of Cisco routers, CCP provides wizards for router, security, Unified Communications, wireless, WAN, and basic LAN configuration.

CCP allows an administrator to graphically deploy Cisco ISRs (Integrated Services Routers) for:

- Dynamic routing
- WAN access
- WLAN
- Firewall
- VPN

- SSL
- VPN
- Intrusion Prevention Systems (IPS)
- Quality of Service (QoS)

The minimum requirements for running CCP include Microsoft Windows 7 - 64 and 32 bit, Microsoft Windows Vista Business Edition, Microsoft Windows Vista Ultimate Edition, Microsoft Windows XP with Service Pack 2 or later, Mac OSX 10.5.6 running Windows XP using VMWare 2.0, 2 GHz processor, minimum 1 GB DRAM/recommended 2 GB DRAM.

CCP can be downloaded from the Cisco Software Center at www.cisco.com. It requires a CCO login, but does not require a support contract.

CCP can be downloaded from the Cisco Software Center at www.cisco.com. It requires a CCO (Cisco Connection Online) login, but does not require a support contract.

Soundthinking Point: What is Cisco Connection Online?

Cisco Connection Online is your link to www.cisco.com. It is your login that, even without a support contract, grants you additional access to Cisco resources. Among the things you can do with a CCO login are:

- Download strong encryption software that doesn't require a service agreement
- View software available for download (although you may not be able to download certain software packages without a service agreement)
- Gain access to technical documentation
- Register online for Cisco seminars

In my opinion, it's well worth it to register for a CCO login. There is no cost for basic access and you gain access to a variety of resources on the Cisco website.

Cisco Router and Security Device Manager (SDM)

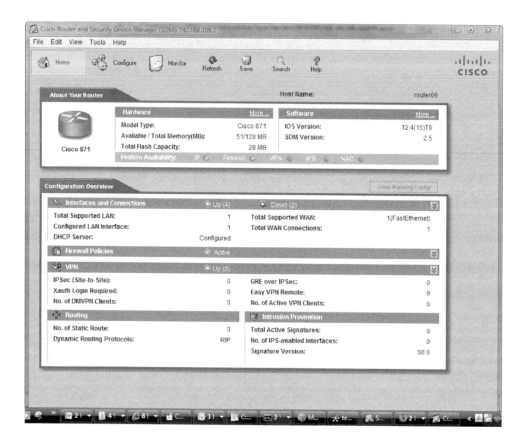

Figure 30: The Cisco SDM home page

The Cisco Router and Security Device Manager (SDM) is a Java-based graphical tool for configuring and managing Cisco routers. You can use SDM to simplify router deployments, and help troubleshoot network and VPN connectivity issues.

SDM can be installed either on a PC, a router, or both.

SDM has been replaced by Cisco Configuration Professional, however it is still available for download from www.cisco.com for use with older routers.

Cisco Network Assistant (CNA)

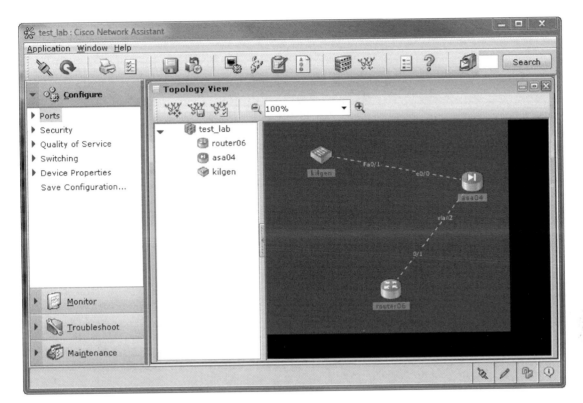

Figure 31: The Cisco Network Assistant utility

The Cisco Network Assistant is a PC-based network management tool that simplifies many routine network management activities. It is optimized for both wired and wireless networks with 40 or fewer routers and switches. The Cisco Network Assistant provides an intuitive, graphical overview of your network and centralized management of Cisco routers, switches, and access points. The Cisco Network Assistant supports the following tasks:

- Configuration management
- File management
- Drag-and-drop Cisco IOS Software upgrades
- Inventory reports

- Event notification
- Troubleshooting advice
- Network security settings
- Task-based menu

The Cisco Network Assistant is a free download, available at www.cisco.com. Search on "Cisco Network Assistant"). It requires a CCO login, but does not require a support contract.

Cisco IOS Software Images

The operating system for your router is known as the Cisco IOS (Internetwork Operating System). You can view the IOS version, along with other information about the hardware and software on your router with the command show version.

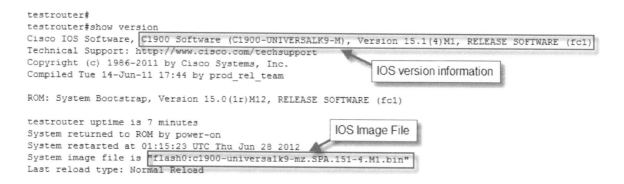

The Cisco IOS image filename includes codes that describe its capabilities. In the screen capture above, the image file provides the following information:

Field	Explanation
Flash0	The image file was loaded from flash memory, partition or disk 0.
C1900	The image file is written for routers in the 1900 series
Universal	Cisco Generation Two ISR (Integrated Services Routers) now ship with a universal image file that contains all the capabilities of the software. Different features are activated depending on the license purchased.
K9	The k9 designation means the software includes strong AES/3DES encryption capability
M	M means the image runs from RAM
Z	Z means the image is zip compressed
SPA	S means the image is digitally signed P means the image is a production image (as opposed to a development image which would designated by an "S" for *special*) A indicates which key version was used to sign the software
151-4.M1	15 is the major release number, 1 is the minor release number, 4 is the new feature release number, M indicates an extended maintenance release, and 1 is the maintenance rebuild number.
Bin	The file is a binary executable.

There are hundreds, perhaps thousands of IOS software image releases. It's not realistic for me to cover them all in this book. Cisco provides several online documents describing the various fields and options in the software releases. Here are a couple of good starting points:

http://www.cisco.com/en/US/prod/collateral/iosswrel/ps8802/ps5460/product_bulletin_c25-557278.html

http://www.cisco.com/en/US/products/sw/iosswrel/ps1834/products_tech_note09186a00800fb9d9.shtml

Also, as of this writing (late summer 2012), Wikipedia has a good article about the Cisco IOS at http://en.wikipedia.org/wiki/Cisco_IOS

The flexibility of the Cisco licensing system allows you to pay for only the features you need. For example, if you're not going to set up a VPN, there's no need to include that capability on your router and no need to pay for it.

Managing the Router: Using the Command Interpreter EXEC

The Cisco command interpreter is EXEC. EXEC is to a router what the Bash shell is to Linux or Unix or what cmd.exe or PowerShell is to Windows. EXEC takes your keyboard input and interprets it for the operating system.

This may seem like splitting hairs, but there is no "exec" mode. There is *privileged EXEC*, which is the administrator mode and there is *user EXEC* which is a read-only mode. In other words, don't let the term EXEC confuse you.

Soundthinking Point: Is it Still Necessary to Use the Command-Line Interface?

It's very important to learn the Cisco CLI (or, for that matter, the command-line interface for any device or system). In spite of the fact that newer graphical tools are much improved over their predecessors, there are still limitations in terms of Java requirements and browser issues. A solid knowledge of the Cisco CLI will allow you to configure and troubleshoot your Cisco network device under all circumstances. The same cannot be said for graphical tools. Additionally, an understanding of CLI commands allows you to automate various administration tasks with scripts.

Interactive Exercise 1.2:
Working in the Command Line Interface

This exercise teaches you the basics of connecting to a Cisco router for administration. You'll also learn how to use the Cisco Internetwork Operating System's context-sensitive help.

Objectives:

1. Understand the basic procedures for logging onto a Cisco router

2. Learn the differences between User EXEC mode and Privileged EXEC mode when using the command line interface

Becoming Familiar with the Cisco Router's Command-Line Interface (CLI)

1. Open a serial console session to your router using PuTTY.

    – In the PuTTY configuration window, push the radio button labeled Serial. Click *Open*. (You may have to specify a port number if you're using a USB-to-Serial adapter or a USB console cable.)

2. Press the Enter key and you should see a user authentication prompt (Username:).

3. Enter the username you created earlier (don) and the password p@ss1234.

4. Disregard the warning about the "one-time" user option.

5. Type the following command to enter User EXEC mode (unprivileged mode):

    – router#*disable*

6. The router returns a User EXEC prompt (>).

7. Enter a question mark to see the commands available in User EXEC: Router>?

8. Some routers, by default, will limit the number of lines on screen to 24. (If your router doesn't limit the number of lines on screen, read through the following three steps, but do not execute them on your router. Later in the book, I'll explain how to configure paging to limit the amount of text that displays at one time.)

    – If your router is configured with limited lines per screen, it will display a --More-- prompt at the bottom of the page. At the --More-- prompt, press the Enter key several times. Notice that the router displays one new line each time your press the Enter key.

    – Now, press the Space Bar at the --More-- prompt. Notice that the router now displays one new page each time you press the Space Bar.

    – Again, enter a question mark at the router prompt. Now, press the letter key "q" on the keyboard. Notice that the router returns to the command prompt. (You can actually press almost any key on the keyboard with the same effect.)

9. Now, type the following commands to enter Privileged EXEC:

   – Router>*enable*[enter]

   – Password:*p@ss5678*[enter]

10. Enter a question mark to display the commands available to you in Privileged EXEC:

    – Router#*?*

11. If necessary, press the space bar each time the router prompts you with --More--. Notice that there are many more commands available to you in Privileged EXEC mode than in User EXEC mode. The router will only display the commands that available within a given mode.

12. Once again, enter the command *"show ip interface brief."* Then enter the command *"show version."* Press the "q" key to return to a prompt. Now, press the "Up Arrow" key at a Privileged Exec prompt. Notice that the router repeats the last command entered. You can cycle through the last few commands by using a combination of the up and down arrow keys. By default, there's a buffer of 10 commands. You can modify it with the privileged EXEC command *terminal history*.

13. The configuration being used by the router is stored in DRAM. It's the current (or active) configuration. You can display it by typing the following command:

    – Router#*show running-config*[enter]

      (Remember the use of the space bar and enter key to display more text after a --More-- prompt.)

14. The saved (or backup) configuration used when you boot the router is stored in NVRAM. You can display it by typing the following command:

    – Router#*show startup-config*[enter]

At this point, the saved configuration (startup-config) should match the current configuration (running-config).

15. Use the following command to exit Privileged Exec:

    – Router#*disable*[enter]

16. While in User EXEC, attempt to display the active configuration file with the command *"show run"* (short for "show running-config"). What happens?

17. Notice that the router displays an "invalid input" message and places a caret under the command at the point where the command becomes invalid. Try typing the command to the point where the caret is placed, then add a question mark to the command (Router>*show r?*). Notice that the router displays available commands. This is a great way to build commands from scratch when you're not sure which commands are available within a particular mode.

18. You can log out of your router with the following command:

    – Router>*logout*[enter]

Initial Configuration

Powering up a router is much like powering up a computer (a router is, after all, simply a specialized computer):

- Diagnostics are run from ROM (POST)
- The bootstrap is executed from ROM
- The configuration register is checked to find the IOS source (boot.ini)
- IOS is loaded into DRAM
- Hardware and software components are inventoried and displayed
- Startup-configuration file is loaded into DRAM and parsed
- If NVRAM is invalid (perhaps due to erasure), a setup script is executed in the Command-Line Interface

In the following interactive exercise, you will erase your configuration and build a new configuration from scratch in the CLI with the assistance of the setup script. The configuration you build using the command-line interface will form the foundation for the router's configuration that will be used for the remainder of the book.

Interactive Exercise 1.3:
Building an Initial Configuration in the CLI

In this exercise, you will use the Cisco IOS Startup Sequence, a question-driven setup dialog, to configure the router. When complete, this is the configuration you'll use as a base configuration for the remainder of the book.

Prepare your router for the exercise

1. Disconnect all Ethernet cables from your router, but leave either the blue console cable attached to the router's console port and your management workstation's serial port (or the USB console cable attached to the router's USB console port and a USB port on your management workstation).

2. If you haven't already, start a terminal session using PuTTY (or any terminal emulation software) on your management workstation.

3. Log on to your router if necessary using the username and password you created earlier (*yourfirstname* and the password *p@ss1234*).

4. Erase your router's configuration with the following command: router#*erase startup-config*

5. Confirm that you wish to erase the startup-config by pressing the enter key on your management workstation.

6. Confirm that the erasure was successful with the following command:
   router#*show startup-config*

```
User Access Verification

Username: don
Password:
testrouter#erase startup-config
Erasing the nvram filesystem will remove all configuration files! Continue? [con
firm]
[OK]
Erase of nvram: complete
testrouter#
May 24 23:33:31.493: %SYS-7-NV_BLOCK_INIT: Initialized the geometry of nvram
testrouter#show startup-config
startup-config is not present
testrouter#
```

Figure 32: Erasing the startup-config in NVRAM

7. Reload your router with the following command: router#*reload* and press enter.
   (If you are asked, do NOT save the modified configuration.)

```
testrouter#reload
Proceed with reload? [confirm]

May 24 23:39:37.165: %SYS-5-RELOAD: Reload requested by don on console. Reload R
eason: Reload Command.
```

Figure 33: Reloading the router

8. If you left the CCP and/or CCP Express windows open in your browser, you will lose those
   connections. Close the browser windows.

9. You will notice a large amount of text scrolling down in your terminal window as the router boots.
   After about a minute and a half, you will see a message saying, "System Configuration Dialog ---
   Would you like to enter the initial configuration dialog? (yes/no):"

10. Type "yes" and press the enter key.

```
Cisco CISCO1941/K9 (revision 1.0) with 491520K/32768K bytes of memory.
Processor board ID FGL1539207J
2 Gigabit Ethernet interfaces
1 terminal line
DRAM configuration is 64 bits wide with parity disabled.
255K bytes of non-volatile configuration memory.
250880K bytes of ATA System CompactFlash 0 (Read/Write)


        --- System Configuration Dialog ---

Would you like to enter the initial configuration dialog? [yes/no]: yes
```

Figure 34: Beginning the system configuration process

Note: Depending on your software version, you may be prompted with: "Press return to get started." In that case, press the Enter key on your keyboard. It's also possible, depending on your software version, that you'll have to manually start the setup script by entering the following commands (Check the prompt. If the prompt is "#", you don't need to use the enable command.):

– Router>*enable*

– Router#*setup*

11. Enter the following responses to each question, paying attention to the information presented onscreen between the questions:

– Would you like to enter basic management setup? [yes/no]: *no*

– First, would you like to see the current interface summary? [yes]: *yes*

– Enter host name [Router]: *testrouter*

– Enter enable secret: *p@ss5678*

12. Enter enable password: *router*

13. Enter virtual terminal password: *p@ss1234*

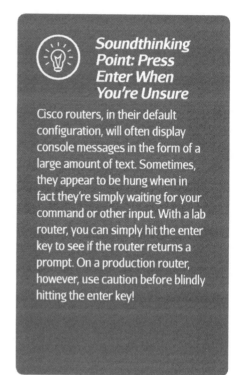

Figure 35:
Configuring the hostname
and passwords

14. Configure SNMP Network Management? [no]: *no*

15. Configure IP? [yes]: *yes*

> **Soundthinking Point: Press Enter When You're Unsure**
>
> Cisco routers, in their default configuration, will often display console messages in the form of a large amount of text. Sometimes, they appear to be hung when in fact they're simply waiting for your command or other input. With a lab router, you can simply hit the enter key to see if the router returns a prompt. On a production router, however, use caution before blindly hitting the enter key!

16. Configure RIP routing? [yes]: *no*

17. Configure CLNS? [no]: *no*

18. Configure bridging? [no]: *no*

19. Configuring interface parameters:

20. Do you want to configure Embedded-Service-Engine0/0 interface? [yes]: *no*

21. Do you want to configure GigabitEthernet0/0 interface? [yes]: *yes*

    – Configure IP on this interface? [yes]: *yes*

22. Do you want to configure GigabitEthernet0/1 interface? [yes]: *no*

23. Would you like to go through AutoSecure configuration? [yes]: *no* (Not all IOS software version will ask this question. For the purpose of this book, if yours does, enter *"no."*

```
 The virtual terminal password is used to protect
 access to the router over a network interface.
 Enter virtual terminal password: p@ss1234
 Configure SNMP Network Management? [yes]: no
Configure IP? [yes]:
    Configure RIP routing? [no]:
Configure CLNS? [no]:
 Configure bridging? [no]:

Configuring interface parameters:

Do you want to configure Embedded-Service-Engine0/0  interface? [yes]: no

Do you want to configure GigabitEthernet0/0  interface? [yes]:
  Configure IP on this interface? [yes]:
    IP address for this interface: 192.168.101.1
    Subnet mask for this interface [255.255.255.0] :
    Class C network is 192.168.101.0, 24 subnet bits; mask is /24

Do you want to configure GigabitEthernet0/1  interface? [yes]: no

Would you like to go through AutoSecure configuration? [yes]: no
AutoSecure dialog can be started later using "auto secure" CLI
```

Figure 36: Interface configuration

24. The router will present the configuration script you just built for your review. Ensure that the configuration matches the steps above. When you're satisfied that it's accurate, enter "2" and press Enter.

```
interface Embedded-Service-Engine0/0
shutdown
no ip address
!
interface GigabitEthernet0/0
ip address 192.168.101.1 255.255.255.0
no mop enabled
!
interface GigabitEthernet0/1
shutdown
no ip address
dialer-list 1 protocol ip permit
!
end


[0] Go to the IOS command prompt without saving this config.
[1] Return back to the setup without saving this config.
[2] Save this configuration to nvram and exit.

Enter your selection [2]:
```

Figure 37: Reviewing and saving the configuration

Note: On some routers, you may see a message about media-type 100BaseX and Invalid input detected at '^' marker. That is due to a default command in the setup script that is not supported on certain routers. In my experience, it can be ignored.

A Sample Configuration

Cisco 1941 Router Sample Configuration

This is the entire configuration process. Your configuration should be similar to this.

--- *System Configuration Dialog* ---

Would you like to enter the initial configuration dialog? [yes/no]: yes
At any point you may enter a question mark '?' for help.

Use ctrl-c to abort configuration dialog at any prompt.

Default settings are in square brackets '[]'.
Basic management setup configures only enough connectivity for management of the system, extended setup will ask you to configure each interface on the system

Would you like to enter basic management setup? [yes/no]: no
First, would you like to see the current interface summary? [yes]: yes
Any interface listed with OK? value "NO" does not have a valid configuration

Interface	IP-Address	OK?	Method	Status	Protocol
Embedded-Service-Engine0/0	unassigned	NO	unset	initializing	down
GigabitEthernet0/0	unassigned	NO	unset	down	down
GigabitEthernet0/1	unassigned	NO	unset	down	down

Configuring global parameters:

Enter host name [Router]: testrouter
The enable secret is a password used to protect access to privileged EXEC and configuration modes. This password, after entered, becomes encrypted in the configuration.

Enter enable secret: p@ss5678
The enable password is used when you do not specify an enable secret password, with some older software versions, and some boot images.

Enter enable password: router
The virtual terminal password is used to protect access to the router over a network interface.

Enter virtual terminal password: p@ss1234
Configure SNMP Network Management? [yes]: no
Configure IP? [yes]: yes
Configure RIP routing? [no]: no
Configure CLNS? [no]: no
Configure bridging? [no]: no
Configuring interface parameters:

```
Do you want to configure Embedded-Service-Engine0/0 interface? [yes]: no
Do you want to configure GigabitEthernet0/0 interface? [yes]: yes
Configure IP on this interface? [yes]: yes
IP address for this interface: 192.168.101.1
Subnet mask for this interface [255.255.255.0] : 255.255.255.0
Class C network is 192.168.101.0, 24 subnet bits; mask is /24

Do you want to configure GigabitEthernet0/1 interface? [yes]: no
Would you like to go through AutoSecure configuration? [yes]: no
AutoSecure dialog can be started later using "auto secure" CLI

The following configuration command script was created:

hostname testrouter

enable secret 5 $1$7EI/$KusRNhno0u00sK2HtWSRN0

enable password router

line vty 0 4

password p@ss1234

no snmp-server

!

ip routing

no clns routing

no bridge 1

!

interface Embedded-Service-Engine0/0

shutdown

no ip address

!

interface GigabitEthernet0/0

ip address 192.168.101.1 255.255.255.0

no mop enabled

!
```

```
interface GigabitEthernet0/1

shutdown

no ip address

dialer-list 1 protocol ip permit

!

end

[0] Go to the IOS command prompt without saving this config.
[1] Return back to the setup without saving this config.
[2] Save this configuration to nvram and exit.

Enter your selection [2]: 2
Building configuration...

[OK]
Use the enabled mode 'configure' command to modify this configuration.
Press RETURN to get started!

Jan 2 12:00:02.331: %IOS_LICENSE_IMAGE_APPLICATION-6-LICENSE_LEVEL: Module name = c1900 Next reboot
level = ipbasek9 and License = ipbasek9

May 25 00:31:13.603: %IFMGR-7-NO_IFINDEX_FILE: Unable to open nvram:/ifIndex-table No such file or directory

May 25 00:31:23.727: %LINK-3-UPDOWN: Interface GigabitEthernet0/0, changed state to down

May 25 00:31:23.727: %LINK-3-UPDOWN: Interface GigabitEthernet0/1, changed state to down

May 25 00:31:24.943: %LINEPROTO-5-UPDOWN: Line protocol on Interface
GigabitEthernet0/0, changed state to down

May 25 00:31:24.943: %LINEPROTO-5-UPDOWN: Line protocol on Interface
GigabitEthernet0/1, changed state to down

May 25 00:33:12.195: %SYS-5-CONFIG_I: Configured from console by console

May 25 00:33:14.459: %LINK-5-CHANGED: Interface Embedded-Service-Engine0/0, changed state to
administratively down

May 25 00:33:14.459: %LINK-5-CHANGED: Interface GigabitEthernet0/1, changed state to administratively down

May 25 00:33:15.459: %LINEPROTO-5-UPDOWN: Line protocol on Interface Embedded-Service-Engine0/0, changed
state to down

May 25 00:33:20.679: %IP-5-WEBINST_KILL: Terminating DNS process May 25 00:33:24.207: %SYS-5-RESTART:
System restarted --
```

```
Cisco IOS Software, C1900 Software (C1900-UNIVERSALK9-M), Version 15.1(4)M1,
RELEASE SOFTWARE (fc1)

Technical Support: http://www.cisco.com/techsupport

Copyright (c) 1986-2011 by Cisco Systems, Inc.

Compiled Tue 14-Jun-11 17:44 by prod_rel_team

May 25 00:33:24.391: %SNMP-5-COLDSTART: SNMP agent on host testrouter is undergoing a cold start

May 25 00:33:25.003: %SYS-6-BOOTTIME: Time taken to reboot after reload = 216 seconds

testrouter>
```

Note: There is a sample configuration from a Cisco 871 router in Appendix F at the end of this book.

Configuring the Router's Outside Interface

Interactive Exercise 1.4:
Configuring the Outside Interface for DHCP

In this exercise you will configure a dynamically assigned address for the router's outside interface.

1. Log on to your router and use the *enable* command to get into privileged mode.

2. Use the command *configure terminal* to move into global configuration mode and the command *interface g0/1* (or whatever interface on your router faces the outside world) to move into interface configuration mode.

3. In interface configuration mode, enter the command *ip address dhcp* and press enter, then enter the command *no shutdown* and press enter to enable the interface as a DHCP client and to turn it on.

4. After a moment or two, you should see console messages indicating that the interface came up and showing the newly assigned IP address.

```
testrouter>enable
Password:
testrouter#configure terminal
Enter configuration commands, one per line.  End with CNTL/Z.
testrouter(config)#interface g0/1
testrouter(config-if)#ip address dhcp
testrouter(config-if)#no shutdown
testrouter(config-if)#
Sep 22 19:54:27.908: %LINK-3-UPDOWN: Interface GigabitEthernet0/1, changed state
 to down
Sep 22 19:54:30.740: %LINK-3-UPDOWN: Interface GigabitEthernet0/1, changed state
 to up
Sep 22 19:54:31.740: %LINEPROTO-5-UPDOWN: Line protocol on Interface GigabitEthe
rnet0/1, changed state to up
Sep 22 19:55:30.556: %DHCP-6-ADDRESS_ASSIGN: Interface GigabitEthernet0/1 assign
ed DHCP address 192.168.1.239, mask 255.255.255.0, hostname testrouter

testrouter(config-if)#
```

Figure 38: Configuring the outside interface as a DHCP client

5. Use the command *show ip interface brief* to review the settings and ensure the interface is functioning properly.

```
testrouter#
testrouter#show ip interface brief
Interface                  IP-Address      OK? Method Status                Prot
ocol
Embedded-Service-Engine0/0 unassigned      YES NVRAM  administratively down down

GigabitEthernet0/0         192.168.101.1   YES NVRAM  down                  down

GigabitEthernet0/1         192.168.1.239   YES DHCP   up                    up

testrouter#
```

Figure 39: Reviewing the IP address configuration on the router

If your router is not connected to a DHCP server on the outside interface, you can manually assign an ip address with the following command sequence:

```
testrouter>
testrouter>enable
Password:
testrouter#configure terminal
Enter configuration commands, one per line.  End with CNTL/Z.
testrouter(config)#interface g0/1
testrouter(config-if)#ip add 192.168.1.239 255.255.255.0
testrouter(config-if)#exit
testrouter(config)#ip route 0.0.0.0 0.0.0.0 192.168.1.1
testrouter(config)#
```

Figure 40:
Configuring a static IP address on the outside interface along with a default gateway

64

In the previous screen capture, I assigned an IP address of 192.168.1.239 with a subnet mask of 255.255.255.0 to the outside interface. I also created a default route to my gateway router at 192.168.1.1. As I'll explain later in the book, the unusual looking address and mask of 0.0.0.0 0.0.0.0 means any route not otherwise known to the router. It's the same as the default gateway on your computer running Microsoft Windows.

Some Miscellaneous Helpful Commands

Configuring your Line Console 0

Line Console 0 is how your control your router through the light blue serial cable. There are several parameters you should configure on line console 0 (line con 0) for security and convenience including a console password, a feature that makes it easy to see a router prompt, a feature that prevents unnecessary DNS lookups, and a feature that minimizes annoying TFTP lookups. In the following steps, you'll do all four.

Interactive Exercise 1.5:
Configuring Line Console 0

Begin by configuring a console password:

1. testrouter>*enable*
   Password: *p@ss5678*

2. testrouter#*conf t*

3. testrouter(config)#*line con 0*

4. testrouter(config-line)#*password p@ss1234*

5. testrouter(config-line)#*login*

Now, force the router to return to a prompt immediately after displaying console messages:

6. testrouter(config-line)#*logging synchronous*

7. testrouter(config-line)#*exit*

Now, prevent unnecessary DNS lookups with the following command:

8. testrouter(config)#*no ip domain-lookup*

Note: If you wish to use a DNS server later for hostname lookups, you will need to enable domain lookups with the command *ip domain-lookup.*

Finally, although this isn't a Line Console 0 command, it will help minimize annoying TFTP lookups during the next few exercises:

9. testrouter(config)#*no service config*

```
testrouter>
testrouter>enable
Password:
testrouter#conf t
Enter configuration commands, one per line.  End with CNTL/Z.
testrouter(config)#line con 0
testrouter(config-line)#password p@ss1234
testrouter(config-line)#login
testrouter(config-line)#logging synchronous
testrouter(config-line)#exit
testrouter(config)#no ip domain-lookup
testrouter(config)#no service config
testrouter(config)#
```

Figure 41: Configuring line console 0

Now, connect your Ethernet cables (inside interface to your PC and outside interface to the lab switch) and test your configuration by attempting to ping another router from your router. Use the exercise diagram to find IP addresses for the test. Try both inside and outside interface addresses, plus computer addresses.

Reminder: Double-check your cables to ensure that your inside interface is connected to your PC and your outside interface is connected to home or office switch or router.

Banners and the Gentle Overlay

Configuring Specific Parameters

- Enter manual configuration mode by using the configure terminal command from the privileged EXEC prompt

- Exit manual configuration mode by entering CTRL-Z after entering all commands

The Command Hierarchy

As you learned earlier, User EXEC provides very limited access to commands while Privileged EXEC provides full access to commands and sub-commands. Privileged EXEC is the portal through which you can access all other command modes. global configuration mode (often referred to simply as "Configuration Mode" is the mode in which you can actually modify the router's configuration.

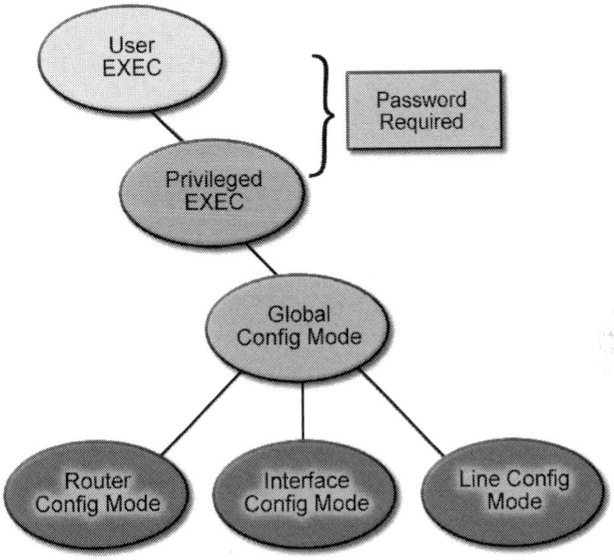

Figure 42:
The Cisco command hierarchy

You can, for example, use configuration mode to set a logon banner to warn users that they're about to access a restricted system or to provide support contact information.

Note: There are other modes under global configuration mode besides those shown in the graphic. The modes available on your router will vary based on the software feature set(s) installed on the router.

The Gentle Overlay

When you're copying configurations from some source into the running-config, the router does what is called a "gentle overlay." When you copy a configuration from, say, a TFTP server into the running-config, the router only overwrites settings in the running-config when a conflict exists between the new configuration and the running-config. Settings in the running-config are left in place unless there is a similar setting in the new configuration.

Interactive Exercise 1.6:
Banners and the Gentle Overlay

In this lab, you'll learn how to use global configuration mode to manually configure various aspects of the Cisco router.

Objectives:

1. Learn how to change the hostname

2. Create a login banner

3. Use the show history command

4. See the results of a "gentle overlay"

Steps:

1. Log in to your router and get to Privileged EXEC mode (Remember the *enable* command?).

2. Display the current configuration file by entering the following privileged EXEC command:

   – testrouter#*show running-config*

3. Find the *hostname* line. Notice that the prompt on your router interface is the same as the hostname line in the output of *show running-config*. The reason for that is because the output of *show running-config* displays the contents of the active configuration being used by the router.

4. Display the backup configuration file by entering the following privileged EXEC command:

   – testrouter#*show startup-config*

5. Find the hostname line. Observe that the prompt on your router interface is once again the same as the hostname line in the output of *show running-config*. It is the same because, when the router booted, it loaded the contents of its backed-up configuration from NVRAM into dynamic RAM where it became the active configuration.

6. Type the following commands to change the hostname of your router:

   – testrouter>*en*

   – Password: *p@ss5678*

   – testrouter#*conf t*

   – testrouter(config)#*hostname Mariners<Enter>*

```
testrouter>en
Password:
testrouter#conf t
Enter configuration commands, one per line.  End with CNTL/Z.
testrouter(config)#hostname Mariners
Mariners(config)#
```

Figure 43: How to modify a router's hostname

7. Display the backup configuration file again (***show startup-config*** or, if you're still in configuration mode, use ***do show startup-config***). Find the *hostname* line. Notice that there is a difference now between the prompt on your router interface and the hostname line. The reason is because, when you issued the hostname command, you modified the active configuration in dynamic RAM (active-config) without saving the changes to NVRAM (startup-config). In order for the change to be reflected in the startup-config, you must save the active-config to the startup-config. Later in this exercise, I'll show you how to save your config.

8. Type the following commands to add a login banner and an exec banner to your router:

    – Mariners(config)# ***banner login #<Enter>*** (Note that there is a space between *login* and "#".)

    – ***This is my login banner # <Enter>*** (Make sure to enter the "#.")

    – Mariners(config)# ***banner exec #<Enter>*** (Note that there is a space between *exec* and "#".)

    – ***This is my exec banner # <Enter>*** (Make sure to enter the "#.")

    – Mariners(config)# ***exit***

```
Mariners(config)#
Mariners(config)#banner login #This is my login banner.#
Mariners(config)#banner exec #This is my exec banner.#
Mariners(config)#exit
Mariners#
May 30 18:44:59.604: %SYS-5-CONFIG_I: Configured from console by console
Mariners#
```

Figure 44: Configuring the login and exec banners on a router

    – Mariners#**logout <Enter>**

9. Now, log back in to your router. You should see your banner during the login process. Notice that the login banner appeared before login and the exec banner appeared after login.

10. Enter privileged mode with the command *enable*, then type the following command to restore the entire configuration file from NVRAM: Mariners# *copy startup-config running-config <Enter>*

    (Some routers will prompt for a destination filename. If your router asks for one, accept the default of [running-config].) Think about what is happening here: You are copying the configuration stored in NVRAM (startup-config) into the router's dynamic RAM (running-config).

11. Notice that the prompt on the router interface changed back to *testrouter* because the copy operation overwrote the hostname value in the running-config with the hostname value in the startup-config. Before you draw conclusions about what happened, continue the exercise. You might be in for a surprise.

12. Display the current configuration file with the following command:

    − testrouter#*show running-config*

    Notice that the hostname line changed from the last time you displayed the current configuration file.

13. Use the following command to display the last ten commands you entered:

    − testrouter# *show history <Enter>*

14. Log out of your router and log back in. Notice that you still see your banners as you log in. You may be thinking, "I copied the startup-config into the running-config which I thought would erase the banners, so why are they still displaying?" The answer is because of what Cisco calls "the gentle overlay." When you copied the startup-config into the running-config, it merged the two files. There was no statement pertaining to banners in the startup-config, so it left the banners in place. There was, however, a statement in the startup-config pertaining to the router's hostname, so it overwrote the existing hostname (Mariners) in the running-config with the saved hostname (testrouter) in the startup-config.

15. Erase your banners with the following command:

    − testrouter# *config t*
    − testrouter(config)# *no banner login <Enter>*
    − testrouter(config)# *no banner exec <Enter>*

16. Copy your router's current configuration to NVRAM by entering the following privileged EXEC command:

    − testrouter#*copy running-config startup-config*

17. Log out of your router with the following command:

    − testrouter#*logout*

Use Aliases to Shorten Commonly-Used Commands

As with Unix and Linux systems, you can create aliases to shorten commonly-used commands. For example, instead of typing *show cdp neighbor detail | include IPv6*, you can create an alias of *sipv6*. When you enter *sipv6i*, the router will respond the same as if you had entered *show cdp neighbor detail | include IPv6*.

To create an alias, in global configuration mode enter the command *alias [command mode] [the alias] [the command]*. For example, to create a privileged mode (exec) alias of proc that will display a sorted list of the top CPU processes, use the following command in global configuration mode:

testrouter(config)#**alias exec proc show processes cpu sorted | exclude 0.00% 0.00% 0.00%**

```
router02#conf t
Enter configuration commands, one per line.  End with CNTL/Z.
router02(config)#alias exec proc show processes cpu sorted | exclude 0.00% 0.00% 0.00%
```

Figure 45: Configuring an alias

Routers come pre-configured with several aliases. You can view all aliases on a router with the command show aliases.

```
router02(config)#do show alias
Exec mode aliases:
  h                   help
  lo                  logout
  p                   ping
  r                   resume
  s                   show
  u                   undebug
  un                  undebug
  w                   where
  proc                show processes cpu sorted | exclude 0.00% 0.00% 0.00%

ATM virtual circuit configuration mode aliases:
  vbr                 vbr-nrt
```

Figure 46: Viewing the aliases on a router

After you configure the alias, you use it by entering it at a command prompt:

```
router02#proc
CPU utilization for five seconds: 0%/0%; one minute: 0%; five minutes: 0%
 PID Runtime(ms)     Invoked      uSecs   5Sec   1Min   5Min TTY Process
  91       1284     66919623          0  0.15%  0.15%  0.15%   0 Ethernet Msec Ti
 116        304     16393045          0  0.07%  0.03%  0.02%   0 IPAM Manager
   1          0            9          0  0.00%  0.00%  0.00%   0 Chunk Manager
   2        108       105006          1  0.00%  0.00%  0.00%   0 Load Meter
   3      23760        17935       1324  0.00%  0.00%  0.00%   0 Exec
   4          0            1          0  0.00%  0.00%  0.00%   0 RO Notify Timers
   5     248848        71059       3501  0.00%  0.06%  0.05%   0 Check heaps
   6          0          108          0  0.00%  0.00%  0.00%   0 Pool Manager
   7          0            1          0  0.00%  0.00%  0.00%   0 DiscardQ Backgro
   8          0            2          0  0.00%  0.00%  0.00%   0 Timers
   9          0          574          0  0.00%  0.00%  0.00%   0 WATCH_AFS
  10          0            1          0  0.00%  0.00%  0.00%   0 License Client N
  11          0            1          0  0.00%  0.00%  0.00%   0 Image License br
  12     334372         8746      38231  0.00%  0.06%  0.05%   0 Licensing Auto U
  13     419712       524597        800  0.00%  0.08%  0.06%   0 Environmental mo
  14        100       104937          0  0.00%  0.00%  0.00%   0 IPC Event Notifi
  15        564         8746         64  0.00%  0.00%  0.00%   0 IPC Dynamic Cach
  16          0            1          0  0.00%  0.00%  0.00%   0 IPC Session Serv
  17          0            1          0  0.00%  0.00%  0.00%   0 IPC Zone Manager
  18         32       512699          0  0.00%  0.00%  0.00%   0 IPC Periodic Tim
  19         20       512699          0  0.00%  0.00%  0.00%   0 IPC Deferred Por
  20          0            1          0  0.00%  0.00%  0.00%   0 IPC Process leve
--More--
```

Figure 47: Using the newly-configured alias

Some aliases that I find helpful include:

sru	show running-config
ss	show startup-config
si	show ip interface brief
sro	show ip route

Summary

In this chapter, you and I covered the fundamentals of Cisco routers. You learned how to log in, you learned how to build a configuration in two different ways, and you learned a lot of the commands we use to manage our routers. You even learned some shortcuts. Now, with the basics in hand, it's time to march boldly into the world of Cisco router configuration! (Am I being too dramatic?)

CHAPTER 2:
Understanding the OSI Reference Model

Chapter Introduction

Sometimes students ask me why they need to know the OSI model. First of all, if you're planning to pursue any networking certification, you'll find questions about it on the tests. Even if you're not interested in certification, however, there are practical applications for understanding the OSI model. When we design a network, we typically start at the top of the model and work down. We consider the needs of the business, how our end-users work, and what applications they need. Those are upper-layer sorts of considerations. Conversely, when we troubleshoot, we start at the bottom and work up. For example, the first step in troubleshooting is always to consider the physical layer. Are you plugged in? Is the device turned on? Then, we move up through the data-link and networking layers.

Oh, and it's fun to memorize the corny mnemonics that help us remember the layers.

Chapter Objectives

- Understand the function of each of the layers of the OSI reference model

- Learn mnemonics to assist in remembering the layers

- See the practical application of the OSI model

Online Companion Resources

Videos: Watch the companion videos for this chapter. They're available at
www.soundtraining.net/videos/cisco-router-training-videos

Web Page: There is a supporting web page with live links and other resources for this book
at www.soundtraining.net/cisco-router-book

Facebook: www.soundtraining.net/facebook

Twitter: www.soundtraining.net/twitter

Blog: www.soundtraining.net/blog

A Brief History of the OSI Reference Model

The Open Systems Interconnection (OSI) reference model was developed by the International Standardization Organization in 1984. It describes standards for inter-computer communication. Many people think of the OSI reference model as "defining" standards for network communication. In fact, the OSI model "describes" how different devices and protocols co-operate within a network (or internetwork) environment. It helps encourage unified, cohesive network development.

How the OSI Reference Model Works

The OSI reference model is a conceptual model, composed of seven layers, each describing particular network functions. It describes how data moves from an application running on one computer on a network to another application on another computer on the network (or, perhaps, a different network).

Name of the Layer	What Happens at the Layer
Layer Seven—Application	Network applications such as FTP, Telnet, SMTP, HTTP, SNMP
Layer Six—Presentation	Data Formatting, Character-Code Conversion, Data Compression, and Data Encryption
Layer Five—Session	Negotiation and Establishment of Connection
Layer Four—Transport	End-to-End Transmission Control
Layer Three—Network	Routing of Packets Across Networks
Layer Two—Data Link	Transfer of Frames, Error Checking, Flow Control
Layer One—Physical	Cabling, Connectors, Signaling, Voltage Levels

Data flows from the sending node down through each layer of the OSI model. Each layer encapsulates the data from the higher layer until the physical layer converts the data into bits and transmits it onto the transmission media. The bits flow across the transmission media to the destination node. At the destination node, each layer strips away its encapsulation until the data is finally delivered to the application layer.

Layer One: The Physical Layer

The physical layer is where voltage levels and the timing of voltage changes are described. Physical data rates, maximum transmission distances, and physical connectors are covered by the physical layer. A basic concept of network troubleshooting is to always start at the physical layer: Is it plugged in and turned on? Are the correct cable types and connectors being used?

Layer Two: The Data Link Layer

Physical addressing is done at the Data Link layer to define how devices are identified. Physical addressing uses a "flat" address space; in other words, there is no distinction made between node IDs and network segments. The physical address is also known as the MAC address, for the Media Access Control sub-layer of the Data Link layer. Other names for the physical layer address include the hardware address, the Ethernet address, and the NIC address. Cisco calls it the BIA (burned-in-address). It's possible to change the hardware address of a router's Ethernet interface, but its BIA will remain the same. Also, at the Data Link layer, network topology describes how devices are to be physically connected (such as in a star, bus, ring, star bus, or star ring topology). At layer two, the data is called a "frame." Basic error-checking and error-correction is done at the Data Link layer.

Layer Three: The Network Layer

Hierarchical addressing schemes such as those used by Internet Protocol version 4 or Internet Protocol version 6 are described at layer three. Telephone numbering is an example of a hierarchical addressing scheme, in which a country code is subdivided into area codes, area codes are subdivided into exchanges, and exchanges support multiple local telephone numbers. Data networks do something similar by dividing an address into a network, subnet, and host sections.

Layer three, the network layer, supports both connection-oriented services such as TCP (Transmission Control Protocol) and connection-less services such as UDP (User Datagram Protocol) from high layer protocols.

Layer Four: The Transport Layer

The Transport layer is like glue that binds upper layers to lower layers. Reliable data conveyance is provided at the Transport layer by TCP (Transmission Control Protocol), while unreliable (but fast) data conveyance is provided at the Transport layer by UDP (User Datagram Protocol). Packets are put in the correct order at the Transport layer and, when supported, message acknowledgement is done at the Transport layer.

Layer Five: The Session Layer

The session layer establishes connections between two applications on different computers. Name recognition and security can occur at the session layer. NetBIOS operates at layer five.

Layer Six: The Presentation Layer

The Presentation layer is where data compression and encryption is done. This is also the layer that prepares the data for "presentation" to the application layer (layer seven) in terms of character representation such as ASCII. Data representation in the form of MPEG and JPEG is also done at the Presentation layer.

Layer Seven: The Application Layer

Network applications operate at layer seven. These applications include mail (Simple Mail Transfer Protocol or SMTP), file transfer (File Transfer Protocol or FTP), web services (Hyper Text Transfer Protocol or HTTP), and management services (Simple Network Management Protocol or SNMP) and should not be confused with desktop applications.

Remember that the OSI reference model attempts to *describe* rather than *define* what happens at each layer. Manufacturers do not have to adhere to the specifications described by the OSI reference model. It is helpful, however, to understand that most networking functions can be described in terms of one or more layers of the OSI reference model.

Remembering the Layers

There are several mnemonics that can help you remember the layers of the OSI reference model. Here are two:

Layer Name	Initial	From top to bottom:	Or, from bottom to top:
Application	A	All	Away
Presentation	P	People	Pizza
Session	S	Seem	Sausage
Transport	T	To	Throw
Network	N	Need	Not
Data Link	D	Data	Do
Physical	P	Processing	Programmers

The OSI Model and Common Network Protocols

	Layer	Name	Protocols
Software	Layer 7	Application	Telnet, SMTP, HTTP, FTP, IMAP, POP3, SNMP
	Layer 6	Presentation	MPEG, ASCII, TLS, SSL
	Layer 5	Session	NetBIOS, SAP
	Layer 4	Transport	TCP, UDP
	Layer 3	Network	IPv4, IPv6, ICMP, IPSec, ARP, MPLS
Hardware	Layer 2	Data Link	MPLS, RARP, Ethernet, 802.11x, PPP, Frame Relay, ATM, FDDI, Fibre Channel
	Layer 1	Physical	RS232, DSL, 10BaseT, 100BaseTX, ISDN, T1

Protocol Data Units (PDUs)

At each layer of the OSI model, a different name is used to refer to the datagrams. As you can see in the following graphic, there are a total of five names used. The reason this is important is because a type of encapsulation is used as the datagram moves through the layers of the OSI model. For example, as upper layer data moves down into the transport layer, it becomes encapsulated in a segment and values such as TCP port numbers are added. As the segment moves down into the network layer, packet encapsulation is added including things like source and destination IP addresses. At the data link layer, frame encapsulation takes place adding MAC address information. Finally, at the physical layer, the datagram is converted into bits and sent out across the network.

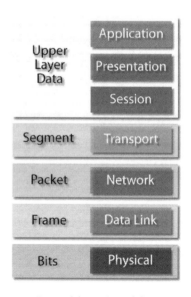

Protocol data units and the layers of the OSI model

Summary

When I was first learning networking, I was kind of intimidated by the OSI model. I'm not sure why. It's not that difficult to learn and the benefits are huge. I now realize that it provides a valuable framework for understanding how data flows across a network.

CHAPTER 3:
Fundamentals of TCP/IP

Chapter Introduction

Many students have also complained about having to learn IP. They complain about the tedious nature of binary conversions. They complain about the amount of time we spend on it. So, why do I devote so much class time and so much of this book to gaining an understanding of the Internet Protocol? The answer is really pretty simple. If you don't understand the structure of IP addresses, you won't be able to configure anything other than the simplest network. You'll blow your static routing configurations. If you use dynamic routing, your routing protocols won't work.

I received a call once from an Accidental Administrator® who was mainly a medical assistant in an orthopedist's office in California. (Someone once saw him typing fast and decided that he could run the network!) He had not been trained as an IT person, but he was doing the best he could to run the office network. He was trying to set up a remote clinic which he wanted to connect to the main office and then to the global Internet. He sent me his router configs and I immediately saw that the problem was in his IP address configurations. He simply didn't understand IP addressing or subnetting. There was no way his networks could talk to each other, let alone the Internet.

IP addressing is to routers and networks what the alphabet is to reading. Yeah, it's really that important. Take your time with this chapter. Watch the companion videos. I've had a lot of students and clients tell me that this technique of learning IP addressing and subnetting works for them, but that doesn't mean it's the only way to learn the subject. Check out YouTube videos. Search the Internet for tutorials. Grant yourself the grace to be confused as you first begin this process. When you get to the point where you understand it, you'll have earned the right to be very proud of yourself!

One final comment as we dive into the fundamentals of TCP/IP: Resist the urge to use an IP subnet calculator as you're working through this chapter. Do the conversions by hand while you're learning so you can gain a more intuitive comprehension of the workings of IP. That will benefit you later when you're in the field trying to figure out why things aren't working.

Chapter Objectives

- Understand the protocols included in the TCP/IP suite

- Understand sockets and ports

- Know the classes of IP addresses

- Understand how to convert an IP address to base-2 numbers

- Know how to identify the dividing line between network, subnet, and host

- Practice designing an IP network with subnets

- Gain familiarity with basic IP troubleshooting tools

Online Companion Resources

Videos: Watch the companion videos for this chapter. They're available at
www.soundtraining.net/videos/cisco-router-training-videos

Web Page: There is a supporting web page with live links and other resources for this book at www.soundtraining.net/cisco-router-book

Facebook: www.soundtraining.net/facebook

Twitter: www.soundtraining.net/twitter

Blog: www.soundtraining.net/blog

The TCP/IP Protocol Suite

TCP/IP is a layered suite of many protocols. The name itself includes two protocols: Transmission Control Protocol and Internet Protocol. There are many other protocols that make up the TCP/IP suite. TCP/IP is sometimes called the DoD protocol because of its development by the Department of Defense.

Protocols in the TCP/IP Suite

Some of the protocols in the TCP/IP suite include:

- IPv4 (Internet protocol version four): Provides addressing and connectionless, best-effort delivery of packets. It is not concerned with content of packets. IPv4 addresses are based on a 32-bit address space.

- IPv6 (Internet protocol version six): Provides addressing and connectionless, best-effort delivery of packets. It is not concerned with content of packets. IPv6 addresses are based on a 128-bit address space.

- TCP (Transmission Control Protocol): A connection-oriented protocol that provides error checking, acknowledgement, and flow control.

- UDP (User Datagram Protocol): A connection-less protocol that is very fast, but unreliable.

- FTP (File Transfer Protocol)

- TFTP (Trivial File Transfer Protocol)

- ICMP (Internet Control Message Protocol): Provides control and messaging capabilities.

- ARP (Address Resolution Protocol): Resolves IP address to MAC address

- RARP (Reverse Address Resolution Protocol): Resolves MAC address to IP address

- HTTP (HyperText Transfer Protocol)

- HTTPS (Secure HyperText Transfer Protocol)

- DHCP (Dynamic Host Configuration Protocol): Dynamically assigns IP addresses and other options to hosts on an IP network.

- Telnet: Used for remote login (can also be used for testing).

- SNMP (Simple Network Management Protocol)

- SMTP (Simple Mail Transfer Protocol)

- POP2 (Post Office Protocol)

- POP3 (Post Office Protocol)

- SNTP (Simple Network Time Protocol)

- NTP (Network Time Protocol)

- Tools in the TCP/IP suite include PING, TraceRoute, DNS, and Telnet.

Socket and Ports

Network sockets connect an application to a network protocol. Sockets are a software object, not a physical object. A socket is the combination of IP address and port number, for example 192.168.0.1:80.

Ports are points of entrance to the TCP/IP stack. TCP and UDP ports are similar to extensions on a telephone switchboard. Some common ports include:

- 80—WWW
- 25—SMTP
- 69—TFTP
- 21—FTP
- 443—HTTPS

There are three broad ranges of port numbers:

- Well-Known Ports (0-1023) are assigned by IANA (Internet Assigned Numbers Authority). They can usually be used only by system (or root) processes or programs when executed by privileged users.
- Registered Ports (1024-49151) are listed by IANA and can typically be used by ordinary user processes and programs when executed by ordinary users. These ports are registered by IANA as a convenience to the community.
- Dynamic and/or Private Ports (49152-65535) available for private use

There are 65,535 TCP port numbers and 65,535 UDP port numbers. For the most part, the TCP and UDP port numbers match. The complete listing of all TCP and UDP port numbers is available at www.iana.org/assignments/port-numbers.

Two Types of IP Nodes

A node is anything in an IP network that has an IP address. There are two types of nodes:

- Host
  - Source or destination of the packets. The term "host" can be a bit confusing to newcomers to the networking world. The name implies that it should be some type of server, but a host can be a desktop workstation, a process control module, a networked printer, an IP phone, a server, or any other IP device.
- Router
  - Directs the packets from one network or subnet to another

Frankly, most of the time, most people use the term host and node interchangeably.

IP Addresses

IP addresses are 32 bits long, composed of four eight-bit octets (also called bytes or fields), and the decimal numbers in each octet can range from 0 to 255 inclusive.

Bits are ones and zeros. A bit that's turned on is represented by a "1" and a bit that's turned off is represented by a "0." There are eight bits in a byte. Each bit has a decimal value that increases from right to left:

Decimal Value	128	64	32	16	8	4	2	1

To determine the decimal value of a byte, add the decimal values of each bit that's turned on (represented by a "1"). The following byte (11010000) converts to decimal by adding 128, 64, and 16 (the bits that are 1s) and ignoring all the other bits (the bits that are 0s). The resulting byte value is 208.

Decimal Value	128	64	32	16	8	4	2	1
Bits	1	1	0	1	0	0	0	0

Decimal Number	208	79	115	3
Binary Conversion	11010000	01001111	01110011	00000011

Classful IP Addresses

IP addresses contain three distinct parts:

The class (A, B, C, D, or E): The class is determined by the value of the first octet. If the first octet falls within the range of 1-126, the address is part of a Class A network. If the first octet falls within the range of 128-191, the address is part of a Class B network. If the first octet falls within the range of 192-223, the address is part of a Class C network.

The network address: The network ID is similar to an area code within the telephone system. Unlike the telephone numbering system, however, the network ID's length changes based on the class of address. In a Class A network, the network ID is eight bits long (or one octet), in a Class B network, the network ID is 16 bits long (or two octets), and in a Class C network, the network ID is 24 bits long (or three octets).

Host ID: The host ID is similar to a local phone number within the telephone system. As with network IDs, the length of the host ID will change based on the class of address. In a Class A network, the host ID is 24 bits long (or three octets), in a Class B network, the host ID is 16 bits long (or two octets), and in a Class C network, the host ID is eight bits long (or one octet).

Of the five classes of IP addresses, three are commonly used in LANs (Class A, B, and C). Class D is used for IP multicasting and Class E is reserved for experimental purposes. Often, IP addresses are compared to telephone numbers in that a network address must be unique to the Internet in much the same way an area code must be unique to the Public Switched Telephone Network, and the host address must be unique to the individual network or subnet in much the same way that a local telephone number must be unique within an area code.

When the Internet was originally designed, Class A addresses were reserved for very large networks, Class B was used for medium sized networks, and Class C was used for smaller networks. Classful IP addresses are still used in LAN environments, so it's important to understand the proper configuration of Classful IP addressing. There is a technology called CIDR (Classless Inter-Domain Routing) (RFC 4632) that has replaced Classful IP address on the Internet. Ultimately, however, IPv6 will replace all IPv4 addressing schemes.

Class	First Part of Address	Maximum # of hosts
A	1-126 (1-126).host.host.host	16,777,214 (2^{24}-2)
B	128-191 (128-191).network.host.host	65,534 (2^{16}-2)
C	192-223 (192-223).network.network.host	254 (2^{8}-2)

IP Addresses

In discussions of IP addresses, the individual octets in an address are sometimes identified as follows: w.x.y.z

- A class A network is represented by the "w" octet
- A class B network is represented by the "w" and "x" octets
- A class C network is represented by the "w", "x", and "y" octets

The Leading Bit Pattern

When an IP address is converted from dotted decimal to binary (base 2) notation, the leading bit patterns identify the class of address.

A router examines each packet, looking at the first bit of its address. If it sees a zero in the first bit position, it knows the address of the packet is a class A address. If it sees a one in the first bit position and a zero in the second bit position, it knows the address is a class B address. If it sees a one in the first two bit positions and a zero in the third bit position, it knows that the address is a class C address.

If you do the math, you'll see that when the leading bit of a byte is a 0, the only possible decimal values for the byte are 0 through 127. Internet rules further restrict the range of first octet values for a Class A address to the 1 through 126 range. Similarly, when the leading bits of a byte are 10, the only possible decimal values for the byte are 128-191 and when the leading bits are 110, the only possible decimal values for the byte are 192-223.

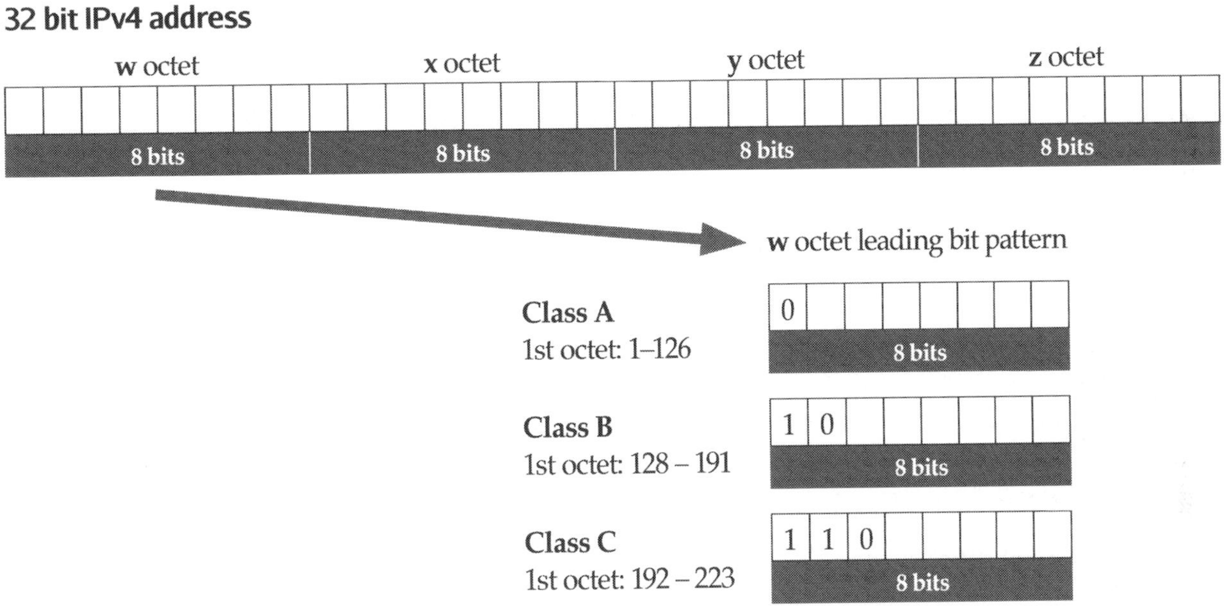

32 bit IPv4 address

Figure 48: How the leading bit pattern determines the class of address

In much the same way that the PSTN (Public Switched Telephone Network) assigns unique numbers to each telephone, TCP/IP assigns unique numbers to each node in an IP network. Although IP addresses are obtained from ISPs, an organization called ICANN is the governing body.

ICANN stands for "Internet Corporation for Assigned Names and Numbers" (www.icann.org). ICANN is the body that, in concert with IANA (Internet Assigned Numbers Authority) (www.iana.org) and InterNIC (Internet Network Information Center) (www.internic.net), controls and manages the IP address space.

IP Addressing: Basic Rules

- Each network must have a unique network ID

- Each workstation on a network must have a unique host ID

- Your IP address must be globally unique in all the world if you are on the public Internet

- Network addresses cannot use the number 127

- The class A network 127 is reserved for loopback testing on hosts

How to Test Your IP Configuration

On a Router

- Use PING to test connectivity with another host (PING is a very common tool for testing connectivity at layer three and below).

- Enter the ping command as follows:

  - *ping [target IP address]*, for example *ping 200.200.200.200*

- You can also control various aspects of ping on a router by entering the command *ping* without an IP address. The router will prompt you for things such as protocol, IP address, source interface, repeat count, and datagram size.

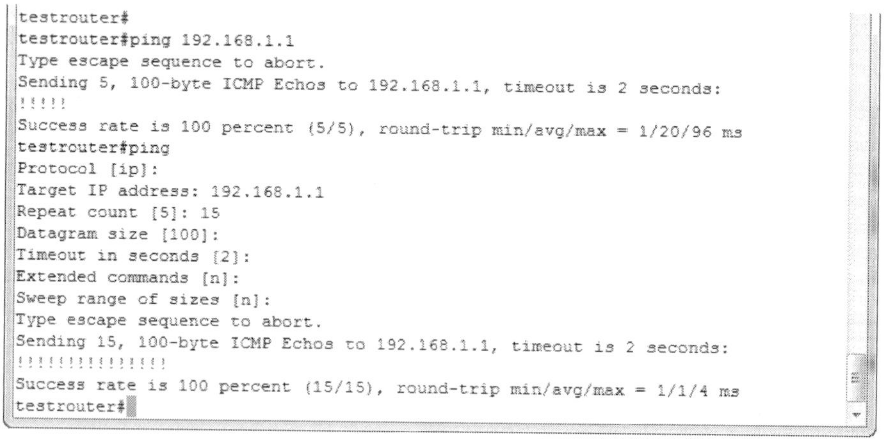

Figure 49:
Using both a standard ping and an extended ping

```
testrouter#
testrouter#ping 192.168.1.1
Type escape sequence to abort.
Sending 5, 100-byte ICMP Echos to 192.168.1.1, timeout is 2 seconds:
!!!!!
Success rate is 100 percent (5/5), round-trip min/avg/max = 1/20/96 ms
testrouter#ping
Protocol [ip]:
Target IP address: 192.168.1.1
Repeat count [5]: 15
Datagram size [100]:
Timeout in seconds [2]:
Extended commands [n]:
Sweep range of sizes [n]:
Type escape sequence to abort.
Sending 15, 100-byte ICMP Echos to 192.168.1.1, timeout is 2 seconds:
!!!!!!!!!!!!!!!
Success rate is 100 percent (15/15), round-trip min/avg/max = 1/1/4 ms
testrouter#
```

On a Computer

The proper procedure for using PING from an IP host follows several logical steps:

- PING 127.0.0.1 to test your IP stack

- PING "localhost" to test for a properly configured HOSTS file

- Run the IPCONFIG utility to determine your host's IP configuration (on a Linux or Unix host, run the command *ifconfig*)

- From the results of IPCONFIG, PING your default gateway

- PING a remote host on the next subnet

The IP Address Rule:

IP addresses, whether network, subnet, or host ID, cannot normally consist of all *binary* ones nor all *binary* zeros.

There are, of course, exceptions to this rule (including the Cisco IOS' support for IP subnet zero). It is, however, an excellent starting point for understanding basics of IP addressing.

A thinking point:

Is 111.111.111.111 a valid IP address? Why or why not?

The answer: It is valid, because it's a decimal number, not binary. If it were a binary representation of an IP address, there would have to be eight 1s or 0s in each section.

Binary Conversion

The easiest way to convert between decimal and binary numbers is, of course, with a calculator. You can use Windows' built-in calculator in scientific mode or download various IP subnet calculators from the Internet. (Search the Internet for IP subnet calculator.) In order to understand the fundamental concepts of IP, however, it's helpful to understand the theory of binary conversion. A table can be used for this purpose in which the columns represent the decimal values of each bit in an eight-bit binary number and the rows represent each of the octets of an IP address to be converted.

Begin by attempting to subtract the decimal value of the leading bit (128) from the value of the first octet (200). Since 128 can be subtracted from 200 (leaving a remainder of 72), put a "1" in the 128s column. Continue by attempting to subtract the decimal value of the next bit (64) from the remainder (72). Since 64 can be subtracted from 72 (leaving a remainder of 8), place a "1" in the 64s column. Next, attempt to subtract the decimal value of the next bit (32) from the remainder (8). Since 32 cannot be subtracted from 8, put a "0" in the 32s column. Continue in this manner until 1s or 0s have been placed in each column.

	128	64	32	16	8	4	2	1
200								
191								
127								
65								

What good does this do?

With every IP address, there is always an associated subnet mask. Notice that the address is a Class C address (its first octet falls within the range of 192-223). How many bits are used for the network portion of any given Class C address? It's the same number as the number of bits that are turned on (represented by 1s) in the subnet mask.

If the bits are turned on in the subnet mask, the corresponding bits in the IP address are network (and/or subnet) bits. In the example, bits 1-24 are turned on in the subnet mask, therefore bits 1-24 of the associated IP address are network bits (and bits 25-32 are host bits).

Now, let's throw a wrench in the works. Suppose that the subnet mask is 255.255.255.192. What happens now?

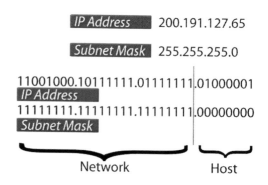

Figure 50: The boundary between network and host in a classful address

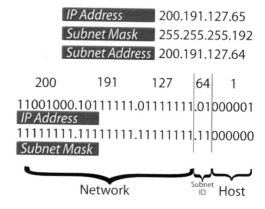

Figure 51: The boundaries between network, subnet, and host in a subnetted address

The dividing line between network and host has moved over two bits, creating a 26 bit network address and a six bit host address. The "major network" address is still actually 24 bits (that's the default for a Class C), but the network designer has taken two bits from the host portion of the address. This creates a subnet of two bits and a subnet mask of 26 bits.

As in the previous example, in order for two hosts to communicate on a network, their network bits in their IP addresses must match, but now there are 26 bits that have to match instead of 24.

Network architects and designers use the practice of subnetting to isolate heavy traffic networks, to minimize broadcasts, and to control excessive WAN traffic.

The purpose of the subnet mask is to identify which bits of the associated IP address are network bits, subnet bits, and host bits.

IP Addressing Design: How Do You Determine the Addresses to Use in Your Network?

The following exercise will help you learn how to design an IP addressing scheme.

Interactive Exercise 3.1:
Home Office and Branches

In this exercise, you will evaluate network needs and design an IP addressing scheme based on your analysis.

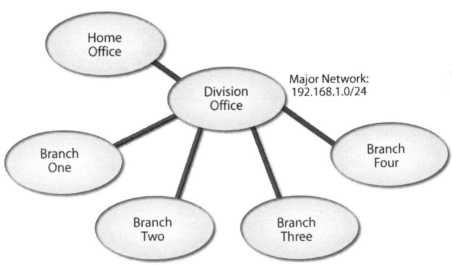

Figure 52: A theoretical network layout

For the purpose of this exercise, assume that each location has no more than 20 hosts at this time and will grow by no more than 50% in the foreseeable future.

- **Step One:** How many subnets are needed? What number of bits borrowed from the host will provide that number?

- **Step Two:** Use the formula of 2^n-2 to determine the number of bits needed to get the necessary number of subnets.

Think of it this way:

- We use "2" because it's the binary number system.

- "N" is the number of bits upon which we're acting.

- We subtract two from the result because we can't use all binary 1's nor or all binary 0's in any Internet address.

Recall the formula 2^n-2: $2^2-2=2$, $2^3-2=6$, $2^4-2=14$, $2^5-2=30$, $2^6-2=62$, etc.

Based on these formulas, we can see that three bits must be borrowed in order to get the needed number of subnets.

- **Step Three:** Create the appropriate subnet mask by turning on three more bits. The default mask is 11111111.11111111.11111111.00000000 or 255.255.255.0. By turning on three more bits we create a mask of 11111111.11111111.11111111.11100000 or 255.255.255.224.

- **Step Four:** Identify the Subnet IDs:

Subnet IDs	128	64	32	16	8	4	2	1
32	0	0	1					
64	0	1	0					
96	0	1	1	Will be used later for host IDs				
128	1	0	0					
160	1	0	1					
192	1	1	0					

- **Step Five:** Add the Subnet IDs to the Major Network Numbers

- Major Network: 192.168.1.0/24

Network Numbers with Subnet IDs:

- 192.168.1.32

- 192.168.1.64

- 192.168.1.96

- 192.168.1.128

- 192.168.1.160

- 192.168.1.192

- **Step Six:** Identify the host IDs

Subnet IDs			Host IDs					
128	64	32	16	8	4	2	1	Decimal Value
			0	0	0	0	1	1
			0	0	0	1	0	2
			0	0	0	1	1	3
	Identified in previous step		0	0	1	0	0	4
			0	0	1	0	1	5
			0	0	1	1	0	6
			0	0	1	1	1	7
			0	1	0	0	0	8

- **Step Seven:** Combine the subnet ID and the host ID to get the fourth octet value:

Subnet IDs			Host IDs					4th Octet Value
128	64	32	16	8	4	2	1	
0	0	1	0	0	0	0	1	

Combine the subnet and the host:

Subnet IDs	1st Host ID	Last Host ID	Range
192.168.1.32	32 + 1 = 33	32 + 30 = 62	192.168.1.33-62
192.168.1.64	64 + 1 = 65	64 + 30 = 94	192.168.1.65-94
192.168.1.96	96 + 1 = 97	96 + 30 = 126	192.168.1.97-126
192.168.1.128	128 + 1 = 129	128 + 30 = 158	192.168.1.128-158
192.168.1.160	160 + 1 = 161	160 + 30 = 190	192.168.1.161-190
192.168.1.192	192 + 1 + 193	192 + 30 = 222	192.168.1.193-222

In a class C network environment, the total number of hosts per subnet will always be two less than the smallest subnet ID number. Note in the example that the lowest subnet ID is 32 (207.201.142.32) and there are 30 hosts per subnet.

Assign to Locations

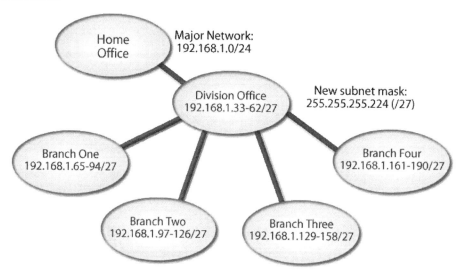

Figure 53: A theoretical network layout with addresses assigned

The Broadcast Address

Broadcasts are used when the unicast address is not known. The broadcast address is determined by turning on all host bits.

Subnet IDs			Host IDs					4th Octet Value
128	64	32	16	8	4	2	1	
1	1	1	1	1	1	1	1	
255								255

A more challenging problem arises when the network is subnetted. It's still the same concept: Turn on all the host bits. The difference is in where the subnet (network) bits end and the host bits begin.

Subnet IDs			Host IDs					4th Octet Value
128	64	32	16	8	4	2	1	
1	0	1	1	1	1	1	1	
160			31					191

Private Range Addresses and Default Subnet Masks

Private Range IPv4 addresses are defined in RFC 1918. You may use these addresses in your private networks and internetworks without fear of conflict with registered host addresses on the public Internet.

- Class A 10.0.0.0/8 (10.h.h.h)

- Class B 172.16.0.0/12 (172.16.h.h-172.31.h.h)

- Class C 192.168.0.0/16 (192.168.0.h-192.168.255.h)

These addresses are known by various names including private space addresses, private range addresses, or RFC 1918 addresses. Some people refer to them as "non-routable" addresses, but that's not really accurate. They're perfectly routable, just not on the public Internet because they will never be included in the Internet routing tables.

Default subnet masks

- Class A is 255.0.0.0 (/8)

- Class B is 255.255.0.0 (/16)

- Class C is 255.255.255.0 (/24)

You must specify at least the default subnet mask.

Notice the use of the "slash" following the above addresses 255.0.0.0/8. Recall from earlier that the slash indicates the number of "1" bits in the mask, so a /8 indicates that the first eight bits are turned on (they're "1s"), resulting in a dotted-decimal mask of 255.0.0.0. A /16 indicates that the first 16 bits are turned on, resulting in a dotted decimal mask of 255.255.0.0. A /24 indicates that the first 24 bits are turned on, resulting in a dotted-decimal mask of 255.255.255.0.

Obtaining an IP Address

IP Addresses are generally obtained through an ISP. For computers that will not be directly connected to the Internet, use private range IP addresses. Do not use any address not assigned to you except for private range addresses.

For more information about IP addresses, visit ICANN.org or InterNIC.net.

Interactive Exercise 3.2:
IP Subnetting and Broadcasts

Calculate the following values for each address on the list below.

- 192.168.1.33/27
- 200.201.193.65/30
- 172.16.66.4/18
- 10.17.0.0/12

> **Bonus Material:** Download my exclusive companion worksheet for this subnetting exercise. It's available at www.soundtraining. net/subnetting-worksheet

1. What is the class of address?

2. What is the address in binary?

3. What is the mask in binary?

4. Calculate the subnet mask (in dotted decimal).

5. What is the subnet ID number? (Remember that the subnet ID and the subnet mask are two totally separate components.)

6. What is the broadcast address?

7. What is the total number of major network bits? Subnet bits? Host bits?

8. How many available subnets? Hosts per subnet?

Example: IP address 207.201.142.65/27 (Remember to convert to binary.)

1. Class of address: C (the first octet is within the range of 192-223, inclusive)

2. Address: 11001111.11001001.10001110.01000001

3. Mask: 11111111.11111111.11111111.11100000

4. Subnet mask: 255.255.255.224

5. Subnet ID #:   64 (You could say "207.201.142.**64**.")

6. Broadcast address: 207.201.142.95

7. Total # of major network bits: 24
   - Total # of subnet bits: 3
   - Total # of host bits: 5

8. Available subnets: 6
   - Hosts per subnet: 30 (Remember 2n-2?)

Internet Protocol Version 6

IPv6 is the replacement for IPv4, the current version of the Internet Protocol. The IPv4 protocol has many limitations including its 32 bit address space which supports only about 4,000,000,000 hosts. In addition, IPv4 is complicated to configure and has no built-in security.

IPv6 is designed to overcome those limitations. Its 128 bit address space supports 2^{128} addresses. That equates to 340 undecillion addresses! IPv6 includes built-in security technologies and supports stateless auto-configuration.

Here is an example of an IPv6 host address: 2001:DB8:3::201/64. The /64 at the end of the address is the subnet mask. It means that the first 64 bits of the address are the network portion and the remaining bits are the host portion. Also, notice the two back-to-back colons (::)? Those indicate a string of zeros. The non-shortened address looks like this: 2001:0DB8:0003:0000:0000:0000:0000:0201/64. Here's an example of an IPv6 network address: 2001:DB8:3::/64. Again, the two back-to-back colons represent a string of zeros. The non-shortened network address looks like this: 2001:0DB:003:0000:0000:0000:0000:0000/64. Again, the /64 represents the subnet mask.

IPv6 is installable as a software upgrade on Internet devices. It is designed for backwards compatibility and interoperability with IPv4 devices. Cisco began limited support for IPv6 in Cisco IOS 12.0S and gradually added full support in subsequent IOS releases. It is also supported by default in most modern computer operating systems.

IPv6 is covered in chapter 14 of this book.

Commands for Configuring IP on Your Router

Commands are available to build a host table linking hostnames to IP addresses, to display the host table, and to assign IP addresses and subnet masks to interfaces.

To assign an IP address and subnet mask (in Interface Configuration Mode): testrouter(config-if)#*ip address [address] [mask]*

For example, if you wanted to assign the address 192.168.101.5 with a mask of 255.255.255.0 to interface Gigabit Ethernet 0/0, you would issue the following sequence of commands:

```
testrouter#
testrouter#conf t
Enter configuration commands, one per line.  End with CNTL/Z.
testrouter(config)#int g0/0
testrouter(config-if)#ip add 192.168.101.5 255.255.255.0
testrouter(config-if)#
```

Figure 54: Assigning an IP address to an interface

You can also tell the router to get its IP address for a particular interface dynamically from a DHCP server with the following command: testrouter(config-if)#*ip address dhcp*

Host Name to IP Address Mapping

A hosts file maps names to IP addresses. To build a host file (in global configuration mode): Router(config)#*ip host [hostname] [IP address]*

```
testrouter#conf t
Enter configuration commands, one per line.  End with CNTL/Z.
testrouter(config)#ip host router01 192.168.0.101
testrouter(config)#ip host router02 192.168.0.102
testrouter(config)#ip host router03 192.168.0.103
testrouter(config)#ip host router04 192.168.0.104
testrouter(config)#ip host computer01 192.168.0.201
```

Figure 55: Configuring static hostname to IP address mapping (a hosts file)

You can display the hosts file on the router with the command *show hosts*.

```
testrouter#show hosts
Default domain is not set
Name/address lookup uses domain service
Name servers are 255.255.255.255

Codes: UN - unknown, EX - expired, OK - OK, ?? - revalidate
       temp - temporary, perm - permanent
       NA - Not Applicable None - Not defined

Host                    Port   Flags      Age Type  Address(es)
router01                None   (perm, OK)  0   IP   192.168.0.101
router02                None   (perm, OK)  0   IP   192.168.0.102
router03                None   (perm, OK)  0   IP   192.168.0.103
router04                None   (perm, OK)  0   IP   192.168.0.104
computer01              None   (perm, OK)  0   IP   192.168.0.201
testrouter#
```

Figure 56: Viewing a router's hosts file

Notice, in the screen capture, that the router shows the name server address as the broadcast address of 255.255.255.255. That means that no name-server is configured and, anytime a host lookup is attempted, the router will do a broadcast looking for a name server. Most networks will include a DNS name server, thus eliminating the need for a static host file like this. You can configure your router to use a DNS server for name lookups with the following command: testrouter(config)#*ip name-server 208.67.222.222*

You can configure up to six name servers on the router.

```
testrouter(config)#ip name-server 208.67.222.222
testrouter(config)#ip name-server 208.67.220.220
testrouter(config)#
```

Figure 57: Configuring name servers on a router

Note: The name servers used in the screen capture are the OpenDNS name servers, which are available for anyone's use.

After you configure name servers on the router, you can ping Internet hosts by name and get a response, as in this example:

Figure 58:
Pinging by host names

```
testrouter#ping www.yahoo.com
Translating "www.yahoo.com"...domain server (208.67.222.222) [OK]

Type escape sequence to abort.
Sending 5, 100-byte ICMP Echos to 72.30.38.140, timeout is 2 seconds:
!!!!!
Success rate is 100 percent (5/5), round-trip min/avg/max = 28/32/36 ms
testrouter#ping www.zombo.com
Translating "www.zombo.com"...domain server (208.67.222.222) [OK]

Type escape sequence to abort.
Sending 5, 100-byte ICMP Echos to 69.16.230.117, timeout is 2 seconds:
!!!!!
Success rate is 100 percent (5/5), round-trip min/avg/max = 76/92/156 ms
testrouter#ping www.ted.com
Translating "www.ted.com"...domain server (208.67.222.222) [OK]

Type escape sequence to abort.
Sending 5, 100-byte ICMP Echos to 72.3.218.115, timeout is 2 seconds:
!!!!!
Success rate is 100 percent (5/5), round-trip min/avg/max = 52/52/52 ms
testrouter#
```

Additionally, when you ping a host after configuring name servers, the hostname-to-IP-address mapping is cached in the router's hosts file, as you can see in the following example:

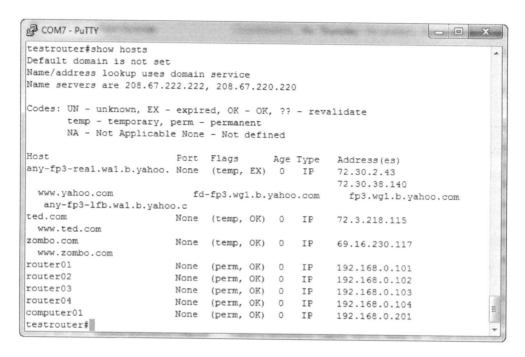

Figure 59: Viewing cached host names on a router

Verifying Address Configuration

Traceroute

Traceroute uses TTL values to generate messages from each router used along the path. "traceroute" shows each router between the source and destination. It probes each router three times and shows the duration of each probe.

PING

PING was created by Mike Muuss of the Army Research Laboratory in December of 1983 in about a day. It was developed in response to network difficulties he encountered.

PING is a very basic testing mechanism that uses ICMP to verify hardware connection and logical address of the network layer. Simple ping works with defaults; extended ping allows custom configuration of the ping. (Use extended ping by entering the command "ping" with no parameters at a privileged EXEC prompt.)

Muuss, the creator of one of the most widely used tools in all of networking, was killed in a car accident on November 20, 2000.

Telnet

Telnet is used to login to a remote site. The successful use of Telnet generally results in the login prompt of the destination host. A successful Telnet attempt verifies application layer software between source and destination stations. Telnet can also be used to test availability of services on a particular port by specifying the port number at the end of the Telnet command: "telnet 192.168.0.1 25" would allow you to connect to an SMTP server. Many administrators today disable Telnet due to security concerns. Here is an example of using Telnet to attempt to retrieve (GET) a file from an HTTP server:

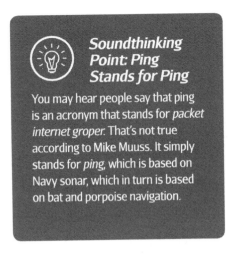

Soundthinking Point: Ping Stands for Ping

You may hear people say that ping is an acronym that stands for *packet internet groper*. That's not true according to Mike Muuss. It simply stands for *ping*, which is based on Navy sonar, which in turn is based on bat and porpoise navigation.

```
testrouter#telnet 192.168.1.1 80
Trying 192.168.1.1, 80 ... Open
GET /index.html HTTP/1.1
host: 192.168.1.1

HTTP/1.0 401 Unauthorized
Date: Tue, 29 May 2012 22:03:00 GMT
Server: Boa/0.94.11
Cache-Control: no-cache
Pragma: no-cache
Expires: 0
Connection: close
WWW-Authenticate: Basic realm="NETGEAR WNR2000"
Content-Type: text/html; charset=UTF-8

<HTML><HEAD><TITLE>401 Unauthorized</TITLE></HEAD>
                                  <BODY><H1>401 Unauthorized</H1
>
  Your client does not have permission to get URL /index.html from this server.
                                                                          </
BODY></HTML>
            [Connection to 192.168.1.1 closed by foreign host]
testrouter#
```

Figure 60: Using telnet to connect via port 80 (HTTP)

In the above example, the HTTP GET request was not successful due to a permissions issue.

Summary

This chapter and chapter fourteen may be the two most important chapters in this book. In my experience, when I receive phone calls asking for help from beginning network admins, the problem is often caused by a lack of understanding of IP addressing. Treat this and chapter fourteen as though you're going to be tested on them, even if you're not. The time you spend understanding IPv4 and IPv6 addressing is time well spent.

CHAPTER 4:
Backing Up and Restoring Configurations

Chapter Introduction

Does this chapter really need an introduction? I mean, don't we all back up our configs and software images? Hmmm, on second thought, perhaps it does need an introduction.

Look, I know the opening paragraph sounds kind of caddy. Here's the thing: In the time that I've been working with Cisco network devices, I've seen several routers, switches, and firewalls fail. I've also seen human frailty (my own as well as that of other people) cause the loss of configs and software images. Once, when I was at a client location (a major enterprise organization), someone accidentally erased the software image from a 3560 switch and they didn't have it backed up. Fortunately, I had a software image on my computer and was able to help them. If I hadn't been on site, they might have had a very expensive doorstop!

Back 'em up!

Chapter Objectives

- Learn how to backup and restore configurations using a terminal window

- Learn how to backup and restore configurations using TFTP

- Learn how to backup and restore the contents of flash memory, including the router's software image, using TFTP

Online Companion Resources

Videos: Watch the companion videos for this chapter. They're available at
www.soundtraining.net/videos/cisco-router-training-videos

Web Page: There is a supporting web page with live links and other resources for this book
at www.soundtraining.net/cisco-router-book

Facebook: www.soundtraining.net/facebook

Twitter: www.soundtraining.net/twitter

Blog: www.soundtraining.net/blog

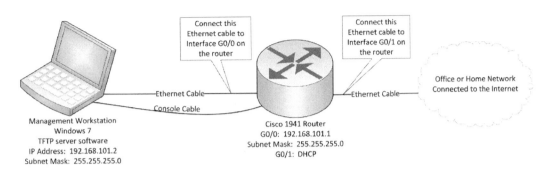

Diagram 2: Backing Up and Restoring Configs and Software Images

How to Backup and Restore Configurations and Software Images

It's easy to backup and restore both configuration files and software images on a Cisco router. The procedures can be done either in the command line environment or in the graphical user interface. In this chapter, I'll show you first how to use the command line interface, then I'll show you how to use the Cisco CP.

Trivial File Transfer Protocol (TFTP)

TFTP is like "FTP-lite" in that it supports basic file transfer operations, but doesn't support much more than that. TFTP operates over UDP port 69. TFTP servers can operate on nearly any platform including Windows and UNIX computers, even another Cisco router. TFTP servers are useful for storing CIOS images, configurations, hosts files, and access control lists.

I recommend the use of tftpd32 or tftpd64, both available for free from http://tftpd32.jounin.net.

Capturing and Sending Text in a Terminal Program

Terminal programs such as HyperTerminal or PuTTY allow you to capture text displayed in their window and save it to a text file. You can also send text from a text file to the programs's window. In addition, you can highlight and copy text anywhere, in any application, and use the paste command to paste text.

When using a terminal program's capture text utility to capture long text files such as a router's running configuration file, you may find it helpful to use the Privileged EXEC mode command "terminal length 0" to eliminate paging the output and preventing "more" statements from being captured. If you don't do this step, you'll need to edit the captured configuration file to remove the "more" statements from the file.

Interactive Exercise 4.1:
Backing Up and Restoring Configurations

This exercise teaches you how to use a terminal program such as PuTTY to capture and restore a router's configuration and a TFTP server to backup and restore a configuration.

Objectives:

- Learn how to save and restore your router's configuration using PuTTY

- Learn how to copy your router's active configuration to a TFTP server

- Learn how to backup and restore configurations using Cisco Configuration Professional

Steps:

You must prepare your computer for the following exercises with these steps:

1. Create a folder called c:\ciscofiles on your computer:

    - Click on Start, then click on My Computer, then double-click on Local Disk (C:) to open the C drive.

    - In the left panel, under File and Folder Tasks, click on "Make a new folder"

    - In the right pane, name the new folder "ciscofiles" and press the Enter key when you're done.

2. For the tftp portion of this exercise, you must first manually configure your management workstation with the IP address indicated on the exercise diagram. If you're not familiar with how to do that, see Appendix A at the end of this book.

Interactive Exercise 4.1.1:
How to Use PuTTY to Capture Text in a Terminal Window

If Your PuTTY Session is Already Running

1. Click on the control button (it's the button in the far upper-left corner of the PuTTY window) to display the control menu.

2. Choose "Change Settings"

3. In the left-hand Category tree, select Logging

4. In the right-hand pane, under "Options controlling session logging", select the radio button for "Printable output."

5. Click on the "Browse…" button to select the location for your log file (perhaps c:\MyConfigs).

6. For the log file name, enter "testrouter&Y&M&D.txt" (That creates a filename of testrouterYearMonthDay.txt, for example, testrouter20120719.txt.)

7. Click "Apply."

8. In the PuTTY terminal window, enter the following commands:

   – testrouter#*terminal length 0* (this prevents the router from paging the output)

   – testrouter#*show run*

   – testrouter#*terminal length 20* (this resets the router to page the output)

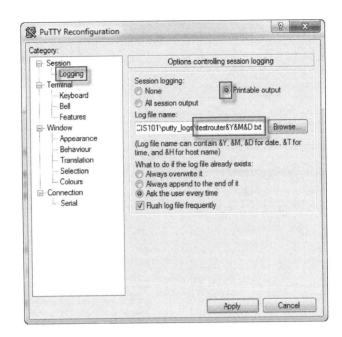

Figure 61: The PuTTY reconfiguration window

9. To stop logging, click on the control button (as before, it's the button in the far upper-left corner of the PuTTY window) to display the control menu.

10. Choose "Change Settings"

11. In the left-hand Category tree, select Logging

12. In the right-hand pane, under "Options controlling session logging", select the radio button for "None."

13. Click "Apply."

If You're Starting a New PuTTY Session

1. Open PuTTY.

2. In the Session window, enter your desired connection information. It is not necessary to click "Apply" at this time.

3. In the left-hand Category tree, select Logging

4. In the right-hand pane, under "Options controlling session logging", select the radio button for "Printable output."

5. Click on the "Browse…" button to select the location for your log file (perhaps c:\MyConfigs).

6. For the log file name, enter "testrouter&Y&M&D.txt" (That creates a filename of testrouterYearMonthDay.txt, for example, testrouter20120719.txt.)

7. Click "Apply."

8. In the PuTTY terminal window, enter the following commands:

    –   testrouter#*terminal length 0* (this prevents the router from paging the output)

    –   testrouter#*show run*

    –   testrouter#*terminal length 20* (this resets the router to page the output)

9. To stop logging, click on the control button (as before, it's the button in the far upper-left corner of the PuTTY window) to display the control menu.

10. Choose "Change Settings"

11. In the left-hand Category tree, select Logging

12. In the right-hand pane, under "Options controlling session logging", select the radio button for "None."

13. Click "Apply."

Interactive Exercise 4.1.2:
Restoring a saved configuration by pasting text in PuTTY

When you have a PuTTY terminal window open, you can paste text into the window starting at the cursor by simply right-clicking with your mouse.

1. Find the file that you backed up in the previous exercise.

2. Clean it up to avoid errors during the restore. The things to remove include the lines at the top of the file before the first exclamation mark and each of the "--more—" statements.

Soundthinking Point: Disable Terminal Paging

One way to simplify the process of restoring a configuration in the terminal window is to disable terminal paging before you start logging with the privileged mode command *terminal length 0*. When you're finished with the logging, you can restore it to the default with the privileged mode command *terminal length 20*.

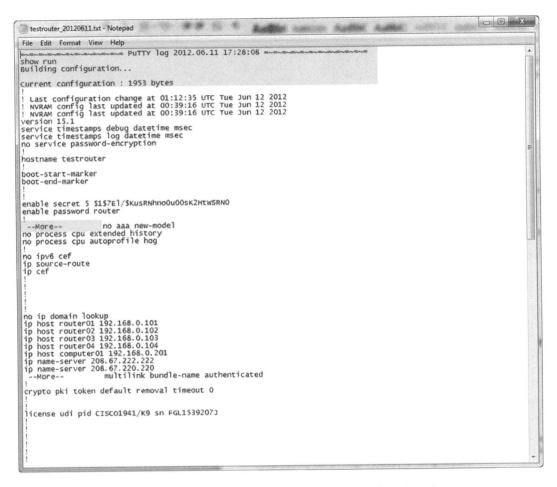

Figure 62: A captured router configuration file before it has been cleaned up

3. Be careful not to remove any parts of the configuration. For example, notice in the screen capture that there is a "--more--" statement on the same line as the statement "no aaa new-model." You want to leave the "no aaa new-model" statement, but remove the "--more--" statement.

4. After you have cleaned up the file, select and copy all of the text (I use the key combination of Ctrl+A in Windows to do that.)

5. Ensure that the router is in global configuration mode (config t)

6. Paste the text into the terminal window by positioning your mouse anywhere within the terminal window and right-clicking with your mouse. (Note: You can right-click anywhere in the terminal window and PuTTY will paste the copied text starting at the cursor position. It is not necessary to carefully position the mouse pointer.)

I've noticed that sometimes the preceding procedure seems to overload a buffer and the terminal window freezes. When that happens, a restart of PuTTY and a repeat of the paste seems to solve the problem.

Interactive Exercise 4.1.3:
Using Trivial File Transfer Protocol

Installing and Configuring the TFTP Server

1. Configure a static IP address and subnet mask on your computer using the address and mask indicated on the network diagram at the beginning of this chapter. It is not necessary to supply any other parameters except an IP address and a mask. (If you're not sure how to manually assign a static IP address, see Appendix A at the end of the book.)

2. On your management workstation, navigate to http://jounin.net, download either tftpd64 or tftpd32 (depending on your platform) and follow the prompts to install the tftpd64 (or tftpd32) server on your computer. (Note: For simplicity, from this point on, I'll refer to the tftpd64 server. You should, obviously, use whichever one is appropriate for your platform.)

3. On your computer, click on Start, then All Programs. Navigate to the folder "tftpd64." Open the folder to find and start tftpd64.

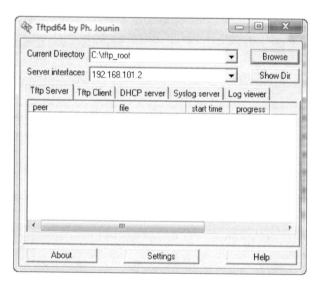

4. In the TFTP Server window, click the button labeled *Browse* and specify the location on your management workstation where you wish to store backups from your router. (I created the folder C:\ tftp_root and chose it for the TFTP server directory.)

5. Leave the TFTP server running for the remainder of the exercises.

Figure 63: The Tftpd64 main window

Note: There are many reasons why I like tftpd64. Among the reasons are its simplicity, its availability for download without complicated registration procedures, and its included DHCP server and syslog server. Click the button labeled *Settings* to see what I mean.

A Rant About Some Websites (You Know Who You Are)

I don't mind registering with a website in order to download valuable tools and other resources, but I get annoyed when I have to jump through a lot of hoops and give up a lot of information. I try to make www.soundtraining.net as easy to use as possible. Yes, you may have to register with your name and email address for some things, but you don't have to re-register over and over again and I won't call you and bug you on the telephone after you register. I'm not namin' names, but you know who you are!

Using TFTP to Backup and Restore Your Router's Configuration

Note: In this exercise, your management workstation is assumed to have an IP address of 192.168.101.2. If it's different, modify the steps in this exercise accordingly.

Use the following commands to backup your router's configuration using TFTP:

1. At the privileged EXEC prompt, type the following command:
    Router#*copy system:running-config tftp://192.168.101.2/testrouter.txt* (all on one line)

2. Accept the prompts for "Address or name of remote host" and "Destination filename."

```
cisco1941#copy system:running-config tftp://192.168.101.2/testrouter.txt
Address or name of remote host [192.168.101.2]?
Destination filename [testrouter.txt]?
!!
5436 bytes copied in 0.176 secs (30886 bytes/sec)

cisco1941#
```

Figure 64: Backing up the router's configuration to a tftp server

3. If you receive an error, confirm that your management workstation's address is 192.168.101.2. If it's not, modify IP address settings, either on the management workstation or in the copy command as necessary to make the exercise work properly.

4. On your management workstation, open the file c:\classfiles\testrouter.txt using Wordpad to review the configuration.

5. Change your router's hostname with the following command:

    - router#*config t*router(config) #*hostname seahawks*

    Enter the following Privileged EXEC command (all on a single line) to restore the backed up configuration from the TFTP server:

    - seahawks#*copy tftp://192.168.101.2/testrouter.txt system:running-config<Enter>*

6. Notice that the prompt has changed to the previous host name because you restored the configuration from your TFTP server.

TFTP can also be used to backup or restore your Cisco IOS in addition to configuration files. Recall from earlier that your router's Cisco IOS is stored in flash memory. You can view the contents of flash memory with the command show flash. The IOS is the file with a name similar to c1900-universalk9-mz. SPA.151-4.M1.bin.

```
cisco1941#show flash
-#- --length-- -----date/time------ path
1     55364328 Sep 18 2011 23:08:28 -08:00 c1900-universalk9-mz.SPA.151-4.M1.bin
2         2903 Sep 18 2011 23:18:14 -08:00 cpconfig-19xx.cfg
3      2941440 Sep 18 2011 23:18:30 -08:00 cpexpress.tar
4         1038 Sep 18 2011 23:18:40 -08:00 home.shtml
5       115712 Sep 18 2011 23:18:48 -08:00 home.tar
6      1697952 Sep 18 2011 23:19:02 -08:00 securedesktop-ios-3.1.1.45-k9.pkg
7       415956 Sep 18 2011 23:19:12 -08:00 sslclient-win-1.1.4.176.pkg

195932160 bytes available (60555264 bytes used)

cisco1941#
```

Figure 65: Viewing the contents of flash memory with the show flash command

Of course, it's always a good idea to maintain backups of your router's IOS, related files, and configuration files. It's an especially good idea to back up the contents of your router's flash memory if you don't maintain a Cisco service contract. Suppose that you accidentally overwrote the IOS image in your router's flash memory. Without a Cisco service contract or a backup, you would have no way of repairing the router, thus rendering the router useless. With a backup, it's a simple matter to restore the router to full functionality.

Interactive Exercise 4.2:
Managing Configurations and Software Images
Using Cisco Configuration Professional

Router configurations and software images can also be managed through Cisco Configuration Professional (CCP), the graphical user interface for Cisco routers. You can download CCP from www.cisco.com. As of this writing, a Cisco.com login is required, but you are not required to have a service contract. As mentioned previously, there is no charge to obtain a Cisco.com login which gives you access to some software such as CCP.

Objectives

- Install Cisco Configuration Professional

- Configure your router to allow connections via HTTP and HTTPS

- Backup router configurations to your management workstation and to your router's NVRAM

Interactive Exercise 4.2.1:
Installing Cisco Configuration Professional

Preparing your router for CCP

In order to run CCP, you must configure your router to allow HTTP and/or HTTPS connections and you must configure a username and password with an admin privilege level.

> **Soundthinking Point: Cisco Privilege Levels**
>
> Many Cisco devices support up to 16 privilege levels, ranging from privilege level 0 to privilege level 15. I'll cover privilege levels in more detail later. For now, you should know the two default privilege levels. Privilege level 1 is user EXEC and privilege level 15 is Privileged EXEC (or admin level). I'll talk more about Cisco privilege levels in chapter 15 when we discuss router security.

1. Configure a username (don) and password (p@ss1234) on the router with admin privilege level (15)

```
testrouter#conf t
Enter configuration commands, one per line.  End with CNTL/Z.
testrouter(config)#username don privilege 15 secret 0 p@ss1234
testrouter(config)#
```

Figure 66:
Configuring a username and password at privilege level 15

2. Enable the http server and the https server on the router with the global configuration mode commands *ip http server* and *ip http secure-server*. Notice, in the screen capture below, how the router generates RSA keys and enables SSH as part of the process.

```
testrouter#conf t
Enter configuration commands, one per line.  End with CNTL/Z.
testrouter(config)#username don privilege 15 secret 0 p@ss1234
testrouter(config)#ip http server
testrouter(config)#ip http secure-server
% Generating 1024 bit RSA keys, keys will be non-exportable...
[OK] (elapsed time was 1 seconds)

testrouter(config)#
Jun 12 23:14:09.939: %SSH-5-ENABLED: SSH 1.99 has been enabled
testrouter(config)#
Jun 12 23:14:10.035: %PKI-4-NOAUTOSAVE: Configuration was modified.  Issue "writ
e memory" to save new certificate
testrouter(config)#
```

Figure 67:
Enabling both the http and the https servers

3. Instruct the router to use the local user database for http authentication and configure http timeout values.

```
testrouter(config)#
testrouter(config)#ip http authentication local
testrouter(config)#ip http timeout-policy idle 60 life 86400 requests 10000
testrouter(config)#
```

Figure 68: Configuring http authentication and timeouts

Interactive Exercise 4.2.2:
Installing CCP on Your Management Workstation

CCP is installed on your management workstation. The following procedures assume that you're installing CCP on a computer running Windows 7. For other operating systems, visit www.cisco.com and search on the term "installing cisco configuration professional."

1. After you have downloaded CCP from cisco.com, you must extract the installer from the .zip file.

2. After the installer has been extracted, you must install it as an administrator. (If you don't install it as an administrator, each time you run it in the future you will have to choose to run it as an administrator.)

3. Right-click on the installer file and choose "Run as administrator"

4. If a previous version of CCP is already installed, the installer will remove it before installing the new version.

5. You must accept the license agreement. Click <**Next**>.

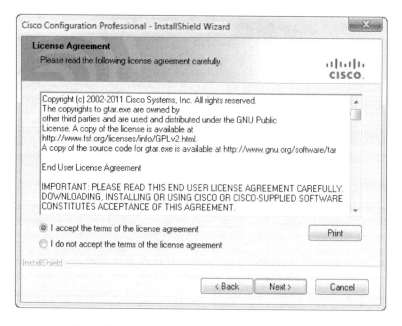

Figure 69: Accept the license agreement to install CCP

6. Confirm the install location and Click **<Next>**.

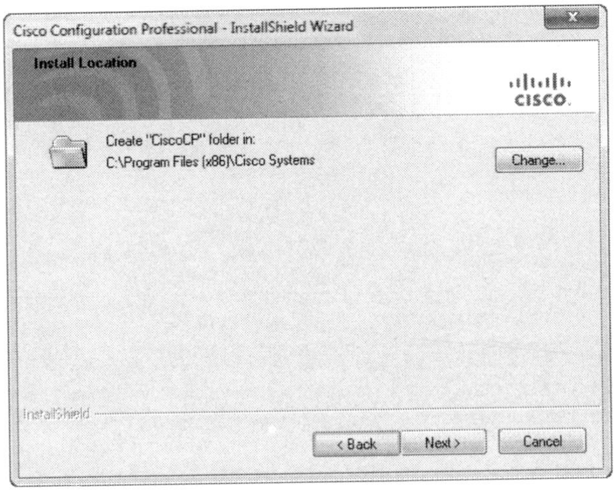

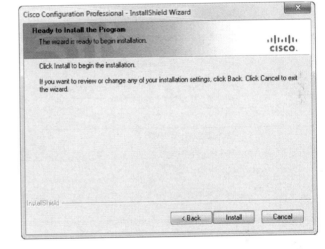

Figure 70:
Confirm the install location

7. Click Install to start the installation process.

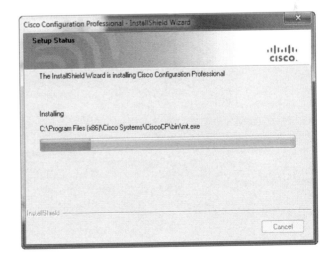

Figure 71:
Starting the installation process

8. The installation process begins.

Figure 72:
The installation process begins

9. The installation process completes.

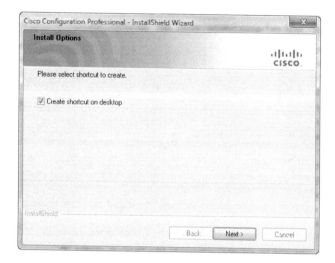

Figure 73:
Install options

10. The installation program performs a system check to ensure your system meets the minimum requirements for CCP. If it doesn't, you will be prompted to install the required software. Assuming your system meets the minimum requirements, Click <Next>.

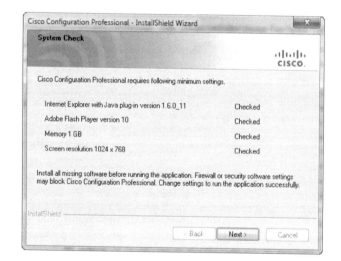

Figure 74:
Installation performs a system check

11. At this point, the installation is complete. Check the box labeled *Run Cisco Configuration Professional* and click Finish.

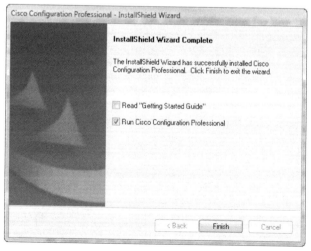

Figure 75:
The installShield Wizard is complete

114

12. Your newly installed CCP will now load.

Figure 76: Starting CCP

Interactive Exercise 4.2.3:
Using CCP to Backup and Restore Configurations

Now that CCP is installed on your management workstation and enabled on your router, you're ready to back up your running-config.

1. If CCP is not already running on your computer, click on the Start button. Navigate on your start menu to Cisco Configuration Professional and click the link to start CCP. (Make sure NOT to click on the demo.)

2. If you receive an error saying "Access denied", kill CCP (you may have to use Task Manager) and restart it by right-clicking on it and choosing "Run as administrator."

3. When CCP opens for the first time, you will have to enter the IP address of your router, along with your username and password (the one you configured earlier).

4. Check the box labeled *Connect Securely* and the box at the bottom labeled *Discover all devices.*

5. Click OK.

Figure 77:
Adding your router to the
CCP default community

6. Accept the Security Certificate Alert. (In the real world, of course, you should confirm that the device you're connecting to is the one to which you planned to connect.) Click the button labeled Yes.

Figure 78:
The CCP Security Certificate Alert

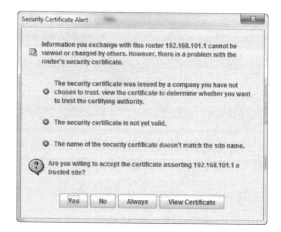

7. In the lower left hand corner of the CCP interface, you'll notice a Utilities section. Click on *Save Configuration to PC*.

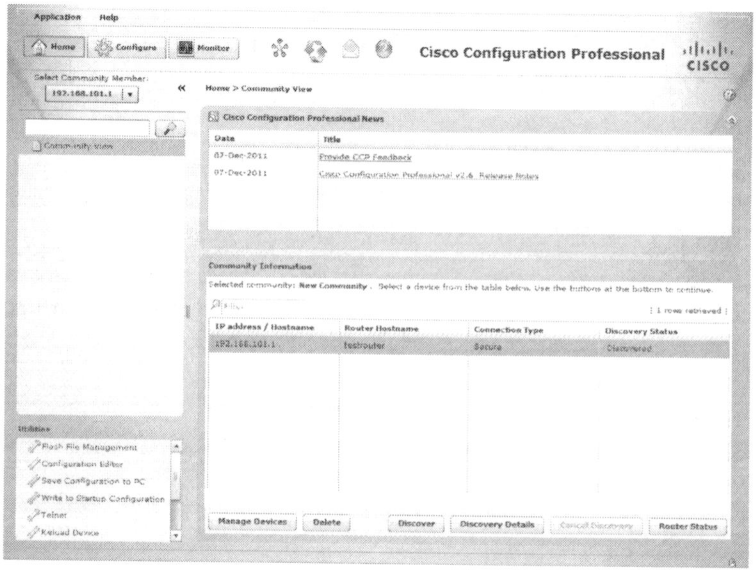

Figure 79:
The CCP interface window

8. A window appears
   with a button
   labeled *Save Running
   Configuration to PC*.
   Click the button.

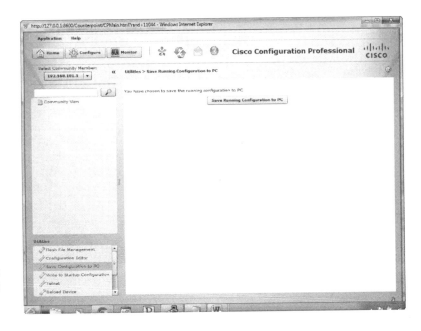

Figure 80:
CCP save running config window

9. A window appears prompting you for
   the location where you wish to save the
   configuration file. Notice that the default
   name of the file is the router's hostname
   combined with the current date. When
   you're satisfied with the save location,
   click the button labeled Save.

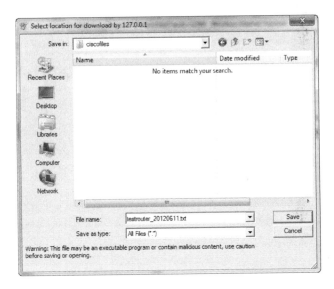

Figure 81:
Choosing a save location for
the configuration file

10. Your configuration is now backed up to the location you chose. You can use a text editor such as
    Notepad, Wordpad, or Notepad++ (my favorite) to view the saved configuration.

11. Save the running-config to the startup-config by using the CCP Utilities. Again, in the lower left-hand corner of the CCP interface, click the link labeled *Write to Startup Configuration*.

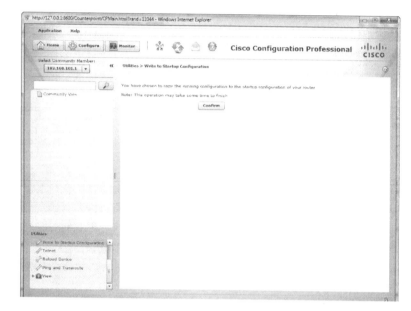

Figure 82:
The CCP "Write to Startup Configuration" window

12. Click the button labeled *Confirm*

Figure 83: Confirming the saved configuration

You have now successfully backed up your router's configuration to both your management workstation and your router's NVRAM.

Summary

I want to make two points in this chapter summary. The first pertains to the importance of performing backups. When you first take your new router out of the box, back up the contents of its flash memory. That way, when something weird happens and you lose the software images, you'll have access to an immediate backup without having to download the software from Cisco. If you don't have a Cisco service contract, you won't be permitted to download the software from Cisco which means that your fancy new router is really just a fancy doorstop. Back up your flash memory. Also, back up your configuration. By the time you put your router into production, you'll probably have a lot of time devoted to building its configuration. It really sucks when something weird happens and you lose your configuration. Back up your configuration from NVRAM.

The second point I want to make is about graphical versus command-line interfaces. As I mentioned before, I believe in learning to operate a network device at its command-line for all the reasons I discussed earlier. Still, you may prefer to use graphical tools such as Cisco Configuration Professional. I won't laugh at you if you choose to do that. There's nothing inherently wrong with using a graphical interface. In this chapter, I've shown you how to install the GUI and how to perform a simple task with it. The rest of book deals with the command-line interface.

At some point in the not-too-distant future, graphical tools such as CCP may come to dominate over CLI-based tools. For now, however, the Cisco CLI offers the best combination of speed, reliability, and power for the network administrator.

CHAPTER 5:
Monitoring Your Router

Chapter Introduction

This chapter is all about the *show* commands. The *show* command may be the most-used of all the Cisco commands. It's available on every platform that I've worked with. Use *show* to find out how your router is configured from both a software and a hardware perspective. If you're not sure what *show* options are available, remember your best friend in Cisco-dom, the question mark. In privileged mode, use *show ?* to see what your options are.

Chapter Objectives

- Learn some of the more frequently used *show* commands

- Analyze the output of various *show* commands

- Learn how to configure and manage the Cisco Discovery Protocol

Online Companion Resources

Videos: Watch the companion videos for this chapter. They're available at
www.soundtraining.net/videos/cisco-router-training-videos

Web Page: There is a supporting web page with live links and other resources for this book
at www.soundtraining.net/cisco-router-book

Facebook: www.soundtraining.net/facebook

Twitter: www.soundtraining.net/twitter

Blog: www.soundtraining.net/blog

The "show" Family of Commands

Show Version

"Show Version" displays the boot ROM version, the IOS version, IOS image file name, interfaces, configuration register, among other things. In the following screen capture, the ROM version is 12.4(13r) T5 and the system has been up for 19 hours and 17 minutes. The router was last started with a reload command. The system image file was loaded from flash memory. The router has 239K of NVRAM and 62720K of CompactFlash memory. The configuration register is a software register value that tells the router how to boot. On this router, it's set to the default of 0x2102 which tells the router to load its IOS image from flash memory and its configuration file from NVRAM.

```
router01#
router01#show version
Cisco IOS Software, 2800 Software (C2800NM-ADVIPSERVICESK9-M), Version 12.3(14)T5, RELEASE SOFTWA
RE (fc2)
Technical Support: http://www.cisco.com/techsupport
Copyright (c) 1986-2005 by Cisco Systems, Inc.
Compiled Mon 24-Oct-05 21:43 by kellythw

ROM: System Bootstrap, Version 12.4(13r)T5, RELEASE SOFTWARE (fc1)

router01 uptime is 19 hours, 17 minutes
System returned to ROM by reload at 21:58:23 UTC Sat Nov 22 2008
System image file is "flash:c2800nm-advipservicesk9-mz.123-14.T5.bin"


This product contains cryptographic features and is subject to United
States and local country laws governing import, export, transfer and
use. Delivery of Cisco cryptographic products does not imply
third-party authority to import, export, distribute or use encryption.
Importers, exporters, distributors and users are responsible for
compliance with U.S. and local country laws. By using this product you
agree to comply with applicable laws and regulations. If you are unable
to comply with U.S. and local laws, return this product immediately.

A summary of U.S. laws governing Cisco cryptographic products may be found at:
http://www.cisco.com/wwl/export/crypto/tool/stqrg.html

If you require further assistance please contact us by sending email to
export@cisco.com.

Cisco 2821 (revision 53.51) with 512000K/12288K bytes of memory.
Processor board ID FTX0943A1UR
2 Gigabit Ethernet interfaces
1 Virtual Private Network (VPN) Module
DRAM configuration is 64 bits wide with parity enabled.
239K bytes of non-volatile configuration memory.
62720K bytes of ATA CompactFlash (Read/Write)

Configuration register is 0x2102

router01#
```

Figure 84: The output from the "show version" command on a Cisco 2821 router

Notice the differences in the output of the same command on a Cisco 871 router. Pay particular attention to the differences in interfaces between the two routers.

```
router04#
router04#show version
Cisco IOS Software, C870 Software (C870-ADVIPSERVICESK9-M), Version 12.4(15)T6, RELEASE SOFTWARE
(fc2)
Technical Support: http://www.cisco.com/techsupport
Copyright (c) 1986-2008 by Cisco Systems, Inc.
Compiled Mon 07-Jul-08 20:49 by prod_rel_team

ROM: System Bootstrap, Version 12.3(8r)YI4, RELEASE SOFTWARE

router04 uptime is 18 hours, 20 minutes
System returned to ROM by power-on
System image file is "flash:c870-advipservicesk9-mz.124-15.T6.bin"


This product contains cryptographic features and is subject to United
States and local country laws governing import, export, transfer and
use. Delivery of Cisco cryptographic products does not imply
third-party authority to import, export, distribute or use encryption.
Importers, exporters, distributors and users are responsible for
compliance with U.S. and local country laws. By using this product you
agree to comply with applicable laws and regulations. If you are unable
to comply with U.S. and local laws, return this product immediately.

A summary of U.S. laws governing Cisco cryptographic products may be found at:
http://www.cisco.com/wwl/export/crypto/tool/stqrg.html

If you require further assistance please contact us by sending email to
export@cisco.com.

Cisco 871 (MPC8272) processor (revision 0x300) with 118784K/12288K bytes of memory.
Processor board ID FHK1231245H
MPC8272 CPU Rev: Part Number 0xC, Mask Number 0x10
5 FastEthernet interfaces
128K bytes of non-volatile configuration memory.
28672K bytes of processor board System flash (Intel Strataflash)

Configuration register is 0x2102

router04#
```

Figure 85: The output from the "show version" command on a Cisco 871 router

Show Processes

"Show processes" is similar to opening the Task Manager in Windows. It allows you to observe information about processes currently running on the router.

The following table explains the meaning of each of the columns in the output. At the very top of the output, "CPU utilization for five seconds" shows CPU utilization for the last five seconds. The second number displays the percent of total CPU time spent at the interrupt level. "One minute" displays CPU utilization for the last minute, and "five minutes" is for the last five minutes.

Column	Description
PID	Process ID
Q	Process queue priority. Possible values include L (low), H (high), and C (critical).
Ty	Scheduler Test
PC	Current program counter
Runtime (uS)	Amount of CPU time, in microseconds, the process has used
Invoked	Number of times the process has been invoked
uSecs	Microseconds of CPU time for each time the process was invoked
Stacks	Low water mark or Total stack space available, expressed in bytes
TTY	The terminal controlling the process
Process	The name of the process

An explanation of the each of the processes displayed in the show processes command is beyond the scope of this book, but is available at www.cisco.com. Search on the term "The show processes command."

```
R1#show processes
CPU utilization for five seconds: 0%/0%; one minute: 0%; five minutes: 0%
 PID QTy       PC Runtime (ms)    Invoked   uSecs   Stacks TTY Process
   1 Cwe 803466B0          0          1        0 5740/6000    0 Chunk Manager
   2 Csp 80320C14       1832        549     3336 2672/3000    0 Load Meter
   3 M*         0        836        126     6634 9872/12000   0 Exec
   4 Lst 80343914       2780        323     8606 5568/6000    0 Check heaps
   5 Cwe 8034C184          0          1        0 5704/6000    0 Pool Manager
   6 Mst 801F6994          4          2     2000 5640/6000    0 Timers
   7 Mwe 800BB820          4          2     2000 5648/6000    0 Serial Backgroun
   8 Mwe 801B2824          0          2        0 5640/6000    0 AAA high-capacit
   9 Lwe 801B76D0          0          1        0 5788/6000    0 AAA_SERVER_DEADT
  10 Mwe 8021CFE8          0          1   011724/12000        0 Policy Manager
  11 Mwe 80278620          0          1   023660/24000        0 Crash writer
  12 Mwe 802F8878          0          1        0 5784/6000    0 RO Notify Timers
  13 Mwe 803F1A88          0         49        0 5720/6000    0 ARP Input
  14 Mwe 80414FB4          0          3        0 5636/6000    0 DDR Timers
  15 Mwe 8076BE18          4        138       28 5776/6000    0 HC Counter Timer
  16 Lwe 80AE2CFC         32          2    16000 5472/6000    0 Entity MIB API
  17 Mwe 80D69A44         24         11     2181 8548/9000    0 EEM ED Syslog
  18 Mwe 8000AE20          0          2        0 5652/6000    0 SMART
  19 Mwe 800C2448          0          1        0 5760/6000    0 SERIAL A'detect
  20 Msp 8024C830          8       2740        2 5680/6000    0 GraphIt
  21 Mwe 80431600          4          2 200011648/12000       0 Dialer event
  22 Mwe 8070D868          0          2   011664/12000        0 XML Proxy Client
  23 Cwe 802ED0D8          0          1        0 5752/6000    0 Critical Bkgnd
  24 Mwe 80290264        308       1079 28510128/12000        0 Net Background
 --More--
```

Figure 86: The output from the "show processes" command on a Cisco 1721 router

Show Flash

Show flash lists bootflash or Flash PC card information, including file code names, version numbers, status, and sizes. If the flash has been partitioned, each partition and its content will also be displayed.

Notice the difference in the output of *show flash* on an old Cisco 2501 router (The 2501 router was end-of-life'd in 2002.) compared to a more modern Cisco 2821 router. The Cisco 2501 router has a single IOS file in its flash memory, while the Cisco 2821 router includes an IOS image file, plus a SDM file, a base configuration file, and a variety of other files. As with computer operating systems, Cisco routers have grown more complex over time and the number of files required for their operation has also grown.

Another interesting point is to compare the file size of the 2501's IOS image to that of the 2821. Notice that the 2501's IOS image (c2500-is-l.122-8.T4.bin) is about 14MB in size, while the 2821's IOS image is about 32 MB. There's actually an even greater disparity that what you see, because the 2821's IOS image is compressed and the 2501's is not. You can tell when an IOS image is compressed because of the "z" in the filename. Notice that there is no "z" in the filename of the IOS on a 2501 router, but the filename of the IOS on a 2821 router (c2800nm-advipservericesk9-mz.123-14.T5.bin) includes a "z", meaning it is zip compressed.

```
router1#show flash

System flash directory:
File  Length    Name/status
  1   13863004  /c2500-is-l.122-8.T4.bin
[13863068 bytes used, 2914148 available, 16777216 total]
16384K bytes of processor board System flash (Read ONLY)
```

Figure 87: The output from the "show flash" command on a Cisco 2501 router

```
router01#
router01#show flash
-#- --length-- -----date/time------  path
1      230754 Nov 06 2007 12:15:14 +00:00 crashinfo_20071106-201515
2        1649 Oct 18 2005 20:11:46 +00:00 sdmconfig-28xx.cfg
3     4052480 Oct 18 2005 20:12:12 +00:00 sdm.tar
4      812032 Oct 18 2005 20:12:28 +00:00 es.tar
5     1007616 Oct 18 2005 20:12:44 +00:00 common.tar
6        1038 Oct 18 2005 20:13:00 +00:00 home.shtml
7      113152 Oct 18 2005 20:13:18 +00:00 home.tar
8      511939 Oct 18 2005 20:13:34 +00:00 128MB.sdf
9    31849272 Dec 16 2005 18:30:38 +00:00 c2800nm-advipservicesk9-mz.123-14.T5.bin
10     230558 May 17 2008 02:28:16 +00:00 crashinfo_20080517-092816

25186304 bytes available (38830080 bytes used)

router01#
```

Figure 88: The output from the "show flash" command on a Cisco 2821 router.

Show Protocols

Show protocols displays the configured transport protocols (such as IP or legacy protocols, like DECNet, AppleTalk, or IPX/SPX, if they've been configured) and the interfaces on which they're running.

Figure 89:
Output from "show protocols on a Cisco 1721 router"

```
router04#show protocols
Global values:
  Internet Protocol routing is enabled
FastEthernet0/0 is up, line protocol is up
  Internet address is 200.200.200.4/29
Serial0/0 is up, line protocol is up
  Internet address is 172.16.1.4/29
FastEthernet0/1 is administratively down, line protocol is down
Serial0/1 is up, line protocol is up
  Internet address is 24.1.1.4/29
FastEthernet1/0 is administratively down, line protocol is down
router04#
```

Show CDP Neighbors

show cdp neighbors uses the Cisco Discovery Protocol, a layer two protocol, which is independent of both media and protocols, to display information about directly connected Cisco devices including routers, switches, bridges, and access servers.

```
router01#
router01#show cdp neighbors
Capability Codes: R - Router, T - Trans Bridge, B - Source Route Bridge
                  S - Switch, H - Host, I - IGMP, r - Repeater

Device ID          Local Intrfce      Holdtme    Capability  Platform   Port ID
router02           Gig 0/0            145        R S I       2821       Gig 0/0
kilgen.soundtraining.local
                   Gig 0/0            128          T S       WS-C2912-XFas 0/3
router04           Gig 0/0            123        R S I       871        Fas 4
router01#
```

Figure 90:
Output from "show cdp neighbors" on a router connected to a 2821 router, an 871 router, and a 2912 switch

In this example, router01 is connected to router04 through its own Gigabit Ethernet 0/0 interface (the Local Interface) and through router04's Fast Ethernet 4 interface (the Port ID). The hold time indicates how long (in seconds) the information is valid for the port. The capability is for the remote device, in this case "R" stands for router. The platform is the device family of the remote device, in this case an 871 router.

Show CDP Neighbor Detail

The *show cdp neighbor detail* command also connects via the layer two Cisco Discovery Protocol to retrieve information about directly connected neighbors. It, however, provides much more detail, including IP and IPv6 addresses, as you can see in the following screen capture.

```
router02#show cdp neighbor detail
-------------------------
Device ID: router03
Entry address(es):
  IP address: 24.1.2.3
  IPv6 address: FE80::222:55FF:FEE2:300  (link-local)
  IPv6 address: 2001:DB8:3:0:222:55FF:FEE2:300  (global unicast)
Platform: Cisco 871,  Capabilities: Router Switch IGMP
Interface: GigabitEthernet0/0,  Port ID (outgoing port): FastEthernet4
Holdtime : 153 sec

Version :
Cisco IOS Software, C870 Software (C870-ADVIPSERVICESK9-M), Version 12.4(15)T6, RELEASE SOFTWAR
E (fc2)
Technical Support: http://www.cisco.com/techsupport
Copyright (c) 1986-2008 by Cisco Systems, Inc.
Compiled Mon 07-Jul-08 20:49 by prod_rel_team

advertisement version: 2
VTP Management Domain: ''
Duplex: full

-------------------------
Device ID: router01
Entry address(es):
  IPv6 address: FE80::21A:E2FF:FE19:AAD  (link-local)
 --More--
```

Figure 91:
The output of the "show cdp neighbor detail" command on a router running both IPv4 and IPv6

Show IP Protocols

Show IP Protocols displays the current state and parameters of active routing protocol processes. This is a very useful command in troubleshooting routing operations.

Figure 92:
Output from "show ip protocols" on a 2501 router with RIP and the legacy IGRP routing protocol enabled (Note: IGRP is deprecated and is no longer supported on current router platforms.)

```
Routing Protocol is "rip"
  Sending updates every 30 seconds, next due in 2 seconds
  Invalid after 180 seconds, hold down 180, flushed after 240
  Outgoing update filter list for all interfaces is not set
  Incoming update filter list for all interfaces is not set
  Redistributing: rip
  Default version control: send version 1, receive any version
    Interface             Send  Recv  Triggered RIP  Key-chain
    Ethernet0             1     1 2
    Serial0               1     1 2
  Automatic network summarization is in effect
  Maximum path: 4
  Routing for Networks:
    10.0.0.0
    192.168.1.0
  Routing Information Sources:
    Gateway         Distance      Last Update
    10.16.0.2            120       00:00:19
    192.168.1.34         120       00:00:20
  Distance: (default is 120)

Routing Protocol is "igrp 1"
  Sending updates every 90 seconds, next due in 39 seconds
--More-- _
```

Show IP Route

Show IP Route displays the current routing table, including static and directly-connected routes, plus routes discovered through routing protocols. I'll spend more time with the *show ip route* command later in the routing section of the book.

I'll also spend time with the similar command *show ipv6 route* in chapter 14 of the book when I focus on Internet Protocol version 6.

Figure 93:
Show IP route on a legacy 2501 router. Note the inclusion of the legacy IGRP protocol routes, identified by an "I" in the routing table

```
router1#show ip rou
Codes: C - connected, S - static, I - IGRP, R - RIP, M - mobile, B - BGP
       D - EIGRP, EX - EIGRP external, O - OSPF, IA - OSPF inter area
       N1 - OSPF NSSA external type 1, N2 - OSPF NSSA external type 2
       E1 - OSPF external type 1, E2 - OSPF external type 2, E - EGP
       i - IS-IS, L1 - IS-IS level-1, L2 - IS-IS level-2, ia - IS-IS inter area
       * - candidate default, U - per-user static route, o - ODR
       P - periodic downloaded static route

Gateway of last resort is not set

I    172.16.0.0/16 [100/8576] via 192.168.1.34, 00:00:53, Serial0
     10.0.0.0/12 is subnetted, 1 subnets
C       10.16.0.0 is directly connected, Ethernet0
I    160.254.0.0/16 [100/8576] via 10.16.0.2, 00:00:04, Ethernet0
     192.168.1.0/27 is subnetted, 1 subnets
C       192.168.1.32 is directly connected, Serial0
```

Show Interfaces

Show Interfaces displays statistics for each interface configured on the router.

```
Serial0 is up, line protocol is up
  Hardware is HD64570
  Internet address is 192.168.1.33/27
  MTU 1500 bytes, BW 1544 Kbit, DLY 20000 usec,
     reliability 255/255, txload 1/255, rxload 1/255
  Encapsulation HDLC, loopback not set
  Keepalive set (10 sec)
  Last input 00:00:05, output 00:00:00, output hang never
  Last clearing of "show interface" counters never
  Input queue: 0/75/0/0 (size/max/drops/flushes); Total output drops: 0
  Queueing strategy: weighted fair
  Output queue: 0/1000/64/0 (size/max total/threshold/drops)
     Conversations  0/1/256 (active/max active/max total)
     Reserved Conversations 0/0 (allocated/max allocated)
     Available Bandwidth 1158 kilobits/sec
  5 minute input rate 0 bits/sec, 0 packets/sec
  5 minute output rate 0 bits/sec, 0 packets/sec
     308 packets input, 19470 bytes, 0 no buffer
     Received 308 broadcasts, 0 runts, 0 giants, 0 throttles
     0 input errors, 0 CRC, 0 frame, 0 overrun, 0 ignored, 0 abort
     312 packets output, 20406 bytes, 0 underruns
     0 output errors, 0 collisions, 2 interface resets
     0 output buffer failures, 0 output buffers swapped out
--More-- _
```

Figure 94:
The output of the "show interfaces"
command on a 2501 router

Show Startup-Config and Show Running-Config

Show startup-config and *show running-config* display the router's configuration files. *show startup-config* displays the saved (or backup) configuration file stored in NVRAM. *show running-config* displays the current (or active) configuration running in the router's dynamic RAM.

```
Current configuration : 1159 bytes
!
version 12.2
service timestamps debug uptime
service timestamps log uptime
no service password-encryption
!
hostname router1
!
enable secret 5 $1$6D6.$wlAHiblymyobBC8fb7eHC/
enable password router
!
ip subnet-zero
no ip domain-lookup
ip host ws4 172.16.66.14
ip host ws3 172.16.65.13
ip host ws2 10.16.0.12
ip host ws1 10.16.0.11
ip host switch4 172.16.66.24
ip host switch3 172.16.65.23
ip host switch2 10.16.0.22
ip host switch1 10.16.0.21
--More-- _
```

Figure 95:
Output from "show startup-config"
or "show running-config"

Show Terminal

Show terminal displays configuration information for the current terminal line.

```
Line 0, Location: "", Type: ""
Length: 24 lines, Width: 80 columns
Status: PSI Enabled, Ready, Active, Automore On
Capabilities: none
Modem state: Ready
Special Chars: Escape  Hold  Stop  Start  Disconnect  Activation
                ^^x     none   -     -      none
Timeouts:      Idle EXEC      Idle Session     Modem Answer  Session    Dispatch
                never          never                          none       not set
                              Idle Session Disconnect Warning
                               never
                              Login-sequence User Response
                               00:00:30
                              Autoselect Initial Wait
                               not set
Modem type is unknown.
Session limit is not set.
Time since activation: 00:39:06
Editing is enabled.
History is enabled, history size is 10.
DNS resolution in show commands is enabled
Full user help is disabled
Allowed input transports are none.
--More-- _
```

Figure 96:
The output of the
"show terminal"
command

Additional Show Commands

In this section, I've covered the most commonly used show commands. As you can imagine, there are many others. You can see which show commands are available on your router by using the question mark with the show command.

```
router02#show ?
  aaa                Show AAA values
  access-expression  List access expression
  access-lists       List access lists
  adjacency          Adjacent nodes
  aliases            Display alias commands
  alignment          Show alignment information
  archive            Archive functions
  arp                ARP table
  async              Information on terminal lines used as router interfaces
  auto               Show Automation Template
  autoupgrade        Show autoupgrade related information
  backup             Backup status
  beep               Show BEEP information
  bgp                BGP information
  bridge             Bridge Forwarding/Filtering Database [verbose]
  buffers            Buffer pool statistics
  calendar           Display the hardware calendar
  call               Show call
  call-home          Show command for call home
  caller             Display information about dialup connections
  capability         Capability Information
  cca                CCA information
  cdapi              CDAPI information
  --More--
```

Figure 97:
Using the question
mark to display "show"
command options

Filter Output from the Show Command

Sometimes the output from the *show* command is so long that it'd difficult to find what you need. The Cisco IOS offers output filtering capabilities to narrow the output. To use the filtering capability, issue a show command as normal, but follow it with the pipe (|) symbol, the filter type, and the filtering term. For example, if you want to use the show run command to view your interface configuration, type the following in privileged mode:

Router#*show run | section interface*

Figure 98:
Filtering output from the
"show run" command

```
router02#show run | section interface
interface Embedded-Service-Engine0/0
 no ip address
 shutdown
 no cdp enable
interface GigabitEthernet0/0
 no ip address
 duplex auto
 speed auto
 ipv6 address dhcp
 ipv6 address 2001:DB8:3::201/64
 ipv6 address autoconfig default
 ipv6 enable
 ipv6 rip process_01 enable
 ipv6 eigrp 61
 no mop enabled
interface GigabitEthernet0/1
 no ip address
 duplex auto
 speed auto
 ipv6 address 2001:DB8:2::201/64
 ipv6 enable
 ipv6 rip process_01 enable
 ipv6 eigrp 61
router02#
```

There are several filtering options, as you can see in the following screen capture.

```
router02#
router02#show run | ?
   append    Append redirected output to URL (URLs supporting append operation only)
   begin     Begin with the line that matches
   exclude   Exclude lines that match
   format    Format the output using the specified spec file
   include   Include lines that match
   redirect  Redirect output to URL
   section   Filter a section of output
   tee       Copy output to URL

router02#show run |
```

Figure 99: Cisco IOS filtering options

Interactive Exercise 5.1:
Router Monitoring

This exercise shows various commands used to monitor and analyze your Cisco router.

Objectives:

- Understand the variety of commands available for analyzing router hardware, software and configuration

- Learn how to use the *show* family of commands to view the hardware, software and memory installed on your router

Steps:

1. Log in to your router and get to either user mode or privileged mode.

2. Use the **show version** command to display hardware and Cisco IOS information about your router. The results of the **show version** command will allow you to identify many aspects of your router's base configuration. For this command, I used the output from "show version" on a 1941 router. Your results may be different. On your router, in either user mode or privileged mode, issue the command **show version**.

```
testrouter#show version
Cisco IOS Software, C1900 Software (C1900-UNIVERSALK9-M), Version 15.1(4)M1, RELEASE SOFTWARE (fc1)
Technical Support: http://www.cisco.com/techsupport
Copyright (c) 1986-2011 by Cisco Systems, Inc.
Compiled Tue 14-Jun-11 17:44 by prod_rel_team

ROM: System Bootstrap, Version 15.0(1r)M12, RELEASE SOFTWARE (fc1)

testrouter uptime is 34 minutes
System returned to ROM by power-on
System restarted at 17:50:01 UTC Thu Jun 2
System image file is "flash0:c1900-universalk9-mz.SPA.151-4.M1.bin"
Last reload type: Normal Reload
```

IOS Version

Boostrap Version

Router has been operating for 34 minutes

IOS was loaded from flash memory

```
This product contains cryptographic features and is subject to United
States and local country laws governing import, export, transfer and
use. Delivery of Cisco cryptographic products does not imply
third-party authority to import, export, distribute or use encryption.
Importers, exporters, distributors and users are responsible for
compliance with U.S. and local country laws. By using this product you
agree to comply with applicable laws and regulations. If you are unable
to comply with U.S. and local laws, return this product immediately.

A summary of U.S. laws governing Cisco cryptographic products may be found at:
http://www.cisco.com/wwl/export/crypto/tool/stqrg.html

If you require further assistance please contact us by sending email to
export@cisco.com.

Cisco CISCO1941/K9 (revision 1.0) with 491520K/32768K bytes of memory.
Processor board ID FGL1539207J
2 Gigabit Ethernet interfaces
1 terminal line
DRAM configuration is 64 bits wide with parity disabled.
255K bytes of non-volatile configuration memory.
250880K bytes of ATA System CompactFlash 0 (Read/Write)


License Info:

License UDI:

--------------------------------------------------
Device#   PID               SN
--------------------------------------------------
*0        CISCO1941/K9      FGL1539207J



Technology Package License Information for Module:'c1900'

----------------------------------------------------------------
Technology    Technology-package        Technology-package
              Current      Type         Next reboot
----------------------------------------------------------------
ipbase        ipbasek9     Permanent    ipbasek9
security      None         None         None
data          None         None         None

Configuration register is 0x2102

testrouter#
```

There are two Gigabit Ethernet Interfaces

The configuration register is 0x2102

Figure 100: The output of the "show version" command on a Cisco 1941 router

133

- What version of the IOS is running?

  - 15.1(4)M1

- What version of the System Bootstrap is in ROM?

  - 15.0(1r)M12

- How long has the router been operating?

  - 34 minutes

- How was the router last restarted (returned to ROM)?

  - Power-on

- The IOS was loaded from where?

  - Flash0

- What are the types and number of interfaces on the router?

  - Two Gigabit Ethernet interfaces

- How much non-volatile configuration memory (NVRAM) is installed on the router?

  - 255 Kilobytes

- How much flash memory is installed on the router?

  - 250880 Kilobytes

- The configuration register tells the router how and from where to load its configuration file. What is the setting for the current software configuration register?

  - 0x2102

3. In much the same way that Windows Task Manager displays running processes, a Cisco router can display running processes by using the "show processes" command. Issue the command *show processes* on your router. (For an explanation of each of the columns, see earlier in this chapter. For an explanation of each of the processes, visit www.cisco.com and search on the term "the show processes command.")

4. Remember that the Cisco IOS is usually loaded from Flash memory. You can display the contents of flash memory with the "show flash" command. From the "show flash" command, you can view the amount of flash memory installed on your router and the size of the Cisco IOS image(s) stored in flash memory. Depending on the naming convention used for your Cisco IOS image, you might also be able to identify the version of the CIOS stored in Flash. Issue the command *show flash*.

```
testrouter#show flash
-#- --length-- -----date/time------ path
1      55364328 Sep 19 2011 07:08:28 +00:00 c1900-universalk9-mz.SPA.151-4.M1.bin
2          2903 Sep 19 2011 07:18:14 +00:00 cpconfig-19xx.cfg
3       2941440 Sep 19 2011 07:18:30 +00:00 cpexpress.tar
4          1038 Sep 19 2011 07:18:40 +00:00 home.shtml
5        115712 Sep 19 2011 07:18:48 +00:00 home.tar
6       1697952 Sep 19 2011 07:19:02 +00:00 securedesktop-ios-3.1.1.45-k9.pkg
7        415956 Sep 19 2011 07:19:12 +00:00 sslclient-win-1.1.4.176.pkg

195932160 bytes available (60555264 bytes used)
```

Figure 101:
The output of
the "show flash"
command on
a 1941 router

- How much Flash memory is in use on the router?

  – 60555264 bytes

- How large is the CIOS image stored in Flash on this router?

  – 55364328 bytes

- How much Flash memory is still available?

  – 195932160 bytes

5. The "show protocols" command displays the transport protocols that are available for routing and summarizes the configuration of each interface. Issue the command **show protocols** (you can abbreviate it with **sho prot**).

Figure 102:
The output of the
"show protocols"
command on
a Cisco 1941
router

```
testrouter#show protocols
Global values:
  Internet Protocol routing is enabled
Embedded-Service-Engine0/0 is administratively down, line protocol is down
GigabitEthernet0/0 is up, line protocol is up
  Internet address is 192.168.101.1/24
GigabitEthernet0/1 is up, line protocol is up
  Internet address is 192.168.1.78/24
testrouter#
```

- What transport protocols are available for routing?

  – Internet Protocol

- Are any of your interfaces administratively down? If so, which one(s)?

  – Yes, the Embedded-Service-Engine0/0 is administratively down.

- You can also look at the state of a single interface with the following command:
  Router#**show prot [interface ID]**, for example "**show prot g0/0**" or "**show prot f4**"
  (depending on your particular router's interface configuration).

6. Cisco Discovery Protocol is used to identify adjacent Cisco devices (routers, switches, etc.). The *"show cdp neighbors"* command will help you identify the IDs of devices that are directly connected, the interface to which they're connected, the platform they're running, their capabilities, and their remote port IDs. CDP is disabled by default and must be started, then enabled on each physical interface where you want to use it. Use the global configuration command *cdp run* to enable CDP on the router and the interface configuration command *cdp enable* to enable CDP on each desired interface on the router. (You can use the following graphic to set up your lab for this exercise, but really all you need are two routers connected together. They don't even have to be on the same IP subnet.)

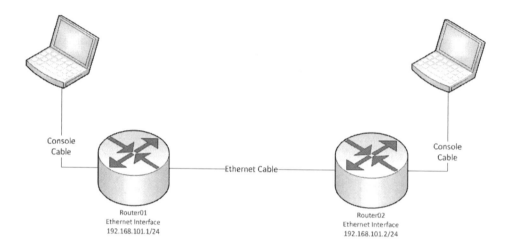

Figure 103: Cisco Discovery Protocol lab configuration

```
testrouter#conf t
Enter configuration commands, one per line.  End with CNTL/Z.
testrouter(config)#cdp run
testrouter(config)#int g0/0
testrouter(config-if)#cdp enable
testrouter(config-if)#int g0/1
testrouter(config-if)#cdp enable
testrouter(config-if)#
```

Figure 104: Enabling Cisco Discovery Protocol (CDP) on a Cisco 1941 router

7. After you have enabled CDP globally on the router and on each desired interface, issue the command *show cdp neighbors* (you can abbreviate it to *show cdp nei*) to view information about your directly connected Cisco neighbors. Your output will be different from the following screen capture.

```
router01#
router01#show cdp neighbors
Capability Codes: R - Router, T - Trans Bridge, B - Source Route Bridge
                  S - Switch, H - Host, I - IGMP, r - Repeater

Device ID          Local Intrfce    Holdtme   Capability  Platform    Port ID
router02           Gig 0/0          145       R S I       2821        Gig 0/0
kilgen.soundtraining.local
                   Gig 0/0          128         T S       WS-C2912-XFas 0/3
router04           Gig 0/0          123       R S I       871         Fas 4
router01#
```

Figure 105: The output of the "sho cdp neighbor" command on a router
connected to two other routers and a 2912 switch

- What are the device ID(s) of your directly connected neighbors?

  - router02, kilgen.soundtraining.local, and router04

- What are the local and remote interfaces being used for the connection (you can identify the remote interfaces in the column labeled Port ID)?

  - The local interfaces are all Gigabit Ethernet 0/0. The remote interfaces are, from top to bottom, Gigabit Ethernet 0/0, Fast Ethernet 0/3, and Fast Ethernet 4.

- What platform are they running?

  - Router02 is running the Cisco 2821 platform, kilgen.soundtraining.local is running the WS-C2912-X platform (It's a Catalyst 2912 switch.), and router04 is running the Cisco 871 platform.

You can use the Privileged EXEC command *clear cdp table* to clear the cdp table. Use the command *show cdp entry <routername>* to display a summary of cdp information. View the CDP status of each of your interfaces with the command *show cdp interface.* You can force a CDP update by using the global configuration mode command *cdp run.* More detailed information, including the neighbor's IP address, is available by using the command *show cdp neighbor detail.*

8. As you can see, CDP discloses quite a bit of information about the devices upon which it is running. For that reason, you'll probably want to disable it especially on outside-facing interfaces. Use the same commands you implemented previously to enable CDP, but precede them with the modifier *no* to disable CDP. Confirm that CDP is disabled with the command *show cdp nei.*

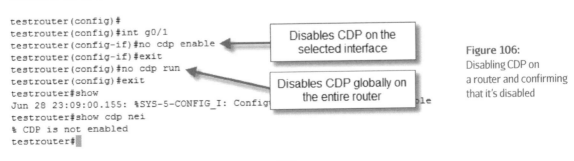

```
testrouter(config)#
testrouter(config)#int g0/1
testrouter(config-if)#no cdp enable ◄──────  Disables CDP on the
testrouter(config-if)#exit                    selected interface
testrouter(config)#no cdp run  ◄────
testrouter(config)#exit                  Disables CDP globally on
testrouter#show                             the entire router
Jun 28 23:09:00.155: %SYS-5-CONFIG_I: Config                 le
testrouter#show cdp nei
% CDP is not enabled
testrouter#
```

Figure 106:
Disabling CDP on
a router and confirming
that it's disabled

9. The "show interfaces" command displays comprehensive information about each of the router's physical interfaces. From the "show interfaces" command, you can determine things such as IP address, subnet mask, bandwidth, queuing method, BIA (Burned In Address), and much more. On your router, you may see some interfaces in use and others that are down. Only answer the questions for the interfaces that are in use.

```
FastEthernet0/0 is up, line protocol is up
  Hardware is AmdFE, address is c805.0b18.0000 (bia c805.0b18.0000)
  Internet address is 8.8.8.1/29
  MTU 1500 bytes, BW 100000 Kbit, DLY 100 usec,
     reliability 255/255, txload 1/255, rxload 1/255
  Encapsulation ARPA, loopback not set
  Keepalive set (10 sec)
  Full-duplex, 100Mb/s, 100BaseTX/FX
  ARP type: ARPA, ARP Timeout 04:00:00
  Last input 00:00:02, output 00:00:01, output hang never
  Last clearing of "show interface" counters never
  Input queue: 0/75/0/0 (size/max/drops/flushes); Total output drops: 0
  Queueing strategy: fifo
  Output queue: 0/40 (size/max)
  5 minute input rate 0 bits/sec, 0 packets/sec
  5 minute output rate 0 bits/sec, 0 packets/sec
     160 packets input, 44598 bytes
     Received 160 broadcasts, 0 runts, 0 giants, 0 throttles
     0 input errors, 0 CRC, 0 frame, 0 overrun, 0 ignored
     0 watchdog
     0 input packets with dribble condition detected
     8 packets output, 801 bytes, 0 underruns
     0 output errors, 0 collisions, 1 interface resets
     0 babbles, 0 late collision, 0 deferred
     0 lost carrier, 0 no carrier
     0 output buffer failures, 0 output buffers swapped out
Serial0/1 is up, line protocol is up
  Hardware is PowerQUICC Serial
  Internet address is 24.1.1.1/29
  MTU 1500 bytes, BW 1544 Kbit, DLY 20000 usec,
     reliability 255/255, txload 1/255, rxload 1/255
  Encapsulation HDLC, loopback not set
  Keepalive set (10 sec)
  Last input 00:00:04, output 00:00:04, output hang never
  Last clearing of "show interface" counters never
  Input queue: 0/75/0/0 (size/max/drops/flushes); Total output drops: 0
  Queueing strategy: weighted fair
  Output queue: 0/1000/64/0 (size/max total/threshold/drops)
     Conversations  0/1/256 (active/max active/max total)
     Reserved Conversations 0/0 (allocated/max allocated)
     Available Bandwidth 1158 kilobits/sec
  5 minute input rate 0 bits/sec, 0 packets/sec
  5 minute output rate 0 bits/sec, 0 packets/sec
     30 packets input, 720 bytes, 0 no buffer
     Received 30 broadcasts, 0 runts, 0 giants, 0 throttles
     0 input errors, 0 CRC, 0 frame, 0 overrun, 0 ignored, 0 abort
     34 packets output, 1260 bytes, 0 underruns
     0 output errors, 0 collisions, 2 interface resets
     0 output buffer failures, 0 output buffers swapped out
     0 carrier transitions
     DCD=up  DSR=up  DTR=up  RTS=up  CTS=up
```

Figure 107: The output of the "show interfaces" command on a Cisco 1721 router

- What is the BIA for the Fast Ethernet 0/0 interface?

  – c805.0b18.0000

- What is the Internet address for the Fast Ethernet 0/0 interface?

  – 8.8.8.1

- What is the subnet mask for the Fast Ethernet 0/0 interface?

  – It's a 29 bit mask which equates to 255.255.255.248 in dotted decimal notation.

- Is there a BIA for the Serial interface?

  – No. The BIA is a MAC (Media Access Control) address which is used on Ethernet interfaces, but not on Serial interfaces. It is possible to manually add a MAC address to a Serial interface with the interface configuration command *mac-address*.

- What queuing strategy is being used on the Fast Ethernet interface?

  – fifo (first-in-first-out)

10. You can narrow the information displayed in the "show interfaces" command by specifying the transport protocol. For example, the command "show ip interface" would display information concerning the IP configuration while the command "show ipv6 interface" would display information concerning the IPv6 configuration. Issue the command *show ip interface* on your router. (You can abbreviate it to *sho ip int*.)

    - Are any interfaces administratively down?

      – Yes. The Embedded-Service-Engine0/0 interface is administratively down. (Administratively down means it has been disabled by an administrator. In this case, this particular interface is not available on this router, therefore it's default condition is administratively down.)

    - What is the IP address of each interface in use on the router?

      – G0/0 is at 192.168.101.1 and G0/1 is at 192.168.1.78.

    - Are there any Access Control Lists configured on any interface?

      – Yes. The access-list BlockLobbyOut is configured as an outbound access-list on Interface G0/0 and the access list 101 is configured as an outbound access-list on Interface G0/1.

    - How were the addresses determined?

      – The address for Interface G0/0 was determined by NVRAM, in other words, it was read from NVRAM when the router booted. The address for Interface G0/1 was assigned by a DHCP server.

Figure 108:
The output of the
"show ip interface" command
on a Cisco 1941 router

11. The command "show ip interface brief" is a handy command to quickly display a summary of your router's IP interface configuration and status. Issue the privileged mode command *show ip interface brief* on your router (it can be abbreviated *sho ip int brie*). Execute the command *show ip interface brief* on your router.

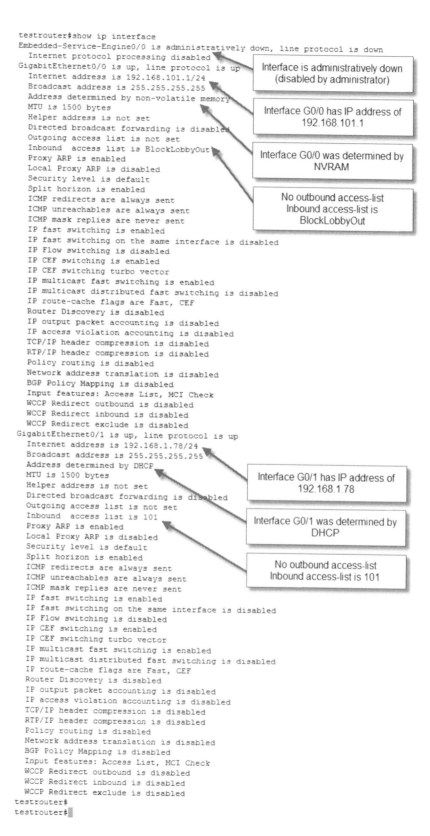

```
testrouter#show ip interface
Embedded-Service-Engine0/0 is administratively down, line protocol is down
  Internet protocol processing disabled
GigabitEthernet0/0 is up, line protocol is up
  Internet address is 192.168.101.1/24
  Broadcast address is 255.255.255.255
  Address determined by non-volatile memory
  MTU is 1500 bytes
  Helper address is not set
  Directed broadcast forwarding is disabled
  Outgoing access list is not set
  Inbound  access list is BlockLobbyOut
  Proxy ARP is enabled
  Local Proxy ARP is disabled
  Security level is default
  Split horizon is enabled
  ICMP redirects are always sent
  ICMP unreachables are always sent
  ICMP mask replies are never sent
  IP fast switching is enabled
  IP fast switching on the same interface is disabled
  IP Flow switching is disabled
  IP CEF switching is enabled
  IP CEF switching turbo vector
  IP multicast fast switching is enabled
  IP multicast distributed fast switching is disabled
  IP route-cache flags are Fast, CEF
  Router Discovery is disabled
  IP output packet accounting is disabled
  IP access violation accounting is disabled
  TCP/IP header compression is disabled
  RTP/IP header compression is disabled
  Policy routing is disabled
  Network address translation is disabled
  BGP Policy Mapping is disabled
  Input features: Access List, MCI Check
  WCCP Redirect outbound is disabled
  WCCP Redirect inbound is disabled
  WCCP Redirect exclude is disabled
GigabitEthernet0/1 is up, line protocol is up
  Internet address is 192.168.1.78/24
  Broadcast address is 255.255.255.255
  Address determined by DHCP
  MTU is 1500 bytes
  Helper address is not set
  Directed broadcast forwarding is disabled
  Outgoing access list is not set
  Inbound  access list is 101
  Proxy ARP is enabled
  Local Proxy ARP is disabled
  Security level is default
  Split horizon is enabled
  ICMP redirects are always sent
  ICMP unreachables are always sent
  ICMP mask replies are never sent
  IP fast switching is enabled
  IP fast switching on the same interface is disabled
  IP Flow switching is disabled
  IP CEF switching is enabled
  IP CEF switching turbo vector
  IP multicast fast switching is enabled
  IP multicast distributed fast switching is disabled
  IP route-cache flags are Fast, CEF
  Router Discovery is disabled
  IP output packet accounting is disabled
  IP access violation accounting is disabled
  TCP/IP header compression is disabled
  RTP/IP header compression is disabled
  Policy routing is disabled
  Network address translation is disabled
  BGP Policy Mapping is disabled
  Input features: Access List, MCI Check
  WCCP Redirect outbound is disabled
  WCCP Redirect inbound is disabled
  WCCP Redirect exclude is disabled
testrouter#
testrouter#
```

Callout boxes:
- Interface is administratively down (disabled by administrator)
- Interface G0/0 has IP address of 192.168.101.1
- Interface G0/0 was determined by NVRAM
- No outbound access-list Inbound access-list is BlockLobbyOut
- Interface G0/1 has IP address of 192.168.1.78
- Interface G0/1 was determined by DHCP
- No outbound access-list Inbound access-list is 101

```
router01#show ip interface brief
Interface              IP-Address    OK? Method Status                Protocol
FastEthernet0/0        8.8.8.1       YES manual up                    up
Serial0/0              10.0.0.1      YES manual up                    down
FastEthernet0/1        unassigned    YES manual administratively down down
Serial0/1              24.1.1.1      YES manual up                    up
FastEthernet1/0        unassigned    YES manual administratively down down
router01#
```

Figure 109: The output of the "show ip interface brief" command on a Cisco 1721 router

In the above screen capture, going from left to right, we see the name of the interface, its IP address (or the fact that no address has been assigned), the OK column concerns the IP address ("yes" indicates that the address is currently valid, while "no" indicates the address isn't currently valid), how the address was determined (manually configured through the router's interface, NVRAM, and DHCP are the most common methods), its status (the hardware condition), and finally protocol which indicates the operational status of the routing protocol on the interface. What's most important to understand is that both status and protocol must be in an "up" condition in order for the router to process packets.

12. You can display the backup configuration file stored in NVRAM with the command "show startup-config." You can display the active configuration file being used to operate the router from DRAM with the command "show running-config." Again, ignore the interfaces that are not in use. Issue the ***show running-config*** command on your router. (It is usually abbreviated to ***show run***.)

Figure 110:
The output of the "show running-config"
command on a Cisco 1721 router

- What is the IP address of the router's Fast Ethernet 0/0 interface?

    – 8.8.8.1

- Does it agree with the address shown by the "show ip interface brief" command?

    – Yes. It should be the same unless the address was modified between the times the two commands were issued.

- What is the IP address of your Serial 0/0 interface?

    – 10.0.0.1

- Does it agree with the address shown by the "show ip interface brief" command?

    – Yes

13. Now issue the *show startup-config* command to display the version of the configuration stored in NVRAM.

```
router01#show running-config
Building configuration...

Current configuration : 982 bytes
!
version 12.3
service timestamps debug datetime msec
service timestamps log datetime msec
no service password-encryption
!
hostname router01
!
boot-start-marker
boot-end-marker
!
enable secret 5 $1$priE$SF7UZYiM6PKdko5pAxFZJ/
enable password password
!
memory-size iomem 15
no aaa new-model
ip subnet-zero
ip cef
!
interface FastEthernet0/0
 ip address 8.8.8.1 255.255.255.248
 speed auto
 half-duplex
!
interface Serial0/0
 mac-address c805.0b18.0001
 ip address 10.0.0.1 255.255.255.0
 clockrate 4000000
!
interface FastEthernet0/1
 no ip address
 shutdown
 duplex auto
 speed auto
!
interface Serial0/1
 ip address 24.1.1.1 255.255.255.248
 clockrate 2000000
!
interface FastEthernet1/0
 no ip address
 shutdown
 duplex auto
 speed auto
!
router rip
 redistribute connected
 network 8.0.0.0
 network 10.0.0.0
 network 24.0.0.0
!
ip http server
ip classless
!
!
dialer-list 1 protocol ip permit
!
line con 0
line aux 0
line vty 0 4
 password p@ss1234
 login
!
!
end
```

Figure 111:
The output of the "show startup-config"
command on a Cisco 1721 router

- How much NVRAM is consumed by the startup-config file?

  – 982 bytes

- Do the parameters displayed by the "show start" command correspond to the parameters displayed by the "show run" command?

  – Yes.

- What would happen if you made a configuration change to the router without saving it to NVRAM? Would the two commands continue to display matching information?

  – The startup-config and the running-config would be different. That's why it is important to save the running-config to the startup-config after making changes and verifying the changes in the router's configuration.

Comparing the Running-Config and Startup-Config (Looking for Differences)

Sometimes you'll want to know the differences between the router's current configuration (running-config) and its saved configuration (startup-config) or other files. Cisco's Contextual Configuration Diff Utility provides a means of comparing files, including the running-config and the startup-config. The syntax is:

show archive config differences [first file] [second file]

```
router01#show startup-config
Using 982 out of 127992 bytes
!
version 12.3
service timestamps debug datetime msec
service timestamps log datetime msec
no service password-encryption
!
hostname router01
!
boot-start-marker
boot-end-marker
!
enable secret 5 $1$priE$SF7UZYiM6PKdko5pAxFZJ/
enable password password
!
memory-size iomem 15
no aaa new-model
ip subnet-zero
ip cef
!
!
!
!
!
!
!
interface FastEthernet0/0
 ip address 8.8.8.1 255.255.255.248
 speed auto
 half-duplex
!
interface Serial0/0
 mac-address c805.0b18.0001
 ip address 10.0.0.1 255.255.255.0
 clockrate 4000000
!
interface FastEthernet0/1
 no ip address
 shutdown
 duplex auto
 speed auto
!
interface Serial0/1
 ip address 24.1.1.1 255.255.255.248
 clockrate 2000000
!
interface FastEthernet1/0
 no ip address
 shutdown
 duplex auto
 speed auto
!
router rip
 redistribute connected
 network 8.0.0.0
 network 10.0.0.0
 network 24.0.0.0
!
ip http server
ip classless
!
!
dialer-list 1 protocol ip permit
!
line con 0
line aux 0
line vty 0 4
 password p@ss1234
 login
!
!
end

router01#
```

Here is an example of the utility being used to compare the running-config and startup-config:

```
router03#show archive config differences system:running-config nvram:startup-config
Contextual Config Diffs:
!No changes were found

router03#conf t
Enter configuration commands, one per line.  End with CNTL/Z.
router03(config)#hostname Seattle
Seattle(config)#do show archive config differences system:running-config nvram:startup-config
Contextual Config Diffs:
+hostname router03
-hostname Seattle

Seattle(config)#
```

Figure 112: Comparing the running-config and the startup-config on a Cisco 871 router

In the above screen capture, I first compared an identical running-config and startup-config. You can see where the output of the router indicated there were no differences (changes) in the two files. I then changed the hostname of the router without saving it to NVRAM (startup-config) and ran the utility again. This time it noted the differences.

Understanding the Output

- A minus symbol (-) means the configuration is present in the first file (running-config), but not in the second file (startup-config).

- A plus symbol (+) means the configuration is present in the second file (startup-config), but not in the first file (running-config).

- An exclamation mark (!) precedes comments in the output.

Remember to use the question mark (?) when you receive an error. Sometimes seemingly minor version changes in the software result in command syntax differences. For example, some of the Cisco documentation says to use the following syntax with the Contextual Configuration Diff Utility:

show archive config differences running-config startup-config

That command syntax won't work on more recent software versions that require the file location as well as its name. If you issue the above command exactly as written, some routers will throw off an error as you can see in the following screen capture.

In the example on the right, I typed the command syntax exactly as shown in Cisco documentation. I received an error saying it couldn't open the file running-config. I then typed the command up to the point of running-config and entered a question mark (?) to see what my options were. The router then told me that it needed not only the file name (running-config), but also the file location (system:) in order to complete the command.

```
Seattle#
Seattle#show archive config differences running-config startup-config
Error: Could not open file running-config for reading

Seattle#show archive config differences ?
  archive:   [file1 path]
  cns:       [file1 path]
  flash:     [file1 path]
  ftp:       [file1 path]
  http:      [file1 path]
  https:     [file1 path]
  null:      [file1 path]
  nvram:     [file1 path]
  rcp:       [file1 path]
  scp:       [file1 path]
  system:    [file1 path]
  tar:       [file1 path]
  tftp:      [file1 path]
  tmpsys:    [file1 path]
  xmodem:    [file1 path]
  ymodem:    [file1 path]
  |          Output modifiers
  <cr>

Seattle#show archive config differences
```

Figure 113: Using the question mark to determine syntax

Network Management Systems

A discussion about monitoring a Cisco router would be incomplete without at least a mention of network monitoring systems (NMS). I'll also mention them in the chapter on security, so please forgive the redundancy. An NMS allows you to centralize monitoring of all your network devices. It works using SNMP (Simple Network Management Protocol). There are a variety of NMSs available, including open-source and commercial products. The benefit of an NMS is that it can monitor your devices and send you alerts whenever certain phenomena occur such as equipment failures or excessive processor utilization. A detailed discussion about NMSs is beyond the scope of this book, but may be the subject of a future book.

For more information about NMSs, see chapter 15.

Summary

Spend some time using *show* commands to familiarize yourself with your router. Especially remember to try the *show* command with your new best friend, the question mark: *show ?*.

CHAPTER 6:
Configuring and Deploying DHCP

Chapter Introduction

Why would someone use a Cisco router as a DHCP server? Isn't that normally the province of a Linux/Unix or Windows server? True, but suppose you have a small branch office with four or five client desktops and no network server. Suppose you really don't want to deal with statically assigned IP addresses. A Cisco IOS-based router can do the job for you. It includes a full-featured DHCP server that can hand out all the usual settings such as an IP address, DNS server address, and default gateway. Unlike that little consumer-grade router you picked up at the big electronics store, however, a Cisco router's DHCP server include enterprise-grade capabilities such as the ability to hand out TFTP server addresses or anything else that can be configured with standard raw DHCP options (RFC 2132).

Chapter Objectives

- Understand the DHCP lease process

- Know how to configure a DHCP logging server

- Understand how to configure a DHCP pool, including DHCP options

- Understand DHCP monitoring options

Online Companion Resources

Videos: Watch the companion videos for this chapter. They're available at
www.soundtraining.net/videos/cisco-router-training-videos

Web Page: There is a supporting web page with live links and other resources for this book
at www.soundtraining.net/cisco-router-book

Facebook: www.soundtraining.net/facebook

Twitter: www.soundtraining.net/twitter

Blog: www.soundtraining.net/blog

DHCP Basics

DHCP stands for Dynamic Host Configuration Protocol. It offers many benefits including lower cost for Internet access, lower cost for IP client configuration, and centralized management.

When a DHCP client comes online, it broadcasts a DHCPDISCOVER packet, which is an IP lease request. A DHCP server then sends the client a DHCPOFFER unicast which offers the client an IP lease (and possibly other parameters). The client selects the first one it receives by sending a DHCPREQUEST packet and the DHCP server then sends an acknowledgement (DHCPACK) to the client.

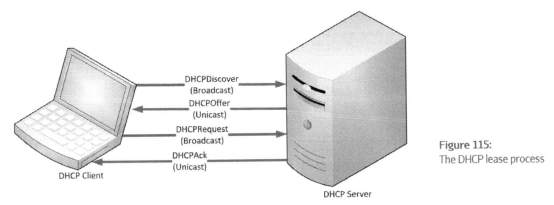

DHCPDiscover
(Broadcast)

DHCPOffer
(Unicast)

DHCPRequest
(Broadcast)

DHCPAck
(Unicast)

DHCP Client

DHCP Server

Figure 115:
The DHCP lease process

Design Considerations

Before configuring DHCP on your Cisco router, you must identify the IP addresses that you will enable the DHCP server to assign and the IP addresses that you will exclude. Additionally, identify necessary DHCP client device options, including: default boot image name, default router(s) (gateways), DNS server(s), NetBIOS name server (WINS), decide on a NetBIOS node type (b, p, m, or h), and decide on a DNS domain name. Once the preliminary design is completed, the steps required to configure DHCP on a Cisco router are fairly simple.

Configure a Logging Server

You can either configure a DHCP logging server to record address conflicts or explicitly disable it. To configure a conflict logging server, use the command: Router(config)#*ip dhcp database [URL] timeout [seconds] write-delay [seconds]*

For example, to configure a conflict database server using FTP with a username of testrouter and a password of p@ss1234 located at 192.168.0.1 with a filename of router-dhcp.txt and a timeout value of 80 seconds, use the following command: Router(config)# *ip dhcp database ftp://testrouter:p@ss1234@192.168.0.1/router-dhcp.txt timeout 80*

To configure a conflict database server using TFTP located at 192.168.0.1 with a filename of router-dhcp.txt and a timeout value of 80 seconds, use the following command: Router(config)#*ip dhcp database tftp://192.168.0.1/router-dhcp.txt timeout 80*

Configuring a DHCP Pool

Configure a DHCP pool name, which also allows you to enter DHCP configuration mode. I recommend using descriptive names such as "net-192.168.0" or "net-12.3.4", etc.

- Router(config)#*ip dhcp pool [name]*. For example, you would issue the following command to create a pool named "net-192.168.0":

  - Router(config)#*ip dhcp pool net-192.168.0*

Configure the DHCP pool network or subnet address and mask. If you don't specify the mask, the DHCP server will assign a mask based on the class of the address. In other words, it will assign an eight-bit mask to class A addresses, a 16-bit mask to class B addresses, and a 24-bit mask to class C addresses. If you don't want to use default values for the subnet mask, you must specify an explicit mask using either dotted decimal notation, such as 255.255.255.0, or CIDR notation, such as /24.

- Router(dhcp-config)#*network [network address] [CIDR mask]*. For example, if you wanted to configure an address pool of 192.168.0.0-192.168.0.254 with a 24-bit subnet mask, you could use any one of the following commands:

  - Router(dhcp-config)#*network 192.168.0.0*

  - Router(dhcp-config)#*network 192.168.0.0 /24*

  - Router(dhcp-config)#*network 192.168.0.0 255.255.255.0*

Configuring DHCP Options

To configure a domain name for the client:

- Router(dhcp-config)#*domain-name [name]*. For example, to configure a domain name of soundtraining.net, use the following command:

  - Router(dhcp-config)#*domain-name soundtraining.net*

To configure DNS server addresses:

- Router(dhcp-config)#*dns-server [address1] [address2]*.

You can configure multiple DNS server addresses. For example, to configure two DNS servers at 208.67.222.222 and 208.67.220.220, use the following command:

- Router(dhcp-config)#*dns-server 208.67.222.222 208.67.220.220*.

Increasingly, WINS (Windows Internet Name Services) servers are not needed. If necessary, however, you can configure WINS server addresses with the following commands:

- Router(dhcp-config)#*netbios-name-server [address]*. For example, to configure a WINS server at 192.168.0.1, issue the following command:

  - Router(dhcp-config)#*netbios-name-server 192.168.0.1*

If necessary, configure the client's NetBIOS node type (If you're not sure which NetBIOS node-type to use, try "h" which attempts NetBIOS name resolution through a server first. If resolution through a server fails, it attempts resolution via a broadcast.):

- Router(dhcp-config)#*netbios-node-type [b,h,m,p]*. For example, to configure a NetBIOS node-type of "h", issue the following command:

  - Router(dhcp-config)#*netbios-node-type h*

To configure the client's default router:

- Router(dhcp-config)#*default-router [address]*. For example, to set the default router as 192.168.101.1, issue the following command:

  - Router(dhcp-config)#*default-router 192.168.101.1*.

Set the address lease time (The lease defaults to one day. In the example, the lease time is set to eight days, fifteen hours, and 20 minutes.):

- Router(dhcp-config)#*lease [(days, hours, minutes) infinite]*. For example, to configure a lease length of eight days, 15 hours, and 20 minutes, issue the following command:

  - Router(dhcp-config)#*lease 8 15 20*

The following is an example configuration from a Cisco 1941 router.

```
testrouter#
testrouter#conf t
Enter configuration commands, one per line.  End with CNTL/Z.
testrouter(config)#ip dhcp database ftp://testrouter:p@ss1234@192.168.0.1/router-dhcp.txt timeout 80
testrouter(config)#ip dhcp pool net-192.168.101
testrouter(dhcp-config)#network 192.168.101.0
testrouter(dhcp-config)#domain-name soundtraining.net
testrouter(dhcp-config)#dns-server 208.67.222.222 208.67.220.220
testrouter(dhcp-config)#netbios-name-server 192.168.0.1
testrouter(dhcp-config)#netbios-node-type h
testrouter(dhcp-config)#default-router 192.168.101.1
testrouter(dhcp-config)#lease 8 0 0
testrouter(dhcp-config)#
Writing router-dhcp.txt !
```

This is where the router wrote to the DHCP conflicts database. It occurred some time following the completion of the configuration.

Figure 116: An example of a DHCP server configuration on a Cisco 1941 router

Although I didn't include it in the above configuration, if you know the option code, you can also configure raw DHCP options while in DHCP configuration mode with the command *option*.

Figure 117:
Configuring DHCP raw options

```
router02(dhcp-config)#option ?
  <0-254>  DHCP option code

router02(dhcp-config)#option
```

Monitoring and Administering DHCP

A variety of commands are available to assist you in administering and troubleshooting the Cisco DHCP server.

The "clear" commands allow you to remove various aspects of DHCP operations, including:

- Binding which removes DHCP address bindings (*clear ip dhcp binding*)
- Conflict which remove DHCP address conflicts
- Pool, which clears objects from a specific pool
- Server statistics, which clears DHCP server statistics
- Subnet, which clears either all leased subnets or a specific address in the subnet
  - Router#*clear ip dhcp binding [address/*]*
  - Router#*clear ip dhcp server statistics*

The family of "debug" commands allows you to see router DHCP messages. (Be careful when using debugging commands. They can quickly eat up router resources and negatively affect the router's ability to process packets.)

Debugging DHCP
- Router#*debug ip dhcp server [events/package/linkage]*

DHCP *Show* Commands
- Router>*show ip dhcp [binding/confict/server statistics]*
- Router#*show ip dhcp database*

Interactive Exercise 6.1:
Configuring and Deploying DHCP

This exercise teaches you how to configure the Dynamic Host Configuration Protocol on a Cisco router.

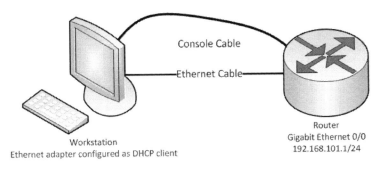

Diagram 3: Configuring and Deploying DHCP

Objectives:

- Determine and configure a DHCP pool

- Determine and configure necessary DHCP client options

- Monitor the DHCP process through logs and console monitoring

Steps:

1. You'll configure DHCP for the Ethernet network that's attached to your router's inside interface. In global configuration mode, enter the command to identify the DHCP pool and start the DHCP service:

    – Router(config)#*ip dhcp pool net-192.168.101*

    – Router(dhcp-config)#*network 192.168.101.0 /24*

2. Configure appropriate options for DHCP clients:

    – Router(dhcp-config)#*domain-name soundtraining.net*

    – Router(dhcp-config)#*dns-server 208.67.222.222 208.67.220.220*

    – Router(dhcp-config)#*default-router 192.168.101.1*

3. Configure a DHCP lease time of eight days, 0 hours, and 0 minutes:

    – Router(dhcp-config)#*lease 8 0 0*

4. Reconfigure your computer for automatic IP address assignment, open a command prompt on your computer, and execute the command "ipconfig /all" at a command prompt to see the results of the router's DHCP address assignment. (You might have to perform an "ipconfig /release" and an "ipconfig /renew" before you can see complete results in an ipconfig /all command.)

5. Back on your router, at a privileged EXEC prompt, try the following commands:

   – Router#*show ip dhcp ?* to see the available DHCP monitoring options.

   – Router#*debug ip dhcp server events*
     To see a DHCP event, renew your IP address on your workstation.

6. Save your configuration:

   – Router#*wr*

7. You can now back up your configuration to your TFTP server. (Be sure to use the correct IP address for your TFTP server. You can check it by using the Windows command environment command "ipconfig.") Use a different file name after each exercise so you'll have a backup from each exercise. Execute the following command on a single line:

   – router#*copy system:running-config tftp://{your computer's IP address}/cfg-dhcp.txt*

Summary

In my experience, you'll normally use a Windows, Linux, or Unix server as the DHCP server. There may be times, however, when you're working with a very small network, perhaps at a branch office. You may not have a server, but you might want to provide centralized IP configuration. That's when a Cisco router can come to the rescue as a DHCP server.

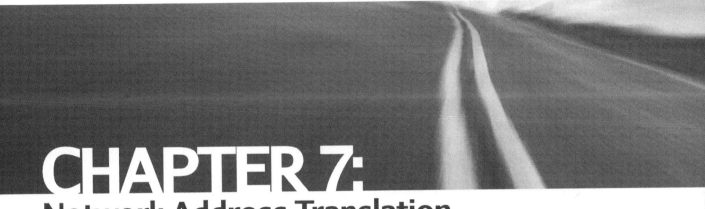

CHAPTER 7:
Network Address Translation

Chapter Introduction

I'm constantly in awe of the engineers who conceived and designed the Internet. NAT is one aspect that is especially impressive to me. When the original IP addressing scheme was conceived back in the early 70s, no one, not even the greatest visionaries of the time, could see the old ARPANET developing into today's global Internet. I'm pretty sure they thought that 4,000,000,000 addresses would suffice. Then, the Internet became a public phenomenon and suddenly we started running out of IP addresses. In 1994, Paul Francis and Kjeld Borch Egevang published RFC 1631 introducing the IP Network Address Translator as a means of dealing with the depletion of the address space.

In this chapter, you'll learn about different types of NAT and I'll show you how to configure the very commonly-used Port Address Translation (PAT). PAT is the many-to-one type of NAT commonly found in networks ranging from the smallest home network to large enterprise networks.

Chapter Objectives

- Gain an understanding of the purpose of Network Address Translation
- Review the different types of Network Address Translation
- Configure Port Address Translation

Online Companion Resources

Videos: Watch the companion videos for this chapter. They're available at
www.soundtraining.net/videos/cisco-router-training-videos

Web Page: There is a supporting web page with live links and other resources for this book
at www.soundtraining.net/cisco-router-book

Facebook: www.soundtraining.net/facebook

Twitter: www.soundtraining.net/twitter

Blog: www.soundtraining.net/blog

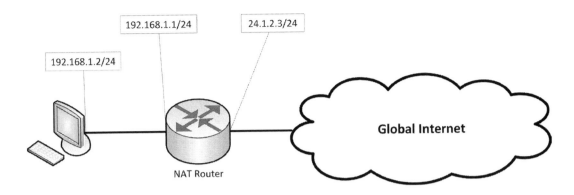

Figure 118: Network Address Translation substitutes one address
for another (usually an outside address for an inside address)

When to Use NAT

Network Address Translation (NAT) substitutes addresses. For example, NAT might substitute a registered public address for a non-registered private address.

Port Address Translation

Suppose you have a private network that uses the 192.168.0/24 network. Addresses that begin with 192.168 are not routable on the public Internet, so if you want your internal hosts to be able to connect to hosts on the public Internet, their private addresses (192.168.0) must be converted to an Internet-routable address. The type of NAT that is most often used to provide this service is called Port Address Translation or PAT.

Static NAT

Another form of NAT allows Internet hosts to connect with a host on a private LAN. This is commonly done when a Web-server, for example, is located behind a firewall on a network using private, non-registered IP address. For example, suppose you have a Web server on your private LAN with an IP address of 10.23.45.1. As you recall from the previous chapter on IP addresses, an address beginning with 10 is a private address, not routable on the public Internet. If you want Internet hosts to be able to connect with your Web server, there has to be a way of providing a registered public address. That's where NAT comes in. This form of NAT is called Static NAT. The router or firewall is configured with two addresses, one public and one private. When a packet arrives at the router's public interface requesting port 80 services, the router forwards it from the public interface to the private address of the Web server.

NAT connects two networks together, one private and one public. NAT is used when private addresses from the LAN need to be converted to public addresses on the Internet (or any external network). NAT allows a device such as a router or proxy server to act as an agent between private and public networks. A single address (or small range of addresses) represents an entire group of IP hosts to the public network. NAT is specified in RFC 1631.

NAT serves several purposes, including the conservation of the limited public IP address space. It also provides security by making it difficult for Internet hosts to initiate connections with internal (LAN) hosts. It allows administrators to control the use of the IP address space, both internally and externally.

Types of Network Address Translation

Static NAT always maps the same unregistered (private) IP address to the same registered (public) IP address. Static NAT is used when computers on private networks needs to be accessible to Internet users, as in the case of a mail or web server.

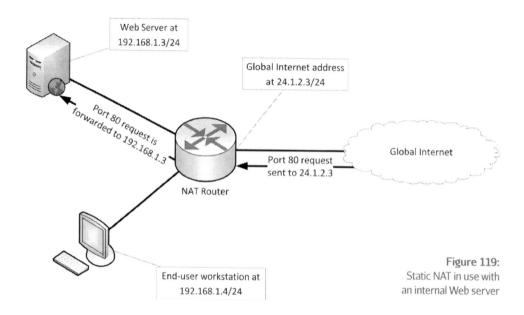

Figure 119:
Static NAT in use with
an internal Web server

Dynamic NAT

Dynamic NAT maps an unregistered (private) address to a registered (public) address from a group of public addresses. It translates to the first available address from the pre-specified group of public addresses.

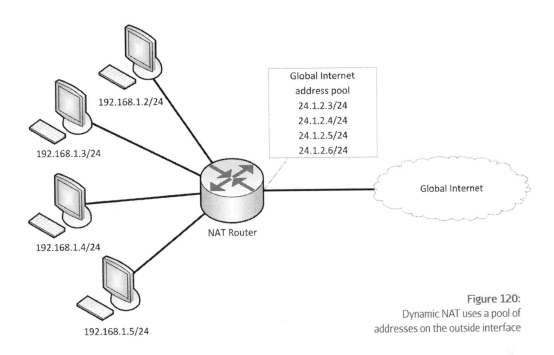

Figure 120:
Dynamic NAT uses a pool of
addresses on the outside interface

NAT Overlapping

Overlapping NAT is used when the private addresses on a LAN are the same as public addresses on another network. The router maintains a "lookup table" of the "overlapping" addresses and overlapping addresses from the LAN are intercepted and replaced with unique public addresses. NAT Overlapping might also be used when two companies, both using the same RFC1918 address space, merge.

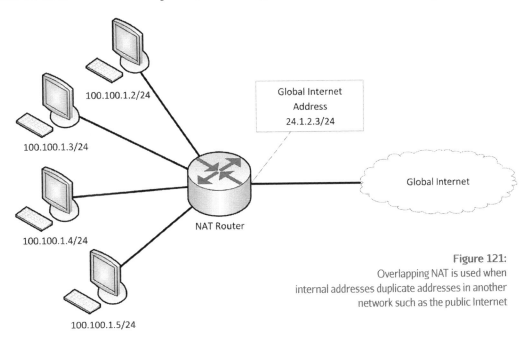

Figure 121:
Overlapping NAT is used when
internal addresses duplicate addresses in another
network such as the public Internet

Port Address Translation (PAT)

Port Address Translation is a form of dynamic NAT. Interior (private) addresses are all mapped to the same public address, but with different port numbers to create unique connections.

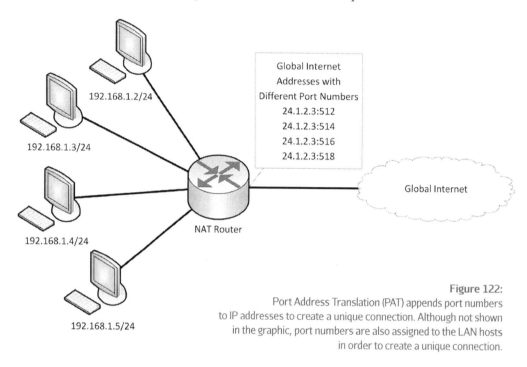

Figure 122:
Port Address Translation (PAT) appends port numbers to IP addresses to create a unique connection. Although not shown in the graphic, port numbers are also assigned to the LAN hosts in order to create a unique connection.

Port Address Translation is also known as:

- NAT Overloading
- Single Address NAT
- Port-level Multiplexed NAT

Port Address Translation utilizes a feature of the TCP/IP stack called "multiplexing", which allows a host to maintain several concurrent connections with a remote computer using different TCP or UDP ports.

When using Port Address Translation, the IP packet header includes:

- Source address
- Source port (TCP or UDP port number assigned by the source computer for this connection)
- Destination address
- Destination port (TCP or UDP port number the source computer is requesting the destination computer to open)

The addresses specify the computers at each end of the connection. The port numbers ensure that the connection has a unique identifier. The combination of the four numbers identifies a unique TCP/IP connection.

Interactive Exercise 7.1:
Configuring Port Address Translation

In this lab, we'll configure Port Address Translation in which all internal interfaces will share one external interface and IP address on the external network.

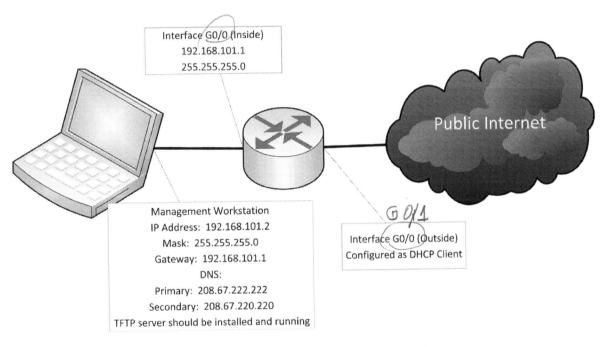

Diagram 4: Configuring Port Address Translation (PAT)

- Ensure that your workstation is configured according to the network diagram.

- On your router, identify which interface will be external and which will be internal. In a real-world setting, the inside interface would normally be an Ethernet connection to a LAN and the outside might be a T1 interface connected to a WAN such as the Internet. For the purpose of this exercise, the internal (inside) interface will be the Gigabit Ethernet 0/0 interface and the external (outside) interface will be the router's Gigabit Ethernet 0/1 interface.

Configure Port Address Translation with the following steps:

1. Identify the inside interface:

    – Router(config)#*int g0/0*

    – Router(config-if)#*ip nat inside*

2. Identify the outside interface:

    – Router(config-if)#*int g0/1*

    – Router(config-if)#*ip nat outside*

```
testrouter#conf t
Enter configuration commands, one per line.  End with CNTL/Z.
testrouter(config)#int g0/0
testrouter(config-if)#ip nat inside

Aug 13 23:24:24.274: %LINEPROTO-5-UPDOWN: Line protocol on Interface NVI0, chang
ed state to up
testrouter(config-if)#int g0/1
testrouter(config-if)#ip nat outside
testrouter(config-if)#
```

Figure 123: Configuring NAT inside and outside interfaces. (NVI0 is the NAT Virtual Interface which is created automatically, but not used in this exercise.)

3. Create an access-control list to identify the traffic permitted to use NAT:

    – Router(config)#*access-list 100 permit ip any any*
    (This access-control list permits all IP traffic from any source address to any destination address. More details on access-control lists later in the book.)

```
testrouter(config)#access-list 100 permit ip any any
testrouter(config)#
```

Figure 124: Configuring an access control list to specify who can use NAT (PAT)

4. Apply the access-control list to the outside interface:

    – Router(config-if)#*ip nat inside source list 100 int g0/1 overload*
    (This statement tells the router to apply the just-created list 100 to interface g0/1 and to implement NAT overloading on the interface.)

```
testrouter(config)#
testrouter(config)#ip nat inside source list 100 int g0/1 overload
testrouter(config)#
```

Figure 125: Turning on Port Address Translation (NAT overloading)

5. Router(config)#*exit*

You can also use *sho ip nat translations* and *show ip nat statistics* to view your NAT configuration.

```
testrouter#show ip nat translations
Pro Inside global        Inside local        Outside local        Outside global
icmp 192.168.1.59:1      192.168.101.2:1     205.210.189.166:1    205.210.189.166:1
udp 192.168.1.59:55434   192.168.101.2:55434 208.67.222.222:53    208.67.222.222:53
testrouter#
```

Figure 126: The output of "show ip nat translations" following a ping to a website

The following table describes each of the fields in the output of the *show ip nat translations* command. (The number following each of the above IP addresses, just after the colon, is the port number. The combination of the four IP addresses and port numbers is what creates a unique connection.

Field Title	Explanation
Pro	The IP protocol in use
Inside global	The actual IP on the outside interface that represents one or more inside local IP address to the outside world or network (In the example above, it's an RFC 1918 address, but in the real world, it will usually be an Internet-routable address.)
Inside local	The actual IP address of an inside host. This is often an RFC1918 address that is not routable on the public Internet.
Outside local	The IP address of an outside host as it appears to hosts on the inside network. This is how the inside host(s) see the outside host.
Outside global	The actual IP address of an outside host, usually assigned by its owner

```
testrouter#show ip nat statistics
Total active translations: 1 (0 static, 1 dynamic; 1 extended)
Peak translations: 298, occurred 00:15:07 ago
Outside interfaces:
  GigabitEthernet0/1
Inside interfaces:
  GigabitEthernet0/0
Hits: 20807  Misses: 0
CEF Translated packets: 19285, CEF Punted packets: 1380
Expired translations: 1096
Dynamic mappings:
-- Inside Source
[Id: 1] access-list 100 interface GigabitEthernet0/1 refcount 1

Total doors: 0
Appl doors: 0
Normal doors: 0
Queued Packets: 0
testrouter#
```

Figure 127:
The output of "show ip nat statistics"

You can watch the address translation taking place with the following command: ***debug ip nat.*** To turn off debugging, issue the following command: ***undebug all***

```
testrouter#debug ip nat
IP NAT debugging is on
testrouter#
Jul 10 00:50:32.562: NAT: s=192.168.101.2->192.168.1.59, d=208.67.222.222 [435]
Jul 10 00:50:32.598: NAT: s=208.67.222.222, d=192.168.1.59->192.168.101.2 [0]
Jul 10 00:50:32.606: NAT*: s=192.168.101.2->192.168.1.59, d=205.210.189.166 [436]
Jul 10 00:50:32.626: NAT*: s=205.210.189.166, d=192.168.1.59->192.168.101.2 [48252]
```

Figure 128: The output of the "debug ip nat" command

In the above screen capture, you can see the time of the NAT translation, the source (s) and the destination (d). The intermediate IP address is the Inside Global address. The number in square brackets at the end of each line is the IP packet number which could be helpful in identifying the same packet in a protocol analyzer's packet stream.

The asterisk indicates the packet is going through the fast path. (The first packet always goes through the slow path, which means it is process switched.)

Back Up Your Configuration

1. Back up your configuration to your TFTP server. (Be sure to use the correct IP address for your TFTP server.) Execute the following command on a single line:

   – router#*copy system:running-config tftp://192.168.101.2/cfg-nat.txt*

2. Remove NAT from your router with the following steps:

   – Router# *conf t*

   – Router(config)# *no access-list 100*

   – Router(config)# *int f4*

   – Router(config-if)# *no ip nat inside source list 100 int f4 overload*

   – Router(config-if)# *no ip nat outside*

   – Router(config-if)# *int vlan1*

   – Router(config-if)# *no ip nat inside*

   – Router(config-if)#

Summary

Network address translation has provided a means to extend the life of IPv4 by overcoming the limitation on the number of available IP addresses. There are issues with NAT, including:

- All internal hosts share the same IP address on the global Internet, thus inhibiting accountability.

- The use of NAT breaks the concept of end-to-end connectivity.

- The use of NAT complicates the process of allowing global Internet hosts to initiate connections with internal hosts.

IPv6, discussed in chapter 14, should eliminate the need for NAT.

CHAPTER 8:
Routing Protocols and Procedures

Chapter Introduction

This is the chapter that hits at the core of why there are routers.

In 1984, husband and wife Leonard Bosack and Sandy Lerner began experimenting with how to connect their two detached networks in separate buildings on the Stanford University campus. They created multiple protocol routers to provide the interconnection. They formed a company called *Cisco*, named for the city to the north of Stanford. Their house was the company headquarters and their startup capital came from their credit cards. Word soon spread about their routers and their infant company began pulling in hundreds of thousands of dollars in revenue each month. Bosack and Lerner left Cisco in 1990. The company they founded, however, has become one of the world's most respected companies. Today, Cisco supplies the bulk of the equipment used to run the global Internet. In 2010, Bosack and Lerner received the 2009 IEEE Computer Society's Computer Entrepreneur Award.

In the early days of Cisco routers, they did indeed have to support multiple protocols such as AppleTalk, DECNet, and IPX/SPX in addition to IP. Today, you most likely will work with IPv4 and perhaps IPv6. In this chapter, we'll focus on IPv4. IPv6 will come later in chapter 14.

Chapter Objectives

- Understand the fundamentals of routing

- Configure static routing

- Configure dynamic routing using RIP, EIGRP, and OSPF

- Configure on-demand routing

- Understand basic routing troubleshooting

Online Companion Resources

Videos: Watch the companion videos for this chapter. They're available at
www.soundtraining.net/videos/cisco-router-training-videos

Web Page: There is a supporting web page with live links and other resources for this book
at www.soundtraining.net/cisco-router-book

Facebook: www.soundtraining.net/facebook

Twitter: www.soundtraining.net/twitter

Blog: www.soundtraining.net/blog

Use the following network diagram to understand the examples and complete the exercises in this chapter. This diagram is designed for educational purposes only. In the real world, the IP addresses would be substantially different from those used in this example. Additionally, you would not often see a circular network like this. Although I'm a big believer in trying to make the learning process mirror the real world whenever possible, there are times when a purely academic exercise can help solidify concepts. This is one of those times.

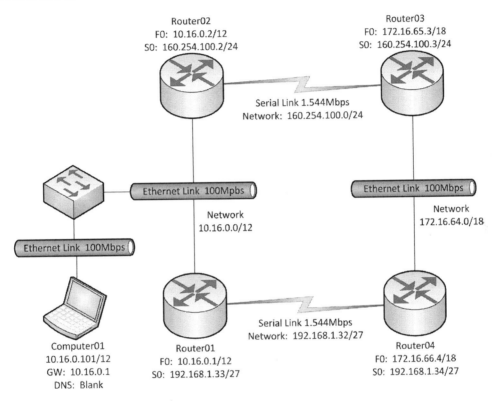

Diagram 5: Network diagram for configuring routing

Fundamentals of Routing

At a basic level, there are two types of routing: static and dynamic. Regardless of whether you're implementing static or dynamic routing, routers require some basic information in order to route packets:

- The target address—You can't get there unless you know where you're going. For the sake of discussion, looking at the chapter network diagram, suppose that you want to ping the fast Ethernet interface on router03 from router01. Your target is 172.16.65.3, which is located on the network 172.16.64.0. Do you understand why the network is 172.16.64.0? The network is 172.16.64.0 because of the 18 bit mask. If you convert the address 172.16.65.3/18 to binary, you'll see that the first 18 bits equal 172.16.64.0. Seriously! Try it.

- Neighboring routers from which they can learn about remote networks—Your neighboring routers know about remote networks and they can share that information with your router. Again, using the example of pinging from router01 to router03, router01's neighbors (router02 and router04) both know how to get to router03. Either router02 or router04 can tell router01 how to get to router03.

- Possible paths to the remote network containing the target address—Just as in an interstate highway system, there are many possible routes to the destination. To send an ping from router01 to router03, the ping could travel either from router01 to router02 to router03 or from router01 to router04 to router03.

- The best path to the remote network containing the target address—Just as in a network of streets and highways, there is usually one best route to the destination. Again, using the streets and highways analogy, the best path is not always the most direct path. In the previous example, either path is equally as good. Both paths have one fast Ethernet link (100Mbps) and one serial link (1.544Mbps), presumably a T1.

- Mechanisms to ensure that routing information is accurate. Still using the streets and highways analogy, you need regular updates to ensure that the routing information you have is accurate. That is one of the functions of a routing protocol such as RIP, OSPF, EIGRP, or BGP. In the absence of a routing protocol, the administrator must manually maintain the accuracy of the routing tables.

Static Routing

With static routing, the routes are manually entered by the administrator and the routing tables must be manually updated whenever topology changes. Static routes are not automatically exchanged with other routers, because they're manually defined by network administrator. Static routes will not change as long as the path is active.

Static Routing Advantages	Static Routing Disadvantages
- Security - Less bandwidth utilization - Less processor utilization	- More administrative overhead - New routes are not discovered automatically

Configuring static routing

```
                 Target Network and Mask              Next Hop (Neighboring) Router

router01#conf t
Enter configuration commands, one per line.   End with CTL/Z.
router01(config)#ip route 160.254.100.0 255.255.255.0 10.16.0.2
router01(config)#ip route 172.16.64.0 255.255.192.0 s0
router01(config)#

                           Interface from which to send packets
```

Figure 129:
Configuring two static routes from router01 to remote networks.
Note that, in the first line, the statement specifies the neighboring router's
address while the second line specifies the interface on the local router
(router01) from which to send the packets.

Gateway of Last Resort

One place where static routing is frequently used is in configuring a "Gateway of Last Resort." A gateway of last resort on a router is similar to a default gateway on a computer running Microsoft Windows. You can think of the gateway of last resort like this: If a router receives a packet and doesn't know what to do with it, it will send it to its gateway of last resort. Such gateways are frequently configured for use with an Internet connection. In the real world, the gateway of last resort could be the address of the ISP's router. In the first of the following examples, the gateway of last resort is the fast Ethernet interface on router02. In the second example, it's the serial interface on router03. Note: You would not normally configure two different gateways of last resort.

- Router01(config)#*ip route 0.0.0.0 0.0.0.0 10.16.0.2*

- Router01(config)#*ip route 0.0.0.0 0.0.0.0 192.168.1.34*

Soundthinking Point: Use Either the Local Interface or the Next-Hop Router

Note in the screen capture that the first line sends the packets to a specific IP address (10.16.0.2), while the second line sends the packets out from a specific interface (s0). The second line's configuration should normally be used only when that interface is connected to a point-to-point link.

Soundthinking Point: Why a Ping Might Not Work

Considering the chapter network diagram, suppose that you enabled the above configuration on router01. What would happen if you were to ping router03 from router01? Would you get a response? The answer is no, because although the ICMP packets from router01 would reach router03, router03 would not know where to send the response because its routing table has not yet been populated with a return route. How would you know this? Execute the "show ip route" command on both routers to see what they know about routes around your internetwork.

Interactive Exercise 8.1:
Static Routing

In this lab, you'll configure static routes to each of the remote networks in the classroom internetwork.

Objectives:

1. Understand how to direct packets to a target network or subnet.

2. Configure static routing statements.

Steps:

Use the chapter network diagram. Ensure that each of the routers in your lab is configured according to the diagram.

Perform the following steps on router01.

1. Save your existing configuration with the following command:

   – router01#*copy run start*

2. Attempt to ping a router in the laboratory internetwork that is not directly connected to your router. The ping is not successful. To understand why the ping is not successful, display your router's routing table with the following command:

   – router#*show ip route*

   Note that the routing table displays only your directly connected networks. The routing table is very important because it tells you what networks and subnets your router knows about. If a network or subnet is not displayed in the routing table, the router has no way of knowing how to reach it.

3. Look at the chapter network diagram. Note that there are several different IP subnets. Your router is directly connected to at least two of the IP subnets (as indicated by the "C" entries in its routing table). All other subnets are considered "remote" subnets. You will now configure static routes to tell your router how to reach each of the remote subnets. (As you enter the configurations, remember that you're configuring network and subnet addresses, not individual interface addresses.) Enter the following commands to configure static routes:

   – router(config)#*ip route <remote network address> <remote network mask> <forwarding router's address>*

The following example is for router01 in the preceding diagram with two remote networks:

```
router01(config)#ip route 172.16.64.0 255.255.192.0 192.168.1.34
router01(config)#ip route 160.254.100.0 255.255.255.0 10.16.0.2
router01(config)#
```

Figure 130: Configuring two static routes to remote networks

(Remember that the forwarding router's address must be an address known to your router. Use the command "show ip route" to see the networks and subnets that are known to your router. (For the forwarding router's address, you should choose your neighboring router that is closest to the remote subnet.)

4. Display router01's routing table with the following command:

   – router#*show ip route*

You should see two directly connected networks (indicated by "C") and two statically configured networks (indicated by "S").

```
router01#show ip route
Codes: C - connected, S - static, R - RIP, M - mobile, B - BGP
       D - EIGRP, EX - EIGRP external, O - OSPF, IA - OSPF inter area
       N1 - OSPF NSSA external type 1, N2 - OSPF NSSA external type 2
       E1 - OSPF external type 1, E2 - OSPF external type 2
       i - IS-IS, su - IS-IS summary, L1 - IS-IS level-1, L2 - IS-IS level-2
       ia - IS-IS inter area, * - candidate default, U - per-user static route
       o - ODR, P - periodic downloaded static route

Gateway of last resort is not set

     172.16.0.0/18 is subnetted, 1 subnets
S       172.16.64.0 is directly connected, Serial0
     10.0.0.0/12 is subnetted, 1 subnets
C       10.16.0.0 is directly connected, FastEthernet0
     160.254.0.0/24 is subnetted, 1 subnets
S       160.254.100.0 [1/0] via 10.16.0.2
     192.168.1.0/27 is subnetted, 1 subnets
C       192.168.1.32 is directly connected, Serial0
router01#
```

Figure 131: The output of "show ip route" after configuring two static routes

5. Attempt to ping each of the interfaces in the network diagram. The ping should be successful to some of the interfaces, but not to others. For example, a ping from router01 to 10.16.0.2 or 192.168.1.34 should be successful. On the other hand, a ping to 172.16.65.3 or even 160.254.100.2 should fail. Go ahead and try it. Why do you think the first two work and the second two fail?

The reason is because, even though you have properly configured router01 with static routes to the remote networks (160.254.100.0/24 and 172.16.64.0/18), router03 has no knowledge of its remote networks (10.16.0.0/12 and 192.168.1.32/27). The packets actually arrive at router03, but router03 doesn't know where to send its ICMP echo reply.

6. Now, on router03, configure static routes back to router01 with the following commands:

   - router03(config)#ip route 10.16.0.0 255.240.0.0 160.254.100.2

   - router03(config)#ip route 192.168.1.32 255.255.255.224 172.16.66.4

7. On router01, attempt the ping again to 160.254.100.3 and 172.16.65.3. This time, it should be successful. Back up your configuration to your TFTP server. (Be sure to use the correct IP address for your TFTP server.) Use a different file name after each exercise so you'll have a backup from each exercise. Execute the following command on a single line (assuming that your TFTP server is located at 10.16.0.101):

   - router#*copy system:running-config tftp://10.16.0.101/cfg-static-route.txt*

8. Now, reload your lab routers without saving the configurations. When they restart, they should be in the same state as they were before you configured the static routes.

Dynamic Routing

Dynamic routing makes use of routing protocols to allow the routers to build their routing tables automatically. Updates are exchanged automatically at regular intervals or whenever new topology information is received (depending on the type of routing protocol). Some routing protocols include RIP, OSPF, IS-IS, EIGRP, and BGP. These protocols allow the routers to exchange information about possible paths (routes) in the internetwork.

Routing vs. Routed Protocols

Routed protocols are transport protocols that include addressing information, data payloads, error-checking. Examples include IPv4 and iPv6.

Routing protocols build and maintain routing tables. They carry routing data from one router to another. Examples include RIP, OSPF.

Two Basic Families of Routing Protocols

Distance Vector: Routers exchange entire routing tables at regular intervals which can create excessive network traffic. Examples include RIP and IGRP.

Link State: Link-state routers maintain a shared view of the network and exchange link information as changes are made which generates minimal network traffic. Examples include OSPF and IS-IS.

Hybrid routing protocols use aspects of both of the above. An example is EIGRP.

Routing Decisions

Metric

The metric is how a routing protocol determines the best route to a destination. Metrics can be based on various criteria, depending on the routing protocol. Some criteria used to determine the metric include hop count, bandwidth, delay, load, reliability, and cost.

Administrative distance

Administrative distance is a measure of the believability of the route. Routers use the administrative distance to choose between similar routes discovered by different routing protocols. Routes with lower administrative distances are believed over routes with higher administrative distances.

Some sample administrative distances:

Route Source	Default Distance	Route Source	Default Distance
Directly Connected Interface	0	IS-IS	115
Static Route	1	RIP	120
EIGRP Summary Route	5	EGP	140
External BGP	20	On Demand Routing	160
Internal EIGRP	90	External EIGRP	170
IGRP	100	Internal BGP	200
OSPF	110	Unknown	255

Modifying Administrative Distance

You can modify the administrative distance on static routes to create what Cisco calls a *floating static route*.

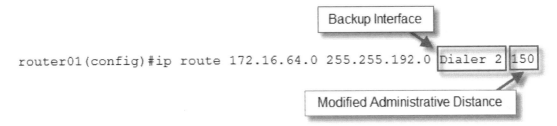

```
router01(config)#ip route 172.16.64.0 255.255.192.0 Dialer 2 150
```

Backup Interface

Modified Administrative Distance

Figure 132:
Creating a floating static route by
modifying the administrative distance

In the previous example, the floating static route was created by assigning an administrative distance of 150 to a static route over an ISDN interface. For the sake of the example, assume that RIP is the routing protocol. RIP-discovered routes, with a default distance of 120, would be preferred over the floating static route with a distance of 150. If, however, the RIP-discovered routes were to fail, the backup route over the ISDN line (Dialer 2) would be used.

Routing Information Protocol (RIP)

RIP is an older routing protocol that is still widely used due to its simplicity of configuration. It uses the distance-vector algorithm to make routing decisions. Routing tables are broadcast every 30 seconds using UDP (User Datagram Protocol) packets. This process is referred to as *advertising*. Routes are marked as unusable when no update is received for 180 seconds. After 240 seconds, the routes are removed from the routing tables. RIP uses the hop count for its metric and has a maximum hop count of 15. RIP's administrative distance is 120.

RIP version 2 supports authentication, route summarization, classless inter-domain routing (CIDR), and variable-length subnet masking (VLSM).

RIP uses a technology called Split horizon to avoid creating routing loops. Split horizon simply keeps a router from advertising a route over the interface from which it learned about that route. Split horizon is turned on by default on Cisco routers.

The Problem with Hop Count

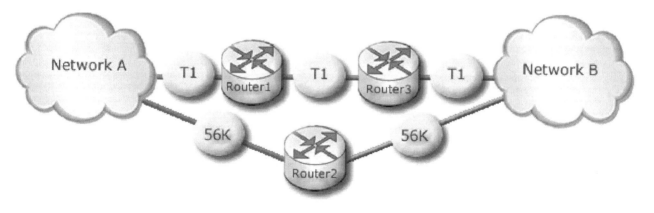

Figure 133: The problem with using hop count as a metric

Notice that there are two possible routes from Network A to Network B. Which one is the fastest? Which one will RIP select? The path through router1 and router3 is faster because the T1 lines operate at 1.544 Mbps compared to the 56 Kbps lines, but RIP will select the more direct path with fewer hops, even though it is much slower (actually, excruciatingly slower!). RIP is documented in RFCs 1058 and 2453.

Open Shortest Path First (OSPF)

OSPF is a link-state protocol, based on the Shortest Path First algorithm, conceived by Dutch computer scientist Edsger Dijkstra in 1956. In fact, it is sometimes known as the Dijkstra algorithm. It is a non-Cisco proprietary, industry standard routing protocol. OSPF is scalable: it's designed for large and growing networks. Its administrative distance is 110. OSPF uses cost to determine metric (cost is determined by 10^8/bandwidth).

OSPF Single Area Configuration Steps

```
router01#
router01#conf t
Enter configuration commands, one per line.  End with CNTL/Z.
router01(config)#router ospf 1
router01(config-router)#network 10.16.0.0 0.15.255.255 area 0
router01(config-router)#network 192.168.1.32 0.0.0.31 area 0
router01(config-router)#
router01#
```

Figure 134: Single-area OSPF configuration example

In the above example, the command "router ospf 1" enables the OSPF routing process and assigns it a process ID (PID) of 1. The PID is local to the router. It is not necessary to use the same PID on all routers in an area, but many administrators do so out of simplicity. (It is possible, but not recommended, to configure multiple OSPF processes on a single router. Doing so taxes router resources.)

The command "network 172.16.64.0 0.0.63.255 area 0" tells the router what networks will be participating in the OSPF routing process and identifies the area to which each network belongs. The "0.0.63.255" portion of the statement is a wildcard mask (an inverse subnet mask) used to mask the network bits from the host bits. Put more simply, it identifies which bits of the address to consider and which bits to ignore. Bits in the address that match a "0" in the wildcard mask are considered, while bits in the address that match a "1" are ignored. The area can be configured as either a simple decimal number (such as that used in the example) or it can be configured in dotted-decimal notation, similar to an IP address. Some routers may require one or the other style of area identification, but Cisco routers accept either one.

Each network that will participate in the OSPF routing process must be configured on a separate line. It is possible to simplify the configuration of OSPF if all interfaces and all networks associated with a router will be participating in the OSPF process in the same area.

```
router04#conf t
Enter configuration commands, one per line.  End with CNTL/Z.
router04(config)#router ospf 1
router04(config-router)#network 0.0.0.0 255.255.255.255 area 0
router04(config-router)#
```

Figure 135: This OSPF configuration automatically assigns all interfaces on the router to area 0

The use of the statement "network 0.0.0.0 255.255.255.255 area 0" tells the router to include all of its interfaces and connected networks in the OSPF routing process and to associate them with area 0.

Intermediate System to Intermediate System (IS-IS)

IS-IS is an ISO routing protocol based on work originally done by Digital Equipment Corporation for use with DECNet. Within the context of IS-IS, it's helpful to understand that an Intermediate System is a router as opposed to an "End System" which could be a computer on a network. IS-IS is a link-state routing protocol.

Enhanced IGRP (EIGRP)

EIGRP is an advanced distance vector routing protocol that uses elements of both distance-vector and link-state routing protocols. It is a Cisco proprietary protocol which cannot be used with non-Cisco devices. EIGRP has an administrative distance is 90. EIGRP offers several benefits including:

- Simple configuration

- Extremely rapid convergence due to DUAL (Diffusing Update Algorithm)

- Multiple protocol support (EIGRP supports IP, IPv6, IPX, and AppleTalk)

- Communication between routers using multicast and unicast instead of broadcast (EIGRP uses the multicast address of 224.0.0.10)

- EIGRP uses a sophisticated metric to make routing decisions based on bandwidth and delay by default. It can also consider reliability, loading, and maximum transmission unit size.

In order to configure EIGRP, you must identify the EIGRP autonomous system number, which is shared amongst all routers. You must also identify the networks that will participate in the EIGRP routing process.

```
router01(config)#router eigrp 10
router01(config-router)#network 10.0.0.0 0.255.255.255
router01(config-router)#network 192.168.1.0 0.0.0.255
router01(config-router)#
```

Figure 136: Enabling EIGRP on a router

Border Gateway Protocol (BGP)

BGP is the routing protocol of the public Internet. It is also used in enterprise networks when redundant links connect the enterprise to multiple ISPs. BGP performs routing between multiple autonomous systems. It exchanges routing information with other BGP systems including reachability information.

BGP is a very complicated routing protocol to configure. Although its configuration is beyond the scope of this book, you should at least be aware of it.

Routing Protocols, Directly Connected Networks, and Static Routes

If a network is directly connected, the router will always use the interface connected to the network. Directly connected networks always have an administrative distance of 0.

Static routes are believed over learned routes and will always have an administrative distance of 1 unless manually configured. As mentioned previously, you might want to manually configure the administrative distance on a static route to create a *floating static route* to act as a backup route.

On-Demand Routing

As mentioned earlier, static routing requires administrative overhead to properly maintain routing tables. The use of dynamic routing with routing protocols requires router processor and bandwidth utilization. An alternative to static routing and dynamic routing is on-demand routing (ODR). On-demand routing can be implemented in a hub-and-spoke network. It uses the Cisco Discovery Protocol (CDP) to exchange information between spoke (stub) routers and the hub router. It can only be used in a hub-and-spoke network. ODR operates with minimal router and network overhead compared to dynamic routing implementations. Similarly, ODR does not require the administrative overhead of static routing implementations.

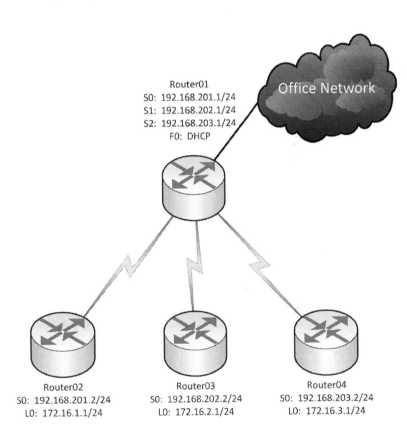

Diagram 6: On-Demand Routing

It's relatively easy to implement ODR. On the hub router, use the global configuration command *router odr.*

179

```
router01(config)#router odr
router01(config-router)#
```

Figure 137: Configure ODR with a single command in global configuration mode on the hub router

After ODR is implemented on the hub router, you can use the ***show ip route*** command to display the routing table on the hub router. Notice that each of the ODR-discovered routes is indicated with a lower-case "o."

```
router01#show ip route
Codes: C - connected, S - static, R - RIP, M - mobile, B - BGP
       D - EIGRP, EX - EIGRP external, O - OSPF, IA - OSPF inter area
       N1 - OSPF NSSA external type 1, N2 - OSPF NSSA external type 2
       E1 - OSPF external type 1, E2 - OSPF external type 2
       i - IS-IS, su - IS-IS summary, L1 - IS-IS level-1, L2 - IS-IS level-2
       ia - IS-IS inter area, * - candidate default, U - per-user static route
       o - ODR, P - periodic downloaded static route

Gateway of last resort is not set

     172.16.0.0/24 is subnetted, 3 subnets
o       172.16.1.0 [160/1] via 192.168.201.2, 00:00:47, Serial0
o       172.16.2.0 [160/1] via 192.168.202.2, 00:00:47, Serial1
o       172.16.3.0 [160/1] via 192.168.203.2, 00:00:47, Serial2
C    192.168.201.0/24 is directly connected, Serial0
C    192.168.202.0/24 is directly connected, Serial1
C    192.168.203.0/24 is directly connected, Serial2
router01#
```

Figure 138: The output of "show ip route" on the ODR hub router

The spoke routers will automatically assign the ODR discovered route as the gateway of last resort (the default gateway) as you can see in the following screen capture.

```
router03>show ip route
Codes: C - connected, S - static, R - RIP, M - mobile, B - BGP
       D - EIGRP, EX - EIGRP external, O - OSPF, IA - OSPF inter area
       N1 - OSPF NSSA external type 1, N2 - OSPF NSSA external type 2
       E1 - OSPF external type 1, E2 - OSPF external type 2
       i - IS-IS, su - IS-IS summary, L1 - IS-IS level-1, L2 - IS-IS level-2
       ia - IS-IS inter area, * - candidate default, U - per-user static route
       o - ODR, P - periodic downloaded static route

Gateway of last resort is 192.168.202.1 to network 0.0.0.0

     172.16.0.0/24 is subnetted, 1 subnets
C       172.16.2.0 is directly connected, Loopback0
C    192.168.202.0/24 is directly connected, Serial0
o*   0.0.0.0/0 [160/1] via 192.168.202.1, 00:00:26, Serial0
router03>
```

Figure 139: The output of "show ip route" on one of the ODR spoke routers

Interactive Exercise 8.2:
Routing Protocols

This exercise uses initial configurations from previous exercises and activates RIP routing for IP. Each router in the exercise must be configured using the specified routing protocols. Use the network diagram at the beginning of the chapter for this exercise.

Objectives:

1. Learn basics of RIP routing, RIPv2 routing, OSPF routing, and EIGRP routing

2. Learn the commands for analyzing the IP routing protocols and routing tables

3. Learn how to debug routing protocols

Steps:

Attempt to ping a router in the classroom that is not directly connected to yours. What happens?

The PING is not successful because your router and the target of the PING have no way of knowing about each other. No static routes have been configured static routes nor have any routing protocols been turned on.

Now, we will turn on a basic routing protocol to allow the routers to exchange information about each of the networks and subnets within our classroom internetwork.

Interactive Exercise 8.2.1:
Routing Information Protocol v1

1. While in privileged EXEC mode, type the following command:

   - Router#*show ip route*

   - Make note of the major networks displayed by the command

2. While in global configuration mode, type the following commands:

   - Router(config)#*router rip*

   - Router(config-router)*network [w.x.y.z]* (where w.x.y.z is the major network to which you are directly connected. You will have to repeat this command for each network to which you are directly connected and each command must go on a separate line.

Figure 140:
Configuring RIP on router01

```
router01(config)#router rip
router01(config-router)#network 10.0.0.0
router01(config-router)#network 192.168.1.0
router01(config-router)#_
```

Figure 141:
Configuring RIP on router02

```
router02(config)#router rip
router02(config-router)#network 10.0.0.0
router02(config-router)#network 160.254.0.0
router02(config-router)#
```

Figure 142:
Configuring RIP on router03

```
router03(config)#router rip
router03(config-router)#network 160.254.0.0
router03(config-router)#network 172.16.0.0
router03(config-router)#
```

Figure 143:
Configuring RIP on router04

```
router04(config)#router rip
router04(config-router)#network 172.16.0.0
router04(config-router)#network 192.168.1.0
router04(config-router)#
```

3. Use the key combination Ctrl-Z to move to Privileged EXEC mode

4. The "show ip protocol" command will provide information about the routing protocol(s) enabled for TCP/IP traffic.

   - Router#*show ip protocol*

```
router01#show ip prot
Routing Protocol is "rip"
  Sending updates every 30 seconds
  Invalid after 180 seconds, hold down 180, flushed after 240
  Outgoing update filter list for all interfaces is not set
  Incoming update filter list for all interfaces is not set
  Redistributing: rip
  Default version control: send version 1, receive any version
    Interface             Send  Recv  Triggered RIP  Key-chain
    FastEthernet0          1     1 2
    Serial0                1     1 2
  Automatic network summarization is in effect
  Maximum path: 4
  Routing for Networks:
    10.0.0.0
    192.168.1.0
  Routing Information Sources:
    Gateway          Distance      Last Update
    10.16.0.2             120      00:00:00
    192.168.1.34          120      00:00:04
  Distance: (default is 120)

router01#
```

Figure 144: The output of the "show ip protocols" command.
Notice the use of the abbreviated version of the command (show ip prot)

- What routing protocol(s) is enabled for IP? You should see RIP as the only routing protocol.

- How often are updates sent? Updates are sent every 30 seconds, by default. It is possible to configure updates to be sent more or less frequently, depending on the needs of the network.

- There are two versions of RIP (version 1 and version 2). What version is being sent? What version can be received? By default, only version 1 is sent, but both versions 1 and 2 can be received.

- Are multiple routing protocols enabled for IP? The answer is no. If other routing protocols were enabled, they would be listed in the output of the "show ip protocols" command.

5. The "show ip route" command shows the IP routing table for the router.

   - Router01#*show ip route*

183

```
router01#show ip route
Codes: C - connected, S - static, R - RIP, M - mobile, B - BGP
       D - EIGRP, EX - EIGRP external, O - OSPF, IA - OSPF inter area
       N1 - OSPF NSSA external type 1, N2 - OSPF NSSA external type 2
       E1 - OSPF external type 1, E2 - OSPF external type 2
       i - IS-IS, su - IS-IS summary, L1 - IS-IS level-1, L2 - IS-IS level-2
       ia - IS-IS inter area, * - candidate default, U - per-user static route
       o - ODR, P - periodic downloaded static route

Gateway of last resort is not set

R    172.16.0.0/16 [120/1] via 192.168.1.34, 00:00:01, Serial0
     10.0.0.0/12 is subnetted, 1 subnets
C       10.16.0.0 is directly connected, FastEthernet0
R    160.254.0.0/16 [120/1] via 10.16.0.2, 00:00:02, FastEthernet0
     192.168.1.0/27 is subnetted, 1 subnets
C       192.168.1.32 is directly connected, Serial0
router01#
```

Figure 145: The output of the "show ip route" command on router01 with RIP enabled

- What major networks do you see? By major network, I mean a non-subnetted, classful network. In the output above, there are four: 172.16.0.0, 10.0.0.0, 160.254.0.0, and 192.168.1.0.

- What subnets do you see? There are two subnets displayed: 10.16.0.0 and 192.168.1.32.

- How are the directly connected subnets connected? 10.16.0.0 is connected via FastEthernet0 and 192.168.1.32 is connected via Serial0.

- What path is used to reach the non-directly-connected subnets? The 172.16.0.0 network is reached via 192.168.1.34 and the 160.254.0.0 network is reached via 10.16.0.2.

- Find the location of each major network and subnet on the chapter network diagram. Remember that you're looking for network addresses, not host or interface addresses.

6. You can monitor the updates being broadcast by RIP with one of the **debug** family of commands.

    – Router#*debug ip rip*

> ⚠ **CAUTION:** Use extreme care when using debugging commands. Debugging can consume significant router resources and can negatively impact router and network performance, especially in a busy production network. In a worst-case scenario, debugging can even render a router useless. Use debugging as a learning tool in a lab network. It is not recommended for use in a production network, except in cases of catastrophic fault conditions as a troubleshooting tool.

```
router01#debug ip rip
RIP protocol debugging is on
router01#
*Mar  1 00:24:47.263: RIP: received v1 update from 192.168.1.34 on Serial0
*Mar  1 00:24:47.267:      160.254.0.0 in 2 hops
*Mar  1 00:24:47.267:      172.16.0.0 in 1 hops
router01#
*Mar  1 00:24:58.403: RIP: sending v1 update to 255.255.255.255 via FastEthernet
0 (10.16.0.1)
*Mar  1 00:24:58.407: RIP: build update entries
*Mar  1 00:24:58.407:    network 172.16.0.0 metric 2
*Mar  1 00:24:58.411:    network 192.168.1.0 metric 1
router01#
```

Figure 146: A sample of the output from "debug ip rip"

Notice in the above screen capture that router01 is receiving a v1 update from its neighbor at 192.168.1.34 on Serial0. That neighbor is saying, "I can reach 160.254.0.0 in 2 hops and 172.16.0.0 in 1 hop." Based on that information and the information it receives from its other neighbor, router01 will decide which routes to inject into its routing table. Recall that RIP uses hop count to choose the best route, so the routes with the least hops will be included in the routing table.

Notice also that the router sends its routing update(s) to the broadcast address of 255.255.255.255. You'll see in the next part of this exercise that RIP v2 uses a multicast address for its updates instead of the 255.255.255.255 broadcast address which sends the updates to all hosts on all networks. RIP v1 is very chatty!

7. Turn off debugging with the following command:

   – Router#*undebug ip rip* or *no debug ip rip*
     (you can also use the command *undebug all* if you prefer to just turn off all debugging.)

```
router01#undebug ip rip
RIP protocol debugging is off
router01#
```

Figure 147:
Disabling IP RIP debugging on router01

Interactive Exercise 8.2.2:
Routing Information Protocol v2

RIPv2 was developed to address several deficiencies of RIPv1. RIPv2 supports authentication, variable-length subnet masking, multicasting, and external route tagging. OSPF is generally preferred over RIPv2, but RIPv2 is simpler to implement.

1. Turn on RIPv2 as follows:

   – Router#*conf t*

   – Router(config)#*router rip*

   – Router(config-router)#*version 2*

```
router01(config)#router rip
router01(config-router)#version 2
router01(config-router)#
```

Figure 148: Enabling RIP version 2 on a router

2. Use the command *show ip protocols* to see the difference between RIP v1 and RIP v2 on the router. Note that, when RIP v2 is enabled, the default settings are for the router to only send and receive version 2 updates. It is possible to configure, on an interface-by-interface basis, the router to send and/or receive either or both types of updates.

```
router01(config-router)#do show ip protocols
Routing Protocol is "rip"
  Sending updates every 30 seconds, next due in 25 seconds
  Invalid after 180 seconds, hold down 180, flushed after 240
  Outgoing update filter list for all interfaces is not set
  Incoming update filter list for all interfaces is not set
  Redistributing: rip
  Default version control: send version 2, receive version 2
    Interface            Send  Recv  Triggered RIP  Key-chain
    FastEthernet0         2     2
    Serial0               2     2
  Automatic network summarization is in effect
  Maximum path: 4
  Routing for Networks:
    10.0.0.0
    192.168.1.0
  Routing Information Sources:
    Gateway          Distance      Last Update
    192.168.1.34          120      00:00:34
  Distance: (default is 120)

router01(config-router)#
```

Figure 149: When RIP v2 is enabled, the default setting allows the router to send and receive only version 2 udates

A version 1 update is considered illegal, as you'll see in the following screen capture of debugging output.

```
router01#debug ip rip
RIP protocol debugging is on
router01#
*Mar  1 00:17:49.675: RIP: sending v2 update to 224.0.0.9 via FastEthernet0 (10.
16.0.1)
*Mar  1 00:17:49.679: RIP: build update entries
*Mar  1 00:17:49.679:    192.168.1.0/24 via 0.0.0.0, metric 1, tag 0
router01#
*Mar  1 00:17:53.799: RIP: sending v2 update to 224.0.0.9 via Serial0 (192.168.1
.33)
*Mar  1 00:17:53.803: RIP: build update entries
*Mar  1 00:17:53.803:    10.0.0.0/8 via 0.0.0.0, metric 1, tag 0
router01#
*Mar  1 00:17:55.875: RIP: ignored v1 packet from 192.168.1.34 (illegal version)
router01#
```

Figure 150: Debugging RIP version 2. Notice that the v1 update packet
from 192.168.1.34 is considered illegal. The update is not included in the routing table.

A couple comments about the screen capture: As I mentioned in the caption, the version 1 update packet from a neighboring router is considered illegal and is not included in router01's routing table. Also, note that RIP version 2 sends updates to the multicast address of 224.0.0.9 instead of the broadcast address of 255.255.255.255. Only other members of the multicast group are required to process the updates, thus improving the efficiency of RIP version 2. The lesson here is that, if you have to use RIP, try to use RIP version 2 instead of version 1.

3. Turn on RIP debugging to see the difference in the RIPv2 updates compared to those in RIPv1. Use the command *debug ip rip* to display the debugging output.

```
router01#debug ip rip
RIP protocol debugging is on
router01#
*Mar  1 00:17:49.675: RIP: sending v2 update to 224.0.0.9 via FastEthernet0 (10.
16.0.1)
*Mar  1 00:17:49.679: RIP: build update entries
*Mar  1 00:17:49.679:    192.168.1.0/24 via 0.0.0.0, metric 1, tag 0
router01#
*Mar  1 00:17:53.799: RIP: sending v2 update to 224.0.0.9 via Serial0 (192.168.1
.33)
*Mar  1 00:17:53.803: RIP: build update entries
*Mar  1 00:17:53.803:    10.0.0.0/8 via 0.0.0.0, metric 1, tag 0
router01#
*Mar  1 00:17:55.875: RIP: ignored v1 packet from 192.168.1.34 (illegal version)
router01#
```

Figure 151: Debugging RIP v2 on router01

(Remember, when you've seen enough of the updates, you can turn off debugging with the command *undebug all.*)

4. Before continuing, enable RIP version 2 on each of the routers in your lab network.

Interactive Exercise 8.2.4:
Enhanced Interior Gateway Routing Protocol

EIGRP is an advanced distance vector routing protocol. Among its features are simple configuration and rapid network convergence. In this exercise, you will implement EIGRP in addition to RIP. Do not disable RIP for this exercise.

1. Enable the EIGRP routing process on each router in your lab network with the global configuration command router eigrp 10 (where "10" is the autonomous system ID which must be the same on each router in the autonomous system).

```
router01(config)#router eigrp 10
router01(config-router)#network 10.0.0.0 0.255.255.255
router01(config-router)#network 192.168.1.0 0.0.0.255
router01(config-router)#
```

Figure 152:
Configuring EIGRP
on router01

```
router02(config)#router eigrp 10
router02(config-router)#network 160.254.0.0 0.0.255.255
router02(config-router)#network 10.0.0.0 0.255.255.255
router02(config-router)#
*Mar  1 00:13:39.983: %DUAL-5-NBRCHANGE: IP-EIGRP(0) 10: Neighbor 10.16.0.1 (Fas
tEthernet0) is up: new adjacency
router02(config-router)#
```

Figure 153:
Configuring EIGRP on router02

```
router03(config)#router eigrp 10
router03(config-router)#network 172.16.0.0 0.0.255.255
router03(config-router)#network 160.254.0.0 0.0.255.255
router03(config-router)#
*Mar  1 00:14:27.715: %DUAL-5-NBRCHANGE: IP-EIGRP(0) 10: Neighbor 160.254.100.2
(Serial0) is up: new adjacency
router03(config-router)#
```

Figure 154:
Configuring EIGRP on router03

```
router04(config)#router eigrp 10
router04(config-router)#network 172.16.0.0 0.0.255.255
router04(config-router)#network 192.168.1.0 0.0.0.255
router04(config-router)#
*Mar  1 00:15:41.679: %DUAL-5-NBRCHANGE: IP-EIGRP(0) 10: Neighbor 172.16.65.3 (F
astEthernet0) is up: new adjacency
*Mar  1 00:15:41.695: %DUAL-5-NBRCHANGE: IP-EIGRP(0) 10: Neighbor 192.168.1.33 (
Serial0) is up: new adjacency
router04(config-router)#
```

Figure 155:
Configuring EIGRP on router04

Notice how, as you enable EIGRP on each router after router01, that the routers establish neighborhood with each other. If you were to run debugging during configuration, you would see them start to exchange route information and hello packets with each other. (That's actually a good idea as a means of understanding what happens in a network running EIGRP. After you do the initial configuration, try going back and undoing the EIGRP configuration. Then, enable debugging before you start configuring EIGRP. You'll see quite a bit of traffic initially as the routers establish neighborhood, then things will quiet down. You can stimulate additional traffic by downing a router or adding another router to the network.)

2. Now that you've configured EIGRP in your network, use the *show ip protocols* command on one of your routers to view the routing protocols that are implemented. (I used router04.)

```
router04#show ip protocols
Routing Protocol is "rip"
  Sending updates every 30 seconds, next due in 25 seconds
  Invalid after 180 seconds, hold down 180, flushed after 240
  Outgoing update filter list for all interfaces is not set
  Incoming update filter list for all interfaces is not set
  Redistributing: rip
  Default version control: send version 2, receive version 2
    Interface              Send  Recv  Triggered RIP  Key-chain
    FastEthernet0          2     2
    Serial0                2     2
  Automatic network summarization is in effect
  Maximum path: 4
  Routing for Networks:
    172.16.0.0
    192.168.1.0
  Routing Information Sources:
    Gateway          Distance      Last Update
    192.168.1.33          120      00:00:16
    172.16.65.3           120      00:00:18
  Distance: (default is 120)

  Routing Protocol is "eigrp 10"
    Outgoing update filter list for all interfaces is not set
    Incoming update filter list for all interfaces is not set
    Default networks flagged in outgoing updates
    Default networks accepted from incoming updates
    EIGRP metric weight K1=1, K2=0, K3=1, K4=0, K5=0
    EIGRP maximum hopcount 100
  --More--
```

Figure 156: The output of the "show ip protocols" command on router04 with both RIP and EIGRP configured

Notice in the above screen capture that both RIP and EIGRP are enabled on the router.

3. Now, issue the *show ip route* command to see which routes the router has included in its routing table.

```
router04#show ip route
Codes: C - connected, S - static, R - RIP, M - mobile, B - BGP
       D - EIGRP, EX - EIGRP external, O - OSPF, IA - OSPF inter area
       N1 - OSPF NSSA external type 1, N2 - OSPF NSSA external type 2
       E1 - OSPF external type 1, E2 - OSPF external type 2
       i - IS-IS, su - IS-IS summary, L1 - IS-IS level-1, L2 - IS-IS level-2
       ia - IS-IS inter area, * - candidate default, U - per-user static route
       o - ODR, P - periodic downloaded static route

Gateway of last resort is not set

     172.16.0.0/16 is variably subnetted, 2 subnets, 2 masks
D       172.16.0.0/16 is a summary, 00:00:55, Null0
C       172.16.64.0/18 is directly connected, FastEthernet0
D    10.0.0.0/8 [90/540160] via 192.168.1.33, 00:00:56, Serial0
D    160.254.0.0/16 [90/540160] via 172.16.65.3, 00:00:56, FastEthernet0
     192.168.1.0/24 is variably subnetted, 2 subnets, 2 masks
C       192.168.1.32/27 is directly connected, Serial0
D       192.168.1.0/24 is a summary, 00:00:56, Null0
router04#
```

Figure 157: The output of "show ip route" on router04 with both RIP and EIGRP configured

Recall in the previous screen capture from the *show ip protocols* command that both RIP and EIGRP are enabled on this router (and all the routers in the lab network, for that matter). In the screen capture from the command *show ip route*, however, you only see EIGRP routes displayed (they're indicated with a "D"). Why don't the RIP routes display? Recall the earlier discussion about administrative distances. EIGRP has an administrative distance of 90, while RIP has an administrative distance of 120. Routes with a lower administrative distance are believed over routes with a higher administrative distance. The router, therefore, chooses the EIGRP-discovered routes for its routing table instead of the RIP discovered routes. That brings up another question: Is there any benefit to running RIP at the same time as EIGRP? Not in this situation. Is there a problem with running RIP and EIGRP at the same time? Yes, most definitely. Think about the cost to the router's performance of running two resource-intensive processes simultaneously, plus consider the bandwidth utilization of RIP and you can understand why we don't generally want to run multiple routing protocols on a single router. Forgive the corny saying, but what we want are "lean, mean routing machines." Corny, yes, but also true. Part of our job as router administrators is to disable all unneeded processes to maximize router performance.

Note: There are some situations where you might have a router connected to one network running RIP and another network running, say OSPF. That type of router is called an *autonomous system boundary router* (ASBR) and it, obviously, would need to run both RIP and OSPF. It acts as a translator using a process called *route redistribution* to exchange routing information between the two networks.

EIGRP Monitoring and Troubleshooting Commands

Several commands are available to aid in monitoring and troubleshooting EIGRP.

- *Show ip eigrp neighbors* displays neighbors discovered by an EIGRP router

- *Show ip eigrp interfaces* displays information about EIGRP-enabled interfaces

- *Show ip eigrp topology* displays the EIGRP topology table

- *Show ip eigrp traffic* displays the number of EIGRP packets both sent and received including a variety of statistical information

The No Auto-Summary Command Allows Routers to Advertise Subnets

Both RIPv2 and EIGRP, by default, enable automatic summarization along classful network boundaries. In other words, if a router is connected to both the 192.168.1.32/27 and 192.168.1.64/27 subnets, automatic summarization will force it to only advertise the major network of 192.168.1.0/24. If you want the router to advertise subnets, you must use the router configuration mode command "no auto-summary". Many network administrators make a habit of disabling automatic summarization, but it really depends entirely on whether you want subnets advertised or summarized.

Interactive Exercise 8.2.5:
Open Shortest Path First

Open Shortest Path First is an industry-standard routing protocol. It is designed for use in large and/or growing internetworks. In this exercise, you will implement single-area OSPF as the sole routing protocol.

1. If you did not write the previous (RIP and EIGRP) configurations to memory, you can remove them by simply restarting your routers. Otherwise, remove RIP by entering the global configuration command *no router rip* on each of the routers in your lab network. Remove EIGRP by entering the global configuration command *no router eigrp 10* on each of the routers in your lab network.

2. Now, enable the OSPF routing process with the following command:

   - Router(config)#*router ospf process-ID*

   Then, define the interface(s) on which you want to run OSPF and configure the area ID for the interface(s):

   - Router(config-router)#*net network address wildcard mask area-ID*

   ```
   router01(config)#
   router01(config)#router ospf 10
   router01(config-router)#network 10.0.0.0 0.255.255.255 area 0
   router01(config-router)#network 192.168.1.0 0.0.0.255 area 0
   router01(config-router)#
   ```

   Figure 158: Configuring OSPF on router01

(The OSPF process ID can be any number between 1 and 65,535. It is specific to the router and does not have to be the same on the other routers in the network. Notice that I used different process IDs on each of the four routers. They can be the same or different, it doesn't matter.)

```
router02(config)#router ospf 20
router02(config-router)#network 160.254.0.0 0.0.255.255 area 0
router02(config-router)#network 10.0.0.0 0.255.255.255 area 0
router02(config-router)#
*Mar  1 00:08:36.775: %OSPF-5-ADJCHG: Process 20, Nbr 192.168.1.33 on FastEthern
et0 from LOADING to FULL, Loading Done
router02(config-router)#
```

Figure 159: Configuring OSPF on router02

```
router03(config)#router ospf 33
router03(config-router)#network 160.254.0.0 0.0.255.255 area 0
router03(config-router)#network 172.16.0.0 0.0.255.255 area 0
router03(config-router)#
```

Figure 160: Configuring OSPF on router03

```
router04(config)#router ospf 44
router04(config-router)#network 172.16.0.0 0.0.255.255 area 0
router04(config-router)#network 192.168.1.0 0.0.0.255 area 0
router04(config-router)#
```

Figure 161: Configuring OSPF on router04

Configuring the network address(es) is how you specify the range of IP addresses you want associated with the OSPF routing process. In a simple configuration, you will configure the network address of each directly connected network, as you can see in each of the above screen captures.

Now, view the router's routing table with the "show ip route" command.

```
router04#show ip route
Codes: C - connected, S - static, R - RIP, M - mobile, B - BGP
       D - EIGRP, EX - EIGRP external, O - OSPF, IA - OSPF inter area
       N1 - OSPF NSSA external type 1, N2 - OSPF NSSA external type 2
       E1 - OSPF external type 1, E2 - OSPF external type 2
       i - IS-IS, su - IS-IS summary, L1 - IS-IS level-1, L2 - IS-IS level-2
       ia - IS-IS inter area, * - candidate default, U - per-user static route
       o - ODR, P - periodic downloaded static route

Gateway of last resort is not set

     172.16.0.0/18 is subnetted, 1 subnets
C       172.16.64.0 is directly connected, FastEthernet0
     10.0.0.0/8 is variably subnetted, 2 subnets, 2 masks
R       10.0.0.0/8 [120/1] via 192.168.1.33, 00:00:02, Serial0
O       10.16.0.0/12 [110/2] via 192.168.1.33, 00:00:25, Serial0
     160.254.0.0/16 is variably subnetted, 2 subnets, 2 masks
O       160.254.100.0/24 [110/2] via 172.16.65.3, 00:00:25, FastEthernet0
R       160.254.0.0/16 [120/1] via 172.16.65.3, 00:00:00, FastEthernet0
     192.168.1.0/27 is subnetted, 1 subnets
C       192.168.1.32 is directly connected, Serial0
router04#
```

Figure 162: The output of "show ip route" with OSPF implemented
as the sole routing protocol

Notice the OSPF routes are indicated by a "O" in the left-hand column of the routing table.

Checking and Debugging the OSPF Configuration

- Router#*show ip ospf* shows OSPF process and related details such as the number of times the router has recalculated the routing table

```
router01#show ip ospf
 Routing Process "ospf 10" with ID 192.168.1.33
 Supports only single TOS(TOS0) routes
 Supports opaque LSA
 Supports Link-local Signaling (LLS)
 Supports area transit capability
 Initial SPF schedule delay 5000 msecs
 Minimum hold time between two consecutive SPFs 10000 msecs
 Maximum wait time between two consecutive SPFs 10000 msecs
 Incremental-SPF disabled
 Minimum LSA interval 5 secs
 Minimum LSA arrival 1000 msecs
 LSA group pacing timer 240 secs
 Interface flood pacing timer 33 msecs
 Retransmission pacing timer 66 msecs
 Number of external LSA 0. Checksum Sum 0x000000
 Number of opaque AS LSA 0. Checksum Sum 0x000000
 Number of DCbitless external and opaque AS LSA 0
 Number of DoNotAge external and opaque AS LSA 0
 Number of areas in this router is 1. 1 normal 0 stub 0 nssa
 Number of areas transit capable is 0
 External flood list length 0
    Area BACKBONE(0)
        Number of interfaces in this area is 2
        Area has no authentication
        SPF algorithm last executed 00:11:58.284 ago
        SPF algorithm executed 8 times
        Area ranges are
        Number of LSA 6. Checksum Sum 0x023C28
```

Figure 163: The output of the "show ip ospf" command.
Note, in particular, that it shows the router ID (192.168.1.33), the area ID (0),
and the number of interfaces on the router in the area (2).

- Router#*show ip ospf database* displays the contents of the OSPF topological database

```
router01#show ip ospf database

            OSPF Router with ID (192.168.1.33) (Process ID 10)

            Router Link States (Area 0)

Link ID         ADV Router      Age      Seq#       Checksum Link count
160.254.100.2   160.254.100.2   831      0x80000004 0x00229F 3
172.16.65.3     172.16.65.3     803      0x80000005 0x005A9F 3
192.168.1.33    192.168.1.33    795      0x80000004 0x005CE2 3
192.168.1.34    192.168.1.34    792      0x80000003 0x00F37C 3

            Net Link States (Area 0)

Link ID         ADV Router      Age      Seq#       Checksum
10.16.0.1       192.168.1.33    932      0x80000001 0x002BE5
172.16.65.3     172.16.65.3     803      0x80000001 0x0042A7
router01#
```

Figure 164: The output of the "show ip ospf database" command.
This command displays the information known to the router about each of the routers in the area.

- Router#*show ip ospf interface* displays the OSPF configuration on each interface.

```
router01#show ip ospf interface
Serial0 is up, line protocol is up
  Internet Address 192.168.1.33/27, Area 0
  Process ID 10, Router ID 192.168.1.33, Network Type POINT_TO_POINT, Cost: 1
  Transmit Delay is 1 sec, State POINT_TO_POINT,
  Timer intervals configured, Hello 10, Dead 40, Wait 40, Retransmit 5
    oob-resync timeout 40
    Hello due in 00:00:09
  Supports Link-local Signaling (LLS)
  Index 2/2, flood queue length 0
  Next 0x0(0)/0x0(0)
  Last flood scan length is 1, maximum is 1
  Last flood scan time is 0 msec, maximum is 0 msec
  Neighbor Count is 1, Adjacent neighbor count is 1
    Adjacent with neighbor 192.168.1.34
  Suppress hello for 0 neighbor(s)
FastEthernet0 is up, line protocol is up
  Internet Address 10.16.0.1/12, Area 0
  Process ID 10, Router ID 192.168.1.33, Network Type BROADCAST, Cost: 1
  Transmit Delay is 1 sec, State DR, Priority 1
  Designated Router (ID) 192.168.1.33, Interface address 10.16.0.1
  Backup Designated router (ID) 160.254.100.2, Interface address 10.16.0.2
  Timer intervals configured, Hello 10, Dead 40, Wait 40, Retransmit 5
    oob-resync timeout 40
--More--
```

Figure 165: The output of the "show ip ospf interface" command.
This command displays interface configuration information, performance statistics, and neighbor information.

- Router#*show ip ospf neighbor* shows information about the router's relationship(s) with its neighbor(s)

```
router01#show ip ospf neighbor

Neighbor ID      Pri   State        Dead Time   Address        Interface
192.168.1.34      0    FULL/  -     00:00:38    192.168.1.34   Serial0
160.254.100.2     1    FULL/BDR     00:00:37    10.16.0.2      FastEthernet0
router01#
```

Figure 166: The output of the "show ip ospf neighbor" command.
This command shows information about each of the router's neighbors.

- router#*debug ip ospf events* show OSPF-related event information including adjacencies, flooding information, shortest path first calculation, and designated router selection

```
router01#debug ip ospf events
OSPF events debugging is on
router01#
*Mar  1 00:22:43.811: OSPF: Send hello to 224.0.0.5 area 0 on Serial0 from 192.1
68.1.33
*Mar  1 00:22:44.143: OSPF: Rcv hello from 192.168.1.34 area 0 from Serial0 192.
168.1.34
*Mar  1 00:22:44.143: OSPF: End of hello processing
router01#
*Mar  1 00:22:45.891: OSPF: Send hello to 224.0.0.5 area 0 on FastEthernet0 from
 10.16.0.1
router01#
```

Figure 167: A debugging trace after enabling "debug ip ospf events."
Notice the sending and receiving of neighbor hello packets. If you were to enable this type of
debugging and then disable and re-enable an interface, you would see a flurry of activity.

Back up your configuration to your TFTP server. (Be sure to use the correct IP address for your TFTP server.) Use a different file name after each exercise so you'll have a backup from each exercise. Execute the following command on a single line:

- router#*copy system:running-config tftp://10.16.0.101/cfg-routing-protocols.txt*

Summary

In this chapter, you learned about routing, both static and dynamic routing. Remember that one is not necessarily better than the other. As with most things in life, it's a matter of choosing the right tool for the job at that particular point in time. Many network admins use a combination of static routes and dynamically discovered routes. It's not a matter of whether one is better than the other, it's a matter of what makes the most sense for your network and the way your end-users work.

CHAPTER 9:
Troubleshooting

Chapter Introduction

I wish I could tell you that you won't ever have to do any troubleshooting. Obviously, that's not true. In this chapter, I'm sharing the troubleshooting techniques that have worked for me in the past. Something that I find helpful is a checklist. One of my training clients is a large service provider in Seattle and, as part of a training program I did for them, they asked me to write a checklist for the techs to use in the field. I've updated it and included it in this chapter. I've also got one you can download as a PDF online at www.soundtraining.net/cisco-router-book.

Look, the most important thing in troubleshooting is this: Don't make assumptions. Don't assume the unit has power. Don't assume the cables are good. Don't assume your partner configured his/her device correctly. For heaven's sake, don't assume you configured your device correctly. You get the idea. Double-check everything starting at the physical layer and work your way up. Good luck!

Chapter Objectives

- Provide a good foundation for troubleshooting basic issues in router troubleshooting

- Provide a checklist for basic router troubleshooting

- Create familiarity with more advanced *show* and *debugging* commands to aid in troubleshooting

- Show how to use logging commands to create system logs to aid in troubleshooting

Online Companion Resources

Videos: Watch the companion videos for this chapter. They're available at
www.soundtraining.net/videos/cisco-router-training-videos

Web Page: There is a supporting web page with live links and other resources for this book
at www.soundtraining.net/cisco-router-book

Facebook: www.soundtraining.net/facebook

Twitter: www.soundtraining.net/twitter

Blog: www.soundtraining.net/blog

Basics of Troubleshooting

Troubleshooting is a great example of how to use the OSI model. Start troubleshooting at layer one and work your way up through the data link and network layers. Most of your router troubleshooting will done at the bottom three layers.

The most fundamental concept in troubleshooting is the importance of starting at the OSI physical layer. Just like a home appliance that's not operating, check to make sure it's getting power and that there are no circuit breakers thrown.

- Are the devices plugged in? If so, are the plugs fully inserted into the sockets? I recently installed a new 1941 router and it seemed to operate erratically. Based on appearances, everything was normal. I tried re-seating plugs and discovered that the power plug was not fully seated, which was causing the problem. It looked normal and it seemed to be fully inserted into the socket, but it actually needed to go in about another quarter of an inch.

- Is there power to the equipment rack? To the room? To the building? Are any circuit breakers thrown?

- Are the correct types of cables being used? This is less of an issue today than in years past, but make sure you're not using a crossover cable where you actually need a straight-through cable. Even though Cisco console ports support an RJ45 connector, you can't use an Ethernet cable to console into your router. You have to use a rollover cable.

- Are the plugs properly oriented? This may seem obvious, but I once spent quite a bit of time troubleshooting a classroom network until I discovered this particular problem. I would often have the students connect the network at the beginning of class. At this time, we were still using serial cables in parts of the classroom network. The serial cables had a DB60 connector which was shaped in such a way that you couldn't (at least in theory) plug it in upside down. Two of the routers interfaces were down, but everything looked normal from a physical standpoint. Finally, I started looking for bent pins in the connectors. That was when I discovered that one of the students had forced a connector on upside down. I have to say that student must have been very strong!

Basic Router Troubleshooting Checklist

Download a PDF of this at www.soundtraining.net/cisco-router-book. When a router isn't functioning, here are some steps to perform to eliminate basic faults as the source of trouble:

1. Check power issues. Look for power lights, check plugs, and circuit breakers.

2. Use the command *show ip interface brief* to ensure that desired interfaces are up.

3. Use the ping and trace commands to check for connectivity.

4. Use the ***show ip route*** command to find out what the router knows. Is there either an explicit route to the remote network or a gateway of last resort?

5. If the problem involves a computer, check to ensure that its firewall is not blocking packets. I've encountered computers at client locations that had two firewalls in operation without the client's knowledge. (They had the Windows firewall enabled, plus they had installed a VPN client that included a firewall which was also enabled. The giveaway was that the computer in question could see other network devices, but none of them could see the computer in question. We disabled the Windows firewall for troubleshooting and still no love. That was when I started looking for another firewall.)

6. If the above steps don't resolve the issue, check for access-control lists that block traffic. As you will learn in the section on access-control lists, there is an implicit "deny any" at the end of every access-control list, so even if you don't see a statement explicitly denying traffic, it might be blocked by an implicit "deny any."

7. If a VPN is part of the connection, check to ensure that it is up. Use the ***show crypto*** family of commands to check VPN connections. With VPN connections, each end of the connection must mirror the other. For example, even something as seemingly inconsequential as a different timeout value or a different key lifetime can prevent a connection.

8. If you are trying to gain remote access to a server, ensure that it supports the protocol you're attempting to use. For example, if the router hasn't been configured to support SSH and you use the default settings in PuTTY which call for SSH, you won't be able to connect. Also, some admins change the default port numbers, so you may expect to use port 22 with SSH, but the admin may have configured it to use a non-standard port.

9. User errors can also be the source of errors. Check to ensure that correct usernames and passwords are being used, that you and the admin on the other end of the connection are using the same network addresses and matching subnet masks.

10. Do not make assumptions. Verify everything!

Often, by using the above steps, you can solve the problem. If that doesn't do it, then proceed to more advanced ***show*** and ***debug*** commands to isolate the problem.

Testing Connectivity with Ping and Traceroute

You've probably used the ping and traceroute (tracert) commands on a computer to test for connectivity. You have access to similar tools on a Cisco router.

The Ping Command

You can perform both standard and extended pings with a router. When using a standard ping, there are no options available to you. You are assumed to be pinging with IPv4 with a hop count of five. Simply enter the ping command with the target (either by IP address or, if name resolution is enabled, the hostname.

```
testrouter#ping 192.168.1.1
Type escape sequence to abort.
Sending 5, 100-byte ICMP Echos to 192.168.1.1, timeout is 2 seconds:
!!!!!
Success rate is 100 percent (5/5), round-trip min/avg/max = 1/1/4 ms
testrouter#
```

Figure 168: The use of a standard ping on a Cisco router

Notice in the above screen capture that the exclamation marks (!) indicate a successful ping. You might also see a period (.) or several other types of responses. The following table explains the possible responses to a ping.

Response	Meaning
!	Each exclamation mark means you received a reply from the target host
.	A period means the router timed out while waiting for a reply
U	Destination unreachable
?	Unknown packet type

You can also perform an extended ping by simply entering the ping command with no parameters. The router will then prompt you for protocol type, target address, and various other information in order to complete the ping. Notice in the screen capture below how I used the question mark to show protocol options with the ping.

Although I didn't choose to use extended commands in the screen capture, one aspect of extended commands that I've found helpful is the ability to specify which interface to use with the ping.

```
testrouter#ping ?
  WORD      Ping destination address or hostname
  atm       ATM echo
  clns      CLNS echo
  ethernet  Ethernet echo
  ip        IP echo
  ipv6      IPv6 echo
  tag       Tag encapsulated IP echo
  <cr>

testrouter#ping
Protocol [ip]: ip
Target IP address: 192.168.1.1
Repeat count [5]: 25
Datagram size [100]:
Timeout in seconds [2]:
Extended commands [n]:
Sweep range of sizes [n]:
Type escape sequence to abort.
Sending 25, 100-byte ICMP Echos to 192.168.1.1, timeout is 2 seconds:
!!!!!!!!!!!!!!!!!!!!!!!!!!!
Success rate is 100 percent (25/25), round-trip min/avg/max = 1/1/4 ms
testrouter#
```

Figure 169: The use of an extended ping on a Cisco router

Using Traceroute

You can use traceroute to find the routes followed by packets on their way from your router to their destination. Traceroute shows each router along the path.

As with ping, there are a variety of possible responses, as shown in the following table.

Response	Meaning
*	Timeout
?	Unknown packet type
A	Prohibited by an administrator, possibly due to an access-control list
H	The host is unreachable
N	The network is unreachable
P	The protocol is unreachable
Q	ICMP source quench, meaning the destination is too busy
T	Also a timeout

```
testrouter#traceroute 208.67.222.222
Type escape sequence to abort.
Tracing the route to resolver1.opendns.com (208.67.222.222)
VRF info: (vrf in name/id, vrf out name/id)
  1 192.168.1.1 0 msec 0 msec 0 msec
  2 73.98.180.1 12 msec 16 msec 8 msec
  3 te-0-0-0-5-ur08.burien.wa.seattle.comcast.net (68.87.206.5) 8 msec 12 msec 8 msec
  4 ae-21-0-ar03.seattle.wa.seattle.comcast.net (69.139.164.141) 12 msec 8 msec 12 msec
  5 he-1-7-0-0-10-cr01.seattle.wa.ibone.comcast.net (68.86.91.165) 24 msec
    he-1-8-0-0-11-cr01.seattle.wa.ibone.comcast.net (68.86.95.249) 16 msec
    he-1-5-0-0-11-cr01.seattle.wa.ibone.comcast.net (68.86.94.65) 16 msec
  6 4.59.234.21 28 msec 8 msec 12 msec
  7 ae-24-52.car4.Seattle1.Level3.net (4.69.147.166) 16 msec 12 msec
    ae-14-51.car4.Seattle1.Level3.net (4.69.147.134) 12 msec
  8 SPLICE-COMM.car4.Seattle1.Level3.net (4.71.156.130) 40 msec 40 msec 36 msec
  9 * * *
 10 * * *
 11 * *
testrouter#
```

Figure 170: Using traceroute to follow the path to a destination

You can break out of traceroute by using the key combination Ctrl+Shift+6. (That's intuitive! (Just kidding.) Where did that come from?)

As with ping, you can perform an extended traceroute by simply entering traceroute with no parameters, the providing information as to protocol, repeat counts, and similar information. Help is available by using the question mark.

```
testrouter#traceroute ?
  WORD      Trace route to destination address or hostname
  appletalk AppleTalk Trace
  clns      ISO CLNS Trace
  ethernet  Ethernet Traceroute
  ip        IP Trace
  ipv6      IPv6 Trace
  ipx       IPX Trace
  <cr>

testrouter#traceroute
```

Figure 171:
Viewing the options for an
extended traceroute

Use of The "show" Command in Troubleshooting

The "show" family of commands displays information about the router's current configuration and performance. I think the two most important commands in troubleshooting router problems are ***show ip interface brief*** and ***show ip route***.

Show ip interface brief displays a summary of the interfaces on the router including whether they are up or down. Interfaces that show "administratively down" have been disabled with the "shutdown" command.

```
router05#show ip interface brief
Interface                IP-Address      OK? Method Status                 Protocol
FastEthernet0            23.4.5.6        YES manual up                     up
Serial0                  192.168.201.2   YES NVRAM  up                     up
Serial1                  192.168.202.2   YES NVRAM  up                     up
Serial2                  192.168.203.2   YES NVRAM  up                     down
Serial3                  192.168.204.2   YES NVRAM  administratively down  down
router05#
```

Figure 172: The output of the "show ip interface brief" command on a router
with one fast Ethernet interface and four serial interfaces

In the above screen shot, going from left to right, the first column indicates the name of the interface, the second column shows its IP address, the third column (OK) indicates whether the IP address is currently valid or not, the fourth column (method) shows how the IP address was obtained, the fifth column (Status) indicates the physical condition of the interface, and the sixth column indicates the routing protocol's operational status.

Things to look for:

- Ensure that the IP address is what you expect. If you need to check the subnet mask, you must use the command ***show ip interface***.

- If the status is administratively down, you must use the ***no shutdown*** command to bring it up

- If the status is just down, check cables and connectors on both ends of the connection

- If the protocol is down, check to ensure that you're using matching protocols on both ends of the connection

Show interfaces displays detailed statistics about the interfaces connected to the router.

```
testrouter#show interface g0/0
GigabitEthernet0/0 is up, line protocol is up
  Hardware is CN Gigabit Ethernet, address is 7081.0570.8500 (bia 7081.0570.8500)
  Internet address is 192.168.101.1/24
  MTU 1500 bytes, BW 100000 Kbit/sec, DLY 100 usec,
    reliability 255/255, txload 1/255, rxload 1/255
  Encapsulation ARPA, loopback not set
  Keepalive set (10 sec)
  Full Duplex, 100Mbps, media type is RJ45
  output flow-control is unsupported, input flow-control is unsupported
  ARP type: ARPA, ARP Timeout 04:00:00
  Last input 00:00:42, output 00:00:10, output hang never
  Last clearing of "show interface" counters never
  Input queue: 0/75/0/0 (size/max/drops/flushes); Total output drops: 6
  Queueing strategy: fifo
  Output queue: 0/40 (size/max)
  5 minute input rate 0 bits/sec, 0 packets/sec
  5 minute output rate 0 bits/sec, 0 packets/sec
    909471 packets input, 179294832 bytes, 0 no buffer
    Received 80730 broadcasts (0 IP multicasts)
    0 runts, 0 giants, 0 throttles
    0 input errors, 0 CRC, 0 frame, 0 overrun, 0 ignored
    0 watchdog, 1887 multicast, 0 pause input
    1214887 packets output, 706491470 bytes, 0 underruns
    0 output errors, 0 collisions, 1 interface resets
    0 unknown protocol drops
    0 babbles, 0 late collision, 0 deferred
    17 lost carrier, 0 no carrier, 0 pause output
    0 output buffer failures, 0 output buffers swapped out
testrouter#
```

Figure 173:
The output of the "show interface g0/0"
command on a Cisco 1941 router

Show ip route displays the routes that the router is aware of. If there is no route to a particular destination in the router's routing table, the packets cannot be forwarded to that destination.

```
router01#show ip route
Codes: C - connected, S - static, R - RIP, M - mobile, B - BGP
       D - EIGRP, EX - EIGRP external, O - OSPF, IA - OSPF inter area
       N1 - OSPF NSSA external type 1, N2 - OSPF NSSA external type 2
       E1 - OSPF external type 1, E2 - OSPF external type 2
       i - IS-IS, su - IS-IS summary, L1 - IS-IS level-1, L2 - IS-IS level-2
       ia - IS-IS inter area, * - candidate default, U - per-user static route
       o - ODR, P - periodic downloaded static route

Gateway of last resort is not set

     172.16.0.0/24 is subnetted, 3 subnets
o       172.16.1.0 [160/1] via 192.168.201.2, 00:00:47, Serial0
o       172.16.2.0 [160/1] via 192.168.202.2, 00:00:47, Serial1
o       172.16.3.0 [160/1] via 192.168.203.2, 00:00:47, Serial2
C    192.168.201.0/24 is directly connected, Serial0
C    192.168.202.0/24 is directly connected, Serial1
C    192.168.203.0/24 is directly connected, Serial2
router01#
```

Figure 174:
The output of the
"show ip route" command
on a hub router with
ODR enabled

```
router01#show ip route
Codes: C - connected, S - static, R - RIP, M - mobile, B - BGP
       D - EIGRP, EX - EIGRP external, O - OSPF, IA - OSPF inter area
       N1 - OSPF NSSA external type 1, N2 - OSPF NSSA external type 2
       E1 - OSPF external type 1, E2 - OSPF external type 2
       i - IS-IS, su - IS-IS summary, L1 - IS-IS level-1, L2 - IS-IS level-2
       ia - IS-IS inter area, * - candidate default, U - per-user static route
       o - ODR, P - periodic downloaded static route

Gateway of last resort is not set

     172.16.0.0/18 is subnetted, 1 subnets
S       172.16.64.0 is directly connected, Serial0
     10.0.0.0/12 is subnetted, 1 subnets
C       10.16.0.0 is directly connected, FastEthernet0
     160.254.0.0/24 is subnetted, 1 subnets
S       160.254.100.0 [1/0] via 10.16.0.2
     192.168.1.0/27 is subnetted, 1 subnets
C       192.168.1.32 is directly connected, Serial0
router01#
```

Figure 175:
The routing table of a router
with two static routes

```
router04(config-router)#do show ip route
Codes: C - connected, S - static, R - RIP, M - mobile, B - BGP
       D - EIGRP, EX - EIGRP external, O - OSPF, IA - OSPF inter area
       N1 - OSPF NSSA external type 1, N2 - OSPF NSSA external type 2
       E1 - OSPF external type 1, E2 - OSPF external type 2
       i - IS-IS, su - IS-IS summary, L1 - IS-IS level-1, L2 - IS-IS level-2
       ia - IS-IS inter area, * - candidate default, U - per-user static route
       o - ODR, P - periodic downloaded static route

Gateway of last resort is not set

     172.16.0.0/16 is variably subnetted, 2 subnets, 2 masks
D       172.16.0.0/16 is a summary, 00:00:23, Null0
C       172.16.64.0/18 is directly connected, FastEthernet0
     10.0.0.0/8 is variably subnetted, 2 subnets, 2 masks
D       10.0.0.0/8 [90/540160] via 192.168.1.33, 00:00:23, Serial0
O       10.16.0.0/12 [110/2] via 192.168.1.33, 00:10:27, Serial0
     160.254.0.0/16 is variably subnetted, 2 subnets, 2 masks
O       160.254.100.0/24 [110/2] via 172.16.65.3, 00:10:27, FastEthernet0
D       160.254.0.0/16 [90/540160] via 172.16.65.3, 00:00:25, FastEthernet0
     192.168.1.0/24 is variably subnetted, 2 subnets, 2 masks
C       192.168.1.32/27 is directly connected, Serial0
D       192.168.1.0/24 is a summary, 00:00:27, Null0
router04(config-router)#
```

Figure 176:
A routing table on a
router with both EIGRP
and OSPF enabled

Show run displays the router's running-configuration. You can filter the output of *show run* by piping the output into various filters, including:

Filter	Effect
Begin	Begin with the line that matches
Exclude	Exclude lines that match
Include	Include lines that match
Section	Filter a section of output

Here are some examples of filtering the output of show run:

```
testrouter#show run | include interface
interface Embedded-Service-Engine0/0
interface GigabitEthernet0/0
interface GigabitEthernet0/1
testrouter#
```

Figure 177:
The include filter is of limited usefulness, but it can be handy in looking at individual lines of a configuration

```
testrouter#show run | begin interface GigabitEthernet0/0
interface GigabitEthernet0/0
 ip address 192.168.101.1 255.255.255.0
 duplex auto
 speed auto
 ipv6 address autoconfig default
 no mop enabled
!
interface GigabitEthernet0/1
 ip address dhcp
 duplex auto
 speed auto
 no cdp enable
!
ip forward-protocol nd
!
ip http server
ip http authentication local
ip http secure-server
ip http timeout-policy idle 60 life 86400 requests 10000
!
ip route 0.0.0.0 0.0.0.0 192.168.1.1 254
ip route 0.0.0.0 0.0.0.0 192.168.1.1 254
ip route 0.0.0.0 0.0.0.0 dhcp
!
 --More--
```

Figure 178:
Notice how the output of "show run" begins with the filtering string specified in the command

```
testrouter#show run | section line con 0
line con 0
 exec-timeout 0 0
 password p@ss1234
 logging synchronous
 login
testrouter#
```

Figure 179:
I use the section filtering a lot. It allows me to look at individual portions of the configuration file

Show access-lists displays Access Control Lists configured on the router.

```
testrouter#show access-lists
Standard IP access list 10
    10 deny   10.1.0.0, wildcard bits 0.0.0.255
Standard IP access list BlockLobbyOut
    10 deny   172.16.0.0, wildcard bits 0.0.0.255
Extended IP access list 100
    10 permit ip any any (116999 matches)
testrouter#
```

Figure 180:
This router has three access-control lists configured including one named list and two numbered lists

Show ip protocols displays the current configuration and state of active routing protocols on the router.

```
testrouter(config)#do show ip prot
*** IP Routing is NSF aware ***

Routing Protocol is "eigrp 1"
  Outgoing update filter list for all interfaces is not set
  Incoming update filter list for all interfaces is not set
  Default networks flagged in outgoing updates
  Default networks accepted from incoming updates
  EIGRP-IPv4 Protocol for AS(1)
    Metric weight K1=1, K2=0, K3=1, K4=0, K5=0
    NSF-aware route hold timer is 240
    Router-ID: 192.168.101.1
    Topology : 0 (base)
      Active Timer: 3 min
      Distance: internal 90 external 170
      Maximum path: 4
      Maximum hopcount 100
      Maximum metric variance 1

  Automatic Summarization: disabled
  Maximum path: 4
  Routing for Networks:
    192.168.1.0
    192.168.101.0
  Routing Information Sources:
    Gateway         Distance      Last Update
  Distance: internal 90 external 170

Routing Protocol is "ospf 1"
  Outgoing update filter list for all interfaces is not set
  Incoming update filter list for all interfaces is not set
  Router ID 192.168.101.1
  Number of areas in this router is 1. 1 normal 0 stub 0 nssa
  Maximum path: 4
  Routing for Networks:
    0.0.0.0 255.255.255.255 area 0
  Routing Information Sources:
    Gateway         Distance      Last Update
  Distance: (default is 110)

Routing Protocol is "odr"
  Sending updates every 60 seconds, next due in 0 seconds
  Invalid after 180 seconds, hold down 0, flushed after 240
  Outgoing update filter list for all interfaces is not set
  Incoming update filter list for all interfaces is not set
  Maximum path: 4
  Routing Information Sources:
    Gateway         Distance      Last Update
  Distance: (default is 160)

testrouter(config)#
```

Figure 181:
The output of the "show ip protocols" command on a router running EIGRP, OSPF, and ODR

Show controllers <interface ID> shows information about the controller state for the interface specified. This command is very useful in identifying DTE or DCE types of interfaces and in identifying the clockrate on DCE interfaces.

Show version displays a summary of the router's hardware and currently installed IOS. At the bottom of the output of show version is the router's configuration register.

Show diag displays a summary of hardware information about the router.

```
testrouter#show diag
Slot 0:
        C1941 Mother board 2GE, integrated VPN and 2W Port adapter, 2 ports
        Port adapter is analyzed
        Port adapter insertion time 4w1d ago
        EEPROM contents at hardware discovery:
        PCB Serial Number        : FOC15330VUX
        Hardware Revision        : 1.0
        Part Number              : 73-11832-06
        Top Assy. Part Number    : 800-30798-02
        Board Revision           : E0
        Deviation Number         : 113332
        Fab Version              : 03
        Product (FRU) Number     : CISCO1941/K9
        Version Identifier       : V02
        CLEI Code                : CMMBS00ARA
        Processor type           : C8
        Chassis Serial Number    : FGL1539207J
        Chassis MAC Address      : 7081.0570.8500
        MAC Address block size   : 96
        Manufacturing Test Data  : 00 00 00 00 00 00 00 00
        EEPROM format version 4
        EEPROM contents (hex):
          0x00: 04 FF C1 8B 46 4F 43 31 35 33 33 30 56 55 58 40
          0x10: 06 19 41 01 00 82 49 2E 38 06 C0 46 03 20 00 78
          0x20: 4E 02 42 45 30 88 00 01 BA B4 02 03 CB 8C 43 49
          0x30: 53 43 4F 31 39 34 31 2F 4B 39 89 56 30 32 20 D9
          0x40: 04 40 C1 CB C2 C6 8A 43 4D 4D 42 53 30 30 41 52
          0x50: 41 09 C8 C2 8B 46 47 4C 31 35 33 39 32 30 37 4A
          0x60: C3 06 70 81 05 70 85 00 43 00 60 C4 08 00 00 00
          0x70: 00 00 00 00 00 F3 00 65 40 00 91 41 00 87 42 00
          0x80: 00 F8 00 28 03 E8 1C 89 07 D0 20 21 0B B8 20 93
          0x90: 0F A0 21 2F 13 88 21 83 17 70 21 A8 1B 58 21 B0
          0xA0: 1F 40 21 AB 23 28 21 79 27 10 21 78 41 00 EB 42
          0xB0: 00 00 F8 00 28 03 E8 1C 20 07 D0 1F 40 0B B8 20
          0xC0: 6C 0F A0 21 34 13 88 21 34 17 70 21 98 1B 58 21
          0xD0: 98 1F 40 21 98 23 28 21 34 27 10 21 34 FF FF FF
          0xE0: FF FF FF FF FF FF FF FF FF FF FF FF FF FF FF FF
          0xF0: FF FF FF FF FF FF FF FF FF FF FF FF FF FF FF FF

Embedded Service Engine 0/0 :
  Total platform memory : 524288K bytes
  Total 2nd core memory : 0K bytes
  Start of physical address for 2nd core : 0x80000000
```

Figure 182:
The output of
"show diag" on
a Cisco 1941 router

Show tech-support is used when reporting a problem. It displays general information about the router, but removes passwords and other security-sensitive information.

Show tcp statistics displays statistical information about TCP connections on the router.

```
testrouter#show tcp statistics
Rcvd: 500 Total, 98 no port
       0 checksum error, 0 bad offset, 0 too short
       152 packets (5133 bytes) in sequence
       0 packets (0 bytes) in CEF
       0 dup packets (0 bytes)
       0 partially dup packets (0 bytes)
       0 out-of-order packets (0 bytes)
       0 packets (0 bytes) with data after window
       0 packets after close
       0 window probe packets, 0 window update packets
       0 dup ack packets, 0 ack packets with unsend data
       211 ack packets (2651 bytes)
       0 ack packets (0 bytes) in CEF
Sent: 7572 Total, 0 urgent packets
       7392 control packets (including 5418 retransmitted)
       133 data packets (2569 bytes)
       0 data packets (0 bytes) in CEF
       0 data packets (0 bytes) retransmitted
       0 data packets (0 bytes) fastretransmitted
       47 ack only packets (0 delayed)
       0 ack only packets in CEF
       0 window probe packets, 0 window update packets
1849 Connections initiated, 0 connections accepted, 43 connections established
1849 Connections closed (including 39 dropped, 1806 embryonic dropped)
5418 Total rxmt timeout, 0 connections dropped in rxmt timeout
0 Keepalive timeout, 0 keepalive probe, 0 Connections dropped in keepalive
testrouter#
```

Figure 183: The output of the "show tcp statistics" command.
You can also use "show tcp brief all" to get a quick summary of TCP connection information.

Show processes displays information about the active processes on the router.

Debugging and Logging

Debugging can be used to diagnose and resolve router and network problems. Debugging, although very helpful, can place high demands on router resources and should therefore be used only as needed and during times of light network and router loads.

> ⚠ CAUTION: As mentioned previously, use extreme care when using debugging commands. Debugging can consume significant router resources and can negatively impact router and network performance, especially in a busy production network. In a worst-case scenario, debugging can even render a router useless. Use debugging as a learning tool in a lab network. It is not recommended for use in a production network, except in cases of catastrophic fault conditions as a troubleshooting tool. Debugging should never be used on a heavily-loaded router in a production environment.

Debugging output is directed to the console by default, but can also be directed to internal buffers or an external syslog server with the use of the "logging" command:

– Router(config)#*logging buffered*

This sends logging information to an internal buffer. You can view the contents of the buffer with the privileged EXEC command "show logging":

– Router#*show logging*

Router(config)#*logging syslog.soundtraining.local* sends logging information to a syslog server on the host "syslog.soundtraining.local." You can use either host names or IP addresses.

How to install syslog on a computer running the Windows operating system

There are several logging servers available for computers running the Windows operating system. I'll mention one that I've used.

Tftp32 is, as the name implies, a TFTP server. It also includes a syslog server and viewer, DHCP, DNS, and SNTP servers. You can download it for free at http://tftpd32.jounin.net/

Configure logging with the logging family of configuration mode commands. For example, tell your router where to send logging messages with the "logging host" command:

– router2(config)#*logging host A.B.C.D*
   (where A.B.C.D is the IP address of the syslog server) Note that you can either include the host command or not. The command *logging host 192.168.1.75* is the same as *logging 192.168.1.75*.

Soundthinking Point: Syslog and Firewalls
Make sure your host-based firewall such as the Windows firewall or ZoneAlarm isn't blocking logging traffic. Syslog transmits data over UDP port 514.

Configure the level of logging with the *logging trap* command (higher levels equal more data written to the log):

```
testrouter(config)#logging trap ?
  <0-7>           Logging severity level
  alerts          Immediate action needed      (severity=1)
  critical        Critical conditions          (severity=2)
  debugging       Debugging messages           (severity=7)
  emergencies     System is unusable           (severity=0)
  errors          Error conditions             (severity=3)
  informational   Informational messages       (severity=6)
  notifications   Normal but significant conditions (severity=5)
  warnings        Warning conditions           (severity=4)
  <cr>
```

Figure 184:
Logging trap levels, displayed alphabetically

Enable logging with the "logging on" command:

– router02(config)#*logging on*

Here is an example of how to configure logging at the level of debugging:

```
testrouter(config)#logging host 192.168.1.75
testrouter(config)#logging trap 7
testrouter(config)#logging on
testrouter(config)#
```

Figure 185:
Configuring logging at severity level 7 (debugging).
This will usually produce a lot of data.

Some Examples of Debugging

Debugging allows you to see the packet traffic on a router. Earlier you saw the use of debugging with routing protocols, but there are myriad debugging commands available to help you with troubleshooting and better understanding your router's operation and performance.

In the example below, you can see the actual ICMP packets in a ping.

```
testrouter#debug ip icmp
ICMP packet debugging is on
testrouter#ping 192.168.1.1
Type escape sequence to abort.
Sending 5, 100-byte ICMP Echos to 192.168.1.1, timeout is 2 seconds:
!!!!!
Success rate is 100 percent (5/5), round-trip min/avg/max = 1/1/4 ms
testrouter#
Aug  3 00:26:05.111: ICMP: echo reply rcvd, src 192.168.1.1, dst 192.168.1.90, topology BASE, dscp 0 topoid 0
Aug  3 00:26:05.111: ICMP: dst (192.168.1.90) port unreachable sent to 192.168.1.1
Aug  3 00:26:05.111: ICMP: echo reply rcvd, src 192.168.1.1, dst 192.168.1.90, topology BASE, dscp 0 topoid 0
Aug  3 00:26:05.111: ICMP: echo reply rcvd, src 192.168.1.1, dst 192.168.1.90, topology BASE, dscp 0 topoid 0
Aug  3 00:26:05.111: ICMP: echo reply rcvd, src 192.168.1.1, dst 192.168.1.90, topology BASE
testrouter#, dscp 0 topoid 0
Aug  3 00:26:05.115: ICMP: echo reply rcvd, src 192.168.1.1, dst 192.168.1.90, topology BASE, dscp 0 topoid 0
testrouter#
```

Figure 186: Monitoring ICMP packets in a ping from the router at 192.168.1.90 to a target at 192.168.1.1

The command ***debug ip packet*** can be overwhelming to a router, but in a lab environment you can use
it to see all IP packets. Notice in the screen capture how you can see the OSPF routing protocol using the
multicast address at 224.0.0.5 to send hello packets and the EIGRP routing protocol using the multicast
address of 224.0.0.10 to send its hello packets.

```
testrouter#debug ip packet
IP packet debugging is on
testrouter#
Aug  3 00:37:09.779: IP: s=192.168.1.90 (local), d=224.0.0.10 (GigabitEthernet0/1), len 60, sending broad/multicast
Aug  3 00:37:09.779: IP: s=192.168.1.90 (local), d=224.0.0.10 (GigabitEthernet0/1), len 60, sending full packet
Aug  3 00:37:10.031: IP: s=192.168.101.1 (local), d=224.0.0.10 (NVI0), len 60, sending broad/multicast
Aug  3 00:37:10.031: IP: s=192.168.101.1 (local), d=224.0.0.10 (NVI0), len 60, output feature, Post-routing NAT NVI Output(23), r
type 0, forus FALSE, sendself FALSE, mtu 0, fw
testrouter#dchk FALSE
Aug  3 00:37:10.031: IP: s=192.168.101.1 (local), d=224.0.0.10 (NVI0), len 60, encapsulation failed
Aug  3 00:37:10.451: IP: s=192.168.101.1 (local), d=224.0.0.10 (GigabitEthernet0/0), len 60, sending broad/multicast
Aug  3 00:37:10.451: IP: s=192.168.101.1 (local), d=224.0.0.10 (GigabitEthernet0/0), len 60, sending full packet
Aug  3 00:37:10.791: IP: s=192.168.1.103 (GigabitEthernet0/1), d=192.168.1.255, len 229, input feature, MCI Check(80), rtype 0, f
orus FALSE, sendself FALSE, mtu 0, fw
testrouter#dchk FALSE
Aug  3 00:37:10.791: IP: tableid=0, s=192.168.1.103 (GigabitEthernet0/1), d=192.168.1.255 (GigabitEthernet0/1), routed via RIB
Aug  3 00:37:10.791: IP: s=192.168.1.103 (GigabitEthernet0/1), d=192.168.1.255 (GigabitEthernet0/1), len 229, rcvd 3
Aug  3 00:37:10.791: IP: s=192.168.1.103 (GigabitEthernet0/1), d=192.168.1.255, len 229, stop process pak for forus packet
Aug  3 00:37:10.791: IP: tableid=0, s=192.168.1.103 (GigabitEthernet0/1), d=192.168.1.255 (GigabitEthernet0/1), routed via RIB
A
testrouter#ug  3 00:37:12.179: IP: s=192.168.101.1 (local), d=224.0.0.5 (GigabitEthernet0/0), len 76, sending broad/multicast
Aug  3 00:37:12.179: IP: s=192.168.101.1 (local), d=224.0.0.5 (GigabitEthernet0/0), len 76, sending full packet
testrouter#
Aug  3 00:37:13.347: IP: s=192.168.1.98 (GigabitEthernet0/1), d=192.168.1.255, len 198, input feature, MCI Check(80), rtype 0, fo
```

Figure 187: A debugging trace from "debug ip packet"

Turn Off Debugging

Use the command ***undebug all*** or ***no debug all*** to disable all debugging. Instead of ***all***, you can specify
which debugging you wish to disable.

If you are seeing a lot of debugging messages on screen, it can be difficult to type the command to stop
debugging. You may just have to do it by feel rather than watching the terminal. I've also had situations
where the debugging activity interfered with the keyboard input. In that situation, I opened a Telnet or
SSH session to the router to issue the command to stop debugging.

```
testrouter#
testrouter#no debug all
All possible debugging has been turned off
testrouter#
testrouter#undebug all
All possible debugging has been turned off
testrouter#
```

Figure 188:
Disabling debugging on a router

Viewing Debugging Messages in a Remote Session (SSH or Telnet)

Before you can see debugging messages when logged in via Telnet or SSH, you must instruct the router
to display the messages with the privileged mode command ***terminal monitor***.

```
192.168.1.90 - PuTTY
This is my login banner.
User Access Verification

Password: This is my exec banner.
testrouter>enable
Password:
testrouter#terminal monitor
testrouter#
```

Figure 189: Enabling an operator to see debugging messages during a virtual terminal (SSH or Telnet) session

Verifying Debugging

Use the command *show debugging* to see which debugging is enabled on the router.

```
testrouter#show debugging
IP routing:
  RIP protocol debugging is on
EIGRP:
  Route Event debugging is on

EIGRP-IPv4: Address-Family:
  Route Event debugging is on


OSPF:
  OSPF events debugging is on for process 1
testrouter#
```

Figure 190: Viewing which debugging has been enabled on a router

> ### Soundthinking Point: Getting Good Info from the Field
>
> How do you react when someone makes a mistake that downs the network? Do you yell and berate the person whose fault it was or do you treat the problem as a learning experience for you and the person at fault? Do you encourage your staff and colleagues to report errors, mistakes, and faults or do you create an atmosphere where they're afraid to come clean? I'm not suggesting that sloppiness or other mistakes should go without some form of consequence. I do feel, however, that most people want to do good work and, unless an individual is an ongoing source of problems, a softer touch will often yield excellent troubleshooting information that can be used to prevent future problems. A hard-nosed approach can discourage people from bringing issues to your attention, thus allowing mistakes to happen again and again.

Summary

There are really three keys to troubleshooting router issues. First, don't make any assumptions about connections, cables, connectors, IP addresses or anything else. Second, start at the physical layer and work up. Third, accept human frailty as part of the equation and review your configurations line-by-line looking for typos and similar errors. Remember that our eyes perform auto-correct. It seems like often, much as I hate to admit it, I'm the source of the problems I'm having with my networks!

CHAPTER 10:
Remote Router Control

Chapter Introduction

Server rooms are very uncomfortable places. They tend to be very loud from all the cooling fans and they're usually pretty cold from the air conditioning. In other words, you probably won't manage your routers very often by sitting in the server room using the serial console port. This chapter is all about connecting remotely. I'll show you how to use Telnet, but don't use it. It's not secure. In fact, you really can't use the word *secure* in the same sentence with *Telnet*. So why am I teaching it? Well, there may be times when you're working on someone else's equipment and they may not have enabled secure remote control connections with SSH, so you're stuck with Telnet. I know, it's a weak excuse, but it's also real. So, I'll show you Telnet, but then I'll show you how to do the same thing securely with SSH. Finally, at the end of the chapter, I'll show you how to enable HTTP and HTTPS connections in case you want to use Cisco Configuration Professional or older HTTP-based management tools such as SDM.

Chapter Objectives

- Learn how to configure Telnet

- Learn how to configure SSH

- Learn how to enable graphical management through Cisco Configuration Professional

Online Companion Resources

Videos: Watch the companion videos for this chapter. They're available at
www.soundtraining.net/videos/cisco-router-training-videos

Web Page: There is a supporting web page with live links and other resources for this book
at www.soundtraining.net/cisco-router-book

Facebook: www.soundtraining.net/facebook

Twitter: www.soundtraining.net/twitter

Blog: www.soundtraining.net/blog

Chapter Network Diagram

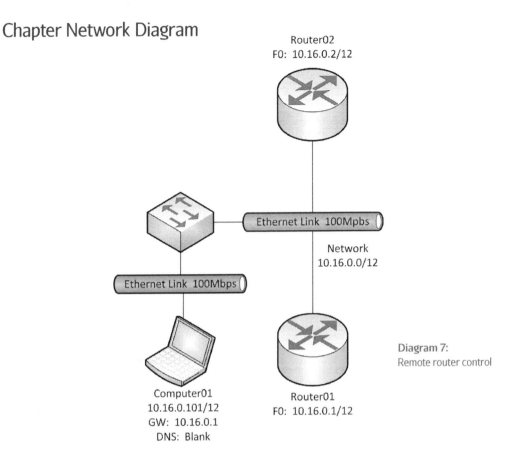

Router02
F0: 10.16.0.2/12

Ethernet Link 100Mpbs

Network
10.16.0.0/12

Ethernet Link 100Mbps

Diagram 7:
Remote router control

Computer01
10.16.0.101/12
GW: 10.16.0.1
DNS: Blank

Router01
F0: 10.16.0.1/12

What is Telnet

Telnet is one of the original IPv4 tools. It is a terminal emulation program that allows remote terminal login. Once the connection is successful, the remote user is prompted for a username and password. Upon successful authentication, the remote user has the same rights and permissions as if they were logged in locally.

Options for Using Telnet

You can access Telnet from either user EXEC or privileged EXEC. It is not necessary to issue the Telnet command. You can simply enter the hostname, if names resolution is enabled, or the IP address:

– Router>*10.16.0.1*

– Router#*router01*

Telnet is widely used to remotely access computer and routers. When you Telnet into a router, you have access to nearly all of the same commands available when you console into a router. If you wish to use the debugging tools while in a Telnet session, you must first execute the "terminal monitor" command to redirect the debugging messages to your Telnet session.

You can also Telnet from a computer into a router. From a Windows computer, issue the command from the "run" dialog on your Start menu or from a command prompt.

Telnet is specified in RFC854 and subsequent RFCs.

> ⚠ **CAUTION: Telnet is a Non-Secure Protocol**
> Although Telnet is handy and easy to use, it should be avoided if possible. When using Telnet, the entire session including authentication is in clear text and can be intercepted by anyone on the network.
>
> For a video demonstrating the dangers of Telnet, visit the soundtraining.net video channel at www.soundtraining.net/videos.

Interactive Exercise 10.1:
Remote Administration Using Telnet

This lab teaches you how to remotely configure a router using Telnet.

Objectives:

- Remotely access and configure the router using Telnet
- Explore your command options when using Telnet between Cisco routers

Steps:

1. Refer to the lab network diagram for the naming convention
2. Log in to router01 and take the necessary steps to get to privileged EXEC mode
3. Type the following command to Telnet router02:
   - router01#**10.16.0.2**
   - Password:**p@ss1234<Enter>**
   - router02>

4. Take the necessary steps to get to the privileged EXEC mode on router02

5. Temporarily suspend your Telnet session by issuing the following command:

    –   router02#*Shift-Ctrl-6*

    –   router02#*x*
        (This command is a little confusing. First, touch the key combination of *Shift-Ctrl-6*
        simultaneously, then release those three keys and touch the "*x*" key.)

6. Now, you can resume your telnet session by simply touching **<Enter>**

    –   router01**<Enter>**

    –   router02#

You can use Telnet to remotely administer any router for which you have permission.

Related commands:

The "show sessions" command will display the remote sessions you have initiated.

  –   Router#*show sessions*

The "show users" command will show sessions initiated remotely into your router.

  –   Router#*show users*

The "send" command will allow you to send a message to another user.

  –   Router#*send con 0* will send a message to the console of the router you're
      remotely administering

  –   Router#*send vty 1* will send a message to the user on Telnet line 1

The "show sessions" command will show the Telnet sessions open from your router.

  –   Router#*show sessions*

The "disconnect" command will disconnect the specified Telnet session(s) displayed in the show
sessions command.

  –   Router#*disconnect 1*

The "show users" command shows the Telnet sessions open into your router from other users.

  –   Router#*show users*

The "clear" command will disconnect Telnet sessions connected to your router:

  –   Router#*clear line <0-4>*

Configuring SSH (Secure Shell) for Remote Login on a Cisco Router

Prior to the introduction of SSH in the Cisco IOS, the only remote login protocol was Telnet. Although quite functional, as mentioned previously, Telnet is a non-secure protocol in which the entire session, including authentication, is in clear text and thus subject to snooping. (See the soundtraining.net YouTube video on Protocol Analysis with Wireshark for a demonstration.)

SSH is both a protocol and an application that replaces Telnet and provides an encrypted connection for remote administration of a Cisco network device such as a router, switch, or security appliance.

The Cisco IOS includes both an SSH server and an SSH client. This document is concerned only with the configuration of the SSH server component.

Prerequisites

Software

The SSH server component requires that you have an IPSec (DES or 3DES) encryption software image from Cisco IOS Release 12.1(1)T or later installed on your router. Advanced IP services images include the IPSec component. This document was written using c2800nm-advipservicesk9-mz.123-14.T5.bin, c1900-universalk9-mz.SPA.151-4.M1.bin, and c870-advipservicesk9-mz.124-15.T6.bin.

Pre-configuration

You must configure a hostname and a domain name on your router. For example:

```
router#conf t
Enter configuration commands, one per line.  End with CNTL/Z.
router(config)#hostname testrouter
testrouter(config)#ip domain-name soundtraining.net
```

Figure 191:
Configuring a hostname and domain name on the router

You must also generate an RSA keypair for your router which automatically enables SSH. In the following example, note how the keypair is named for the combination of hostname and domain name that were previously configured. The modulus represents the key length. Cisco recommends a minimum key length of 1024 bits (even though the default key length is 512 bits):

```
testrouter(config)#crypto key generate rsa
The name for the keys will be: testrouter.soundtraining.net
Choose the size of the key modulus in the range of 360 to 4096 for your
  General Purpose Keys. Choosing a key modulus greater than 512 may take
  a few minutes.

How many bits in the modulus [512]: 1024
% Generating 1024 bit RSA keys, keys will be non-exportable...
[OK] (elapsed time was 1 seconds)
```

Figure 192:
Using the crypto family of commands to generate the RSA keypair

Finally, you must either use an AAA server such as a RADIUS or TACACS+ server or create a local user database to authenticate remote users and enable authentication on the terminal lines. For the purpose of this document, I'll create a local user database on the router. In the following example, the user "user15" was created with a privilege level of 15 (the maximum allowed) and given an encrypted password of "p@ss5678." (The command "secret" followed by "0" tells the router to encrypt the following plaintext password. In the router's running configuration, the password would not be human readable.) I also used line configuration mode to tell the router to use its local user database for authentication (login local) on terminals lines 0-4.

```
testrouter(config)#username user15 privilege 15 secret 0 p@ss5678
testrouter(config)#line vty 0 4
testrouter(config-line)#login local
```

Figure 193: Configuring a username and local authentication

Enabling SSH

To enable SSH, you must tell the router which keypair to use. Optionally, you can configure the SSH version (it defaults to SSH version 1), authentication timeout values, and several other parameters. In the following example, we told the router to use the previously created keypair and to use SSH v 2:

```
testrouter(config-line)#ip ssh version 2
testrouter(config)#ip ssh rsa keypair-name testrouter.soundtraining.net
testrouter(config)#
```

Figure 194: Configuring the router to use SSH v2 and telling it which keypair to use

You can now log on to your router securely using an SSH client. The SSH client I recommend is PuTTY, available at www.putty.org. There are many others available, if you want to use something different.

Soundthinking Point: Deleting RSA Keypairs

To delete the RSA key-pair, use the global configuration command ***crypto key zeroize rsa***. Deleting the RSA key-pair automatically disables the SSH server.

Viewing SSH Configurations and Connections

You can use the privileged mode commands "view ssh" and "view ip ssh" to view SSH configurations and connections (if any).

```
testrouter#show ip ssh
SSH Enabled - version 2.0
Authentication timeout: 120 secs; Authentication retries: 3
Minimum expected Diffie Hellman key size : 1024 bits
IOS Keys in SECSH format(ssh-rsa, base64 encoded):
ssh-rsa AAAAB3NzaC1yc2EAAAADAQABAAAAgQCzUpqPLH3o9UBgOBteKmSIxi/Ydqqw8EmmCnejp3XX
gILZ760sEqFR52zxsW2vl+gW7ABHPriuQW6UyC4k0/Saaos3nnLAOa2MFBrROYY1Dk64pBVsNxfJzMGS
wUvGWVXWY/mP0T7GX8dPfG7AuzgUNELRUqX7eXgr5P5yX6eBMw==
testrouter#show ssh
%No SSHv2 server connections running.          No SSH connections are open
%No SSHv1 server connections running.
testrouter#show ssh
Connection Version Mode Encryption  Hmac       State            Username
0          2.0     IN   aes256-cbc  hmac-sha1  Session started  user15
0          2.0     OUT  aes256-cbc  hmac-sha1  Session started  user15
%No SSHv1 server connections running.
testrouter#                                    After opening a SSH connection
```

Figure 195: Verifying the router's SSH configuration

Interactive Exercise 10.2:
Enabling SSH on a Cisco Router for Secure Remote Login

Goals:

- Generate an RSA keypair

- Configure SSH

- Log in remotely through a secure connection

Steps:

1. Configure a hostname on your router:

   - Router#*conf t*

   - Router(config)#*hostname testrouter*

2. You must also configure a domain name:

   - Router(config)#*ip domain-name soundtraining.net*

3. Generate an RSA keypair with a key length of 1024 bits using the following sequence
   of commands:

   - router(config)#

   - router(config)#*crypto key generate rsa*

The name for the keys will be: testrouter.soundtraining.net

Choose the size of the key modulus in the range of 360 to 2048 for your General Purpose Keys. Choosing a key modulus greater than 512 may take a few minutes.

How many bits in the modulus [512]: *1024*

% Generating 1024 bit RSA keys ... [OK]

4. Create a username in the router's local database for SSH authentication using the following command (for the purpose of the exercise, use the username "user15"):

   – router01(config)#*username user15 privilege 15 secret 0 p@ss5678*

5. Enable login authentication against the local database when logging in to a terminal line with the following commands:

   – router01(config)#*line vty 0 4*

   – router01(config-line)#*login local*

6. Enable SSHv2 and the previously configured keypair with the following commands:

   – router01(config-line)#*ip ssh version 2*

   – router01(config)#*ip ssh rsa keypair-name testrouter.soundtraining.net*

7. Attempt to login to your router using the PuTTY SSH client. (If you haven't already downloaded and installed it, it's available at www.putty.org.)

```
router#
router#conf t
Enter configuration commands, one per line.  End with CNTL/Z.
router(config)#hostname testrouter
testrouter(config)#ip domain-name soundtraining.net
testrouter(config)#crypto key generate rsa
The name for the keys will be: testrouter.soundtraining.net
Choose the size of the key modulus in the range of 360 to 4096 for your
  General Purpose Keys. Choosing a key modulus greater than 512 may take
  a few minutes.

How many bits in the modulus [512]: 1024
% Generating 1024 bit RSA keys, keys will be non-exportable...
[OK] (elapsed time was 1 seconds)

testrouter(config)#username user15 privilege 15 secret 0 p@ss5678
testrouter(config)#line vty 0 4
testrouter(config-line)#login local
testrouter(config-line)#ip ssh version 2
testrouter(config)#ip ssh rsa keypair-name testrouter.soundtraining.net
testrouter(config)#
```

Figure 196: Configuring a router to accept incoming SSH connections

Configuring Your Router to Support the Cisco Configuration Professional Graphical User Interface

Cisco Configuration Professional (CCP) is a graphical user interface (GUI) management tool for Cisco routers. It is included on an accompanying CD with many routers or it can be downloaded from http://www.cisco.com/go/ciscocp. It requires a Cisco login, but does not require a support contract.

CCP can use either HTTP or HTTPS to connect to the router. Perform the following steps to configure your router to accept HTTP and/or HTTPS connections.

1. In global configuration mode, enter the following commands to enable the server:

    – router(config)#*ip http server*

    – router(config)#*ip http secure-server*

2. While still in global configuration mode, enter the follow commands to configure the router for local authentication and to set the HTTP timeout policy:

    – router(config)#*ip http authentication local*

    – router(config)#*ip http timeout-policy idle 60 life 86400 requests 10000*

```
testrouter#
testrouter#conf t
Enter configuration commands, one per line.  End with CNTL/Z.
testrouter(config)#ip http server
testrouter(config)#ip http secure-server
testrouter(config)#ip http authentication local
testrouter(config)#ip http timeout-policy idle 60 life 86400 requests 10000
testrouter(config)#
```

Figure 197: Configuring the router for local authentication of HTTP access requests, such as CCP or SDM

After the http server is configured on the router, you can use either Cisco Configuration Professional Express to connect by pointing your browser to the router (using either HTTP or HTTPS, depending on how you configured it) or you can use the Cisco Configuration Professional (CCP) application to connect. In order to use CCP, you must first install it on your management workstation.

CCP provides a more complete set of configuration options, while CCP Express is very limited. CCP Express is oriented more toward initial configuration. CCP is oriented toward comprehensive router management.

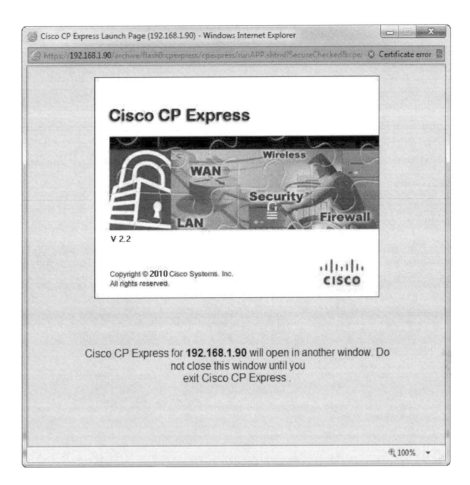

Figure 198: The CP Express splash page. Note that a browser is being used
to make the connection using CP Express.

Summary

How should you manage your routers? Other than avoiding Telnet because of the inherent security risks, I don't think it really matters. I tend to prefer working in the command-line interface. I know a lot of administrators today who prefer working in the GUI. My only comment is that there are occasionally things in the GUI that don't work as expected. That rarely happens in the command-line interface. The GUI is also pretty slow to load. If the task is something you do repeatedly, you can probably do it faster in the command-line. If it's something that's new to you, you may find the GUI easier and less error-prone.

CHAPTER 11:
Understanding Cisco IPv4 Access-Control Lists

Chapter Introduction

When I ask students why they enrolled in my Cisco router class, many respond that they want to learn more about access lists, or as they're formally known, access-control lists. There's even an acronym for them: ACLs. Regardless of what you call them, they are something you must understand in order to master router configuration. You'll encounter them, not only in routers, but also with the Cisco ASA Security Appliance. Their behavior is similar on both platforms.

Here some things to remember about ACLs: Keep them as simple as possible. Write them out on paper or in a text editor before you apply them to the router and think through each line of the list to ensure you know what it's going to do. Finally, as you'll read in a moment, make sure you understand both their *implicit* operations as well as their *explicit* operations.

Chapter Objectives

- Understand what an access-control list is

- Know the two different types of access-control lists

- Understand how to build and manage named access-control lists

Online Companion Resources

Videos: Watch the companion videos for this chapter. They're available at
www.soundtraining.net/videos/cisco-router-training-videos

Web Page: There is a supporting web page with live links and other resources for this book
at www.soundtraining.net/cisco-router-book

Facebook: www.soundtraining.net/facebook

Twitter: www.soundtraining.net/twitter

Blog: www.soundtraining.net/blog

Access-Control Lists Defined

Access Control Lists (ACLs) are sequential lists of permit and deny statements, known as Access Control Entries (ACEs) which can be applied to traffic flows. The ACEs are simply lines within the ACL. Such traffic flows could apply to a router interface, a VPN tunnel, or a function such as logging.

Rules for Access-Control Lists

Read these three rules over and over again until you dream about them. Most of the problems I've seen with access-control lists are because somebody overlooked one of these three rules. I'm serious. Make them a mantra.

1. Each packet is compared with each access-control entry (line) of the access-control list in sequential order until it matches a line.

2. The packet is compared with lines of the Access Control List only until a match is made. Lines of an access-control list after a match are ignored.

3. There is an implicit *deny any* at the end of each access-control list. If packet doesn't match up to any entries in the list, it is discarded. You can't see the *deny any* statement, but it is there. On a consulting project, I even saw the administrator include an explicit *deny any* at the end of his access-control lists just to make sure he didn't forget it was there.

Two Types of IPv4 Access-Control Lists

Note: IPv6 access-control lists are quite similar to IPv4 access-control lists. There is enough difference, however, that I decided to include IPv6 access-control lists in the IPv6 chapter (chapter 14). For the sake of simplicity, please assume that any references to IP access-control lists are referring to IPv4.

Standard IP Access Control Lists

Standard IP access-control lists are numbered 1-99 and 1300-1999 (expanded range). Standard IP access-control lists use only the source IP address for filtering.

```
access-list 10 deny 192.168.101.0 0.0.0.255
access-list 10 deny 192.168.102.0 0.0.0.255
access-list 10 deny 192.168.103.0 0.0.0.255
access-list 10 permit any
```

Figure 199:
An IP standard Access Control List

Extended Access Control Lists

Extended Access Control Lists (100-199 and 2000-2699 (expanded range)) can filter on source and destination address, protocol type, and port number at transport or upper layers.

```
access-list 100 deny tcp any 192.168.101.0 0.0.0.255 eq telnet
access-list 100 deny icmp any host 192.168.0.101 echo
access-list 100 permit ip 192.168.101.0 0.0.0.255 any
access-list 100 permit ip any any
```

Figure 200: An IP extended access-control list

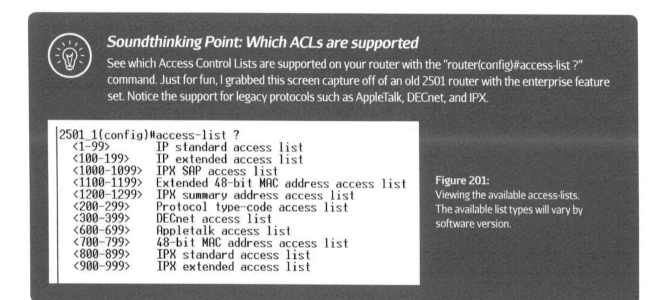

Soundthinking Point: Which ACLs are supported

See which Access Control Lists are supported on your router with the "router(config)#access-list ?" command. Just for fun, I grabbed this screen capture off of an old 2501 router with the enterprise feature set. Notice the support for legacy protocols such as AppleTalk, DECnet, and IPX.

```
2501_1(config)#access-list ?
  <1-99>        IP standard access list
  <100-199>     IP extended access list
  <1000-1099>   IPX SAP access list
  <1100-1199>   Extended 48-bit MAC address access list
  <1200-1299>   IPX summary address access list
  <200-299>     Protocol type-code access list
  <300-399>     DECnet access list
  <600-699>     Appletalk access list
  <700-799>     48-bit MAC address access list
  <800-899>     IPX standard access list
  <900-999>     IPX extended access list
```

Figure 201:
Viewing the available access-lists. The available list types will vary by software version.

Masks and Wildcard Bits

Masks are used with IP addresses to identify which part of the address is network, subnetwork, or host. In a conventional mask, the largest numbers are on the left-hand side. For example, in our classroom network diagram, router01's inside network ID is 192.168.101.0 and the mask is 255.255.255.0 (/24). As you learned previously, the mask indicates which bits are network and which bits are host. In this example, bits 1-24 are network bits and bits 25-32 are host bits. If we want to allow all traffic from the 192.168.101 network, we would tell the router to permit any traffic flow whose first 24 bits equal 192.168.101 (11000000.10101000.01100101) regardless of what the last eight bits are.

In a Cisco IP access-control list, an inverse subnet mask is used, also known as wildcard bits, to identify which bits must be matched and which bits should be ignored. It's similar to a conventional mask except that, instead of matching 1s, we match 0s. A conventional 24-bit mask of 255.255.255.0 (11111111.11111111.11111111.00000000) becomes an inverse mask of 0.0.0.255 (00000000.00000000.00000000.111111110). In this example, the first 24 bits must match and the last eight bits are ignored.

A conventional 18-bit mask of 255.255.192.0 (11111111.11111111.11000000.00000000) becomes 0.0.63.255 (00000000.00000000.00111111.11111111). In this example, the first 18 bits must match and the last 14 bits are ignored. Notice in both examples that we simply invert the 1s and 0s from the conventional mask.

An easy way of dealing with this is to first look at the CIDR notation mask (for example, /24). To determine the inverse mask, count out 24 zeroes and fill in the remaining places with 1s.

Does Order Matter in an ACL?

Yes it does! The important thing to remember about order in an ACL is this: Always go from most specific to most general. Take a look at the following example:

```
testrouter(config)#access-list 10 deny 192.168.0.0 0.0.0.255
testrouter(config)#access-list 10 permit host 192.168.0.1
```

Figure 202: Configuring an ACL with the most general statement first, followed by the most specific statement. This list will not work as written.

In the above screen capture, the list goes from most general to most specific, which won't work. Packets from host 192.168.0.1 are included in the network statement in the first line, so they'll be denied. The packets from host 192.168.0.1 will never make it to the second line.

Newer versions of the IOS actually won't permit you to order from most general to most specific. If you attempt to do so, the router complains and won't accept the command, as you can see in the following screen capture from a 1941 router:

```
testrouter(config)#access-list 10 deny 192.168.0.0 0.0.0.255
testrouter(config)#access-list 10 permit host 192.168.0.1
% Access rule can't be configured at higher sequence num as it is part of the existing rule at sequence num 20
testrouter(config)#
```

Figure 203: Modern routers throw off an error when list entries are created out-of-order

Soundthinking Point: Use Remarks to Document Your ACLs

While in access-list configuration mode, you can use remarks to document the ACL. As with everything in IT, the more you document, the simpler it is to figure things out in the future. Add remarks describing what the ACL does or why you added it.

```
router01(config)#access-list 100 remark Block traffic from sales
router01(config)#access-list 100 remark Requested by R&D
router01(config)#
```

Figure 204: Adding remarks to an ACL

Applying Access Control Lists

Once you've created an Access Control List, you must apply it to an interface. Specify the interface where you want to apply the list:

- router01#*conf t*

- router01(config)#*int e0*

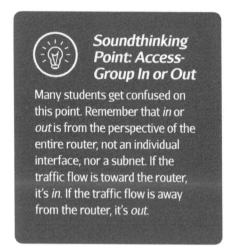

Soundthinking Point: Access-Group In or Out

Many students get confused on this point. Remember that *in* or *out* is from the perspective of the entire router, not an individual interface, nor a subnet. If the traffic flow is toward the router, it's *in*. If the traffic flow is away from the router, it's *out*.

Use the *ip access-group* statement, followed by the number of the list, and the direction of the traffic flow from the perspective of the router. Traffic going away from the router is *out*, traffic coming toward the router is *in*.

- router01(config-if)#*ip access-group 10 out*

Interactive Exercise 11.1:
Blocking One Subnet

Objectives:

- Deny Sales LAN access to the R&D LAN, but allow access to the Internet and Managers

- Allow all other networks full access all other networks.

- In this example, we are asking you to allow users from the Internet to access all of your LANs. Of course, in the real world, that would rarely happen (if ever!).

Steps:

1. Write the above access-control list on a piece of paper to accomplish the objective.

2. Decide where to place the list and in which direction to place it.

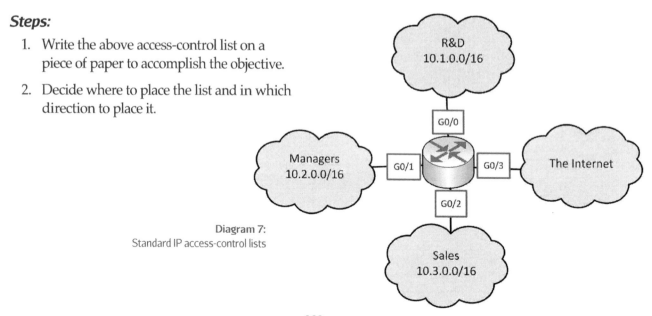

Diagram 7:
Standard IP access-control lists

Solution

I find it easier to work with an access-control list by first creating the list, then deciding where to place it. Since the objective is to block Sales from R&D, I created a list that denies the Sales LAN:

– router(config)#*access-list 10 deny 10.3.0.0 0.0.255.255*

– router(config)#*access-list 10 permit any*

It's not necessary to create any statements explicitly dealing with the other subnets, nor the Internet. The *permit any* statement in the second entry allows them to gain access.

Now, I need to decide where to place it. The only option is to place it on the interface connected to R&D and block outbound traffic.

– router(config)#*interface g0/0*

– router(config-if)#*ip access-group 10 out*

Access Control List Maintenance

It's possible to build an Access Control List in the router's console interface. It's not possible, however, to edit a traditional numbered Access Control List in the console interface because you cannot delete individual lines of an Access Control List in the console interface. Each new line is appended to the end of the Access Control List. As an alternative, you can use Named Access Lists to edit lists within a router interface. Named Access Lists are covered later in this book.

For simplicity, create Access Control Lists in text editors, then apply them to the router. Open Notepad or Wordpad in Windows; vi or emacs in Linux/UNIX. Create your entire Access Control List in the text editor. Select it and copy it to the clipboard, then return to the router's console interface. Ensure that the router is in global configuration mode ("configure terminal" or "conf t"). Paste the contents of the clipboard into the router (In PuTTY, you can simply right-click with your mouse anywhere in the terminal window. PuTTY will paste the contents of the clipboard at the cursor. If you're using HyperTerminal, use the "Paste to Host" command. Alternatively, you can use HyperTerminal's "send text" utility from the Transfer menu to apply the Access Control List to the router.) Regardless of which technique you use, maintaining your Access Control Lists in a text editor provides much greater flexibility than attempting to maintain them by using the router's console interface.

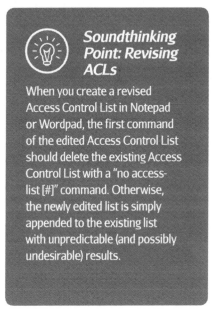

Soundthinking Point: Revising ACLs

When you create a revised Access Control List in Notepad or Wordpad, the first command of the edited Access Control List should delete the existing Access Control List with a "no access-list [#]" command. Otherwise, the newly edited list is simply appended to the existing list with unpredictable (and possibly undesirable) results.

Named ACLs

IP named ACLs were introduced beginning with CIOS version 11.2. An IP named ACL permits the use of names instead of numbers. IP named ACLs also permit more controlled editing within the router's CLI than numbered lists.

Creating a Named Access Control List

To create a Named ACL, in global configuration mode, enter the following command:

– Router(config)#*ip access-list [standard or extended] nameOfTheList*

The router will switch to named ACL configuration mode. You then enter the permit and deny conditions. For example, to permit traffic from the 192.168.1.0/24 subnet, enter the following command:

– Router(config-std-nacl)#*permit 192.168.1.0 0.0.0.255*

The following screen capture shows how I created a standard Named ACL to block traffic form the 10.16.0.0/16 subnet.

```
testrouter(config)#ip access-list standard BlockSales
testrouter(config-std-nacl)#deny 10.16.0.0 0.0.255.255
testrouter(config-std-nacl)#permit any
testrouter(config-std-nacl)#int g0/0
testrouter(config-if)#ip access-group BlockSales out
```

Figure 205: Creating and applying a named access-control list

This example shows how I created an extended named ACL to permit only Telnet traffic to a host located at 10.16.0.1.

```
testrouter(config)#ip access-list extended PermitTelnetOnly
testrouter(config-ext-nacl)#permit tcp any host 10.16.0.1 eq 23
```

Figure 206: An example of a named ACL

This example shows how I created an extended named ACL to deny HTTP and HTTPS traffic while permitting all other types of traffic.

```
testrouter(config)#ip access-list extended DenyWebTraffic
testrouter(config-ext-nacl)#deny tcp 192.168.1.0 0.0.0.255 any eq 80
testrouter(config-ext-nacl)#deny tcp 192.168.1.0 0.0.0.255 any eq 443
testrouter(config-ext-nacl)#permit ip any any
testrouter(config-ext-nacl)#
```

Figure 207: Another example of a named ACL

Using named ACLs offers the benefits of a name instead of a number, thus making it easier to tell at a glance the purpose of the list. Additionally, named ACLs offer flexible editing options within the command-line interface that are not available with traditional numbered lists. It is possible, however, to edit a traditional numbered list using named ACL commands.

Editing a Named ACL

```
testrouter(config)#do show access-list
Standard IP access list BlockSales
    10 deny   10.16.0.0, wildcard bits 0.0.255.255
    20 permit any
testrouter(config)#ip access-list standard BlockSales
testrouter(config-std-nacl)#15 deny 10.32.0.0 0.0.255.255
testrouter(config-std-nacl)#do show access-list
Standard IP access list BlockSales
    10 deny   10.16.0.0, wildcard bits 0.0.255.255
    15 deny   10.32.0.0, wildcard bits 0.0.255.255
    20 permit any
testrouter(config-std-nacl)#
```

Figure 208:
Editing a named ACL

In the above screen capture, I first displayed the existing access-list. Doing so allowed me to see the line numbers in the list. I had to precede the *show access-list* command with the modifier *do* because I was in global configuration mode, not privileged mode. Then, I switched to access-list configuration mode with the command *ip access-list standard BlockSales*.

I specified where in the sequence of access-control entries I wanted the new entry to appear by using a number between the two existing entries (10 and 20). I followed the sequence number (15) with the new access-control entry which denies traffic from the 10.32.0.0/16 network.

Finally, just to prove my point, I used the *show access-list* command to display the ACL with the new entry, sandwiched between the two previous entries.

Interactive Exercise 11.2:
Configuring IP Standard Access Control Lists

This exercise teaches you how to configure filtering using standard Access Control Lists on your router.

Objectives:

- Learn how to control network traffic using a standard access-control list based only on source IP addresses

- Learn how to use the router's interface configuration mode to apply access-control lists to specific interfaces

Steps:

1. Write an Access Control List to block the Seattle office from going out onto the Internet, but allow all other access. All the information you need is in the following diagram.

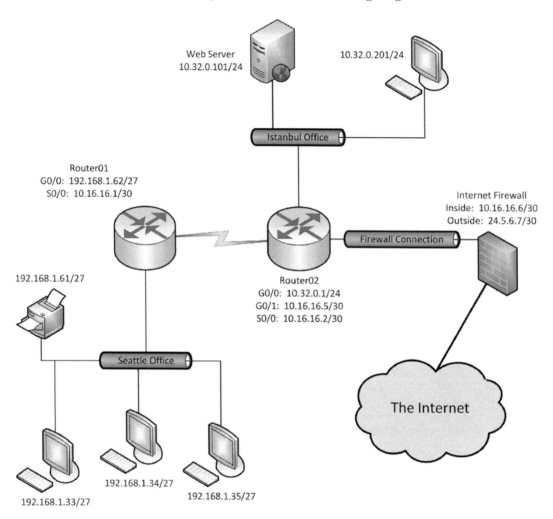

Diagram 8: Standard IP access-control lists, part 2

Solution

Begin by creating a list to identify the traffic to be blocked. Be sure to permit all other traffic, since that's one of the objectives of the exercise:

- Router01(config)#*access-list 10 deny 192.168.1.32 0.0.0.31*

- router01(config)#*access-list 10 permit any*

Now, think about where to place it. If you place it on either interface on router01, users in Seattle will not be able to reach Istanbul. If you place it on router02 on either g0/0 outbound or s0/0 inbound, users in Seattle will still not be able to reach Istanbul. It must be place outbound on router02, interface g0/1. (How do you know interface g0/1 is connected to the Internet? Simple. It's address is on the same subnet as the Internet firewall's inside address.)

– Router01(config)#*int g0/1*

– router01(config-if)#*ip access-group 10 out*

Commands for configuring and applying Access Control Lists:

To configure a standard (simple) Access Control List:

– Router(config)#*access-list [1-99] [permit/deny] [source address] [inverse subnet mask]*

To apply the list to an interface:

– Router(config-if)#*ip access-group [# of corresponding list] [in/out]*

To view the Access Control List:

– Router#*show access-list*

To verify that the Access Control List is properly applied to an interface:

– Router#*show ip interface*

To remove an Access Control List:

– Router#*no access-list [1-99]*

(**Note:** This command will completely remove an entire Access Control List. Access Control Lists cannot be edited within the router interface. In the past, ACLs could not be edited within the router interface, so a common practice was to create and edit Access Control Lists within a text editor such as Notepad or WordPad, then apply the Access Control List to the router.)

To remove an Access Control List from an interface:

– router(config-if)#*no ip access-group [1-99] [in/out]*

Extended Access Control Lists

Extended Access Control Lists can filter on source and destination addresses, TCP and UDP port numbers, and protocol. Extended IP Access Control Lists are numbered 100-199 and 2000-2699 (expanded range). Extended ACLs are also available as a named ACL.

Building an Extended IP Access Control List

Extended IP Access Control Lists offer tremendous flexibility in filtering. What follows is a simple example of how to filter all Telnet traffic from any source to the destination of 10.16.0.3, while permitting all other types of traffic.

- Router#*conf t*

- Router(config)#*access-list 100 deny tcp any host 10.16.0.3 eq 23*

- Router(config)#*access-list 100 permit ip any any*

The meaning of each part of the statement:

- access-list 100—specifies an IP extended Access Control List

- deny—tells the router to block packets. Other options include permit, dynamic, and remark.

- tcp—tells the router to operate on packets within the TCP protocol. Other options include:

  - IP protocol number (0-255)

  - ahp (authentication header protocol)

  - eigrp (Enhanced Interior Gateway Routing Protocol)

  - esp (Encapsulation Security Payload)

  - gre (Generic Routing Encapsulation)

  - icmp (Internet Control Message Protocol)

  - igmp (Internet Gateway Message Protocol)

  - ip (Internet Protocol)

  - ipinip (IP in IP tunneling)

  - nos (KA9Q NOS compatible IP over IP tunneling)

  - object-group (Service object group)

  - ospf (OSPF routing protocol)

  - pcp (Payload Compression Protocol)

  - pim (Protocol Independent Multicast)

  - udp (User Datagram Protocol)

- any—tells the router to operate on packets from any source

- host 10.16.0.3—tells the router to operate on packets destined for the IP address 10.16.0.3 (it could also be expressed as 10.16.0.3 0.0.0.0)

- eq 23—tells the router to operate on packets destined for port 23 (Telnet)). In addition to *eq*, other options include:

  - ack (Match on the ACK bit)

  - dscp (Match packets with given dscp value)

  - eq (Match only packets on a given port number)

  - established (Match established connections)

  - fin (Match on the FIN bit)

  - fragments (Check non-initial fragments)

  - gt (Match only packets with a greater port number)

  - log (Log matches against this entry)

  - log-input (Log matches against this entry, including input interface)

  - lt (Match only packets with a lower port number)

  - neq (Match only packets not on a given port number)

  - option (Match packets with given IP Options value)

  - precedence (Match packets with given precedence value)

  - psh (Match on the PSH bit)

  - range (Match only packets in the range of port numbers)

  - rst (Match on the RST bit)

  - syn (Match on the SYN bit)

  - time-range (Specify a time-range)

  - tos (Match packets with given TOS value)

  - urg (Match on the URG bit)

- Other options for the port number include many TCP and UDP protocols by name or you can specify any port number in the range of 0-65535.

Without the statement permitting all other types of IP traffic, all traffic would be blocked.

The list must, of course, be applied to an interface:

  - Router(config)#*interface e0*

  - Router(config-if)#*ip access-group 100 out*
    (This applies the list to outbound traffic from the router's Ethernet 0 interface.)

Using Object-Groups with ACLs

Object-groups provide a way for you to simplify access-control list configuration, especially in large or frequently changing networks. Object-groups allow you to organize protocols, users, or devices into groups in much the same way that a directory service allows you to classify users into groups to simplify user management.

There are two types of object-groups: network and service object groups.

Network Object-Groups

You can create network object-groups based on the following criteria:

- Network and subnet IP addresses
- Host IP addresses
- Hostnames (if names resolution is enabled)
- Ranges of IP addresses
- Other network object-groups

Service Object-Groups

You can create service object-groups based on the following criteria:

- Source and/or destination protocol port numbers such as 80 (WWW) or 194 (IRC)
- ICMP message types including echo, echo-reply, source-quench, or host-unreachable
- Top-level protocols, including TCP and UDP
- Other service object-groups

Creating Object-Groups

In global configuration mode, enter the command *object-group [network|service] name*, then add a description if desired, followed the objects you want included in the group.

For a network object, include either the host IP address, the network address, the range of addresses, the statement *any* to mean any network, or another group-object.

For a service object, include either the IP protocol number or name, the TCP/UDP port number, the ICMP type, or another group-object.

When you are finished, enter the command *end*.

Here is a screen capture showing the creation of the network object *Accounting*, including one subnet address, plus an individual host address.

```
testrouter(config)#object-group network Accounting
testrouter(config-network-group)#description Main Accounting Office plus Satellite
testrouter(config-network-group)#host 10.32.0.28
testrouter(config-network-group)#10.16.0.1 255.255.255.0
testrouter(config-network-group)#end
testrouter#
```

Figure 209: Creating a network object-group

Here is a screen capture showing the creation of the service object-group *Web*, including both HTTP and HTTPS protocols.

```
testrouter(config)#object-group service WorldWideWeb
testrouter(config-service-group)#description Secure and Non-Secure Web Traffic
testrouter(config-service-group)#tcp eq 80
testrouter(config-service-group)#tcp eq 443
testrouter(config-service-group)#end
```

Figure 210: Creating a service object-group

View the object-groups configured on a router with the command *show object-group*:

```
testrouter#show object-group
Network object group Accounting
 Description Main Accounting Office plus Satellite
 host 10.32.0.28
 10.16.0.0 255.255.255.0

Service object group WorldWideWeb
 Description Secure and Non-Secure Web Traffic
 tcp eq www
 tcp eq 443
```

Figure 211:
Viewing the object-groups
on a router

Here's how you use an object-group within a named access-list:

```
testrouter(config)#ip access-list extended WebRestrict
testrouter(config-ext-nacl)#deny object-group WorldWideWeb any any
testrouter(config-ext-nacl)#permit ip any any
testrouter(config-ext-nacl)#exit
testrouter(config)#
```

Figure 212: Building a named access-control list using object-groups

This is how you use an object-group within a numbered access-list:

```
testrouter(config)#access-list 101 deny object-group WorldWideWeb any any
testrouter(config)#access-list 101 permit ip any any
testrouter(config)#
```

Figure 213: Building a numbered access-control list using object-groups

Here is an example of how to use both a service object-group and a network object-group in a numbered access-list:

```
testrouter(config)#access-list 101 deny object-group WorldWideWeb object-group Accounting any
testrouter(config)#access-list 101 permit ip any any
testrouter(config)#
```

Figure 214: Incorporating both service and network object-groups in a numbered access-control list

Considerations when Using Object-Groups

- Object-groups can be used only in extended ACLs (named or numbered)

- ACLs based on object-groups support only IPv4 addresses as of this writing (summer 2012)

- Object-group-based ACLs support only layer three interfaces.

- IPSec is not supported by object-group-based ACLs

Interactive Exercise 11.3:
Using IP Extended Access Control Lists

Objectives:

- Deny Sales LAN Telnet access to the R&D server

- Allow all other access to the R&D LAN and unrestricted access to the Internet and Managers

- Allow all other subnets full access all other subnets.

Steps:

1. Write an access-control list on paper that accomplishes the objectives of the exercise

2. Determine where and in which direction to place the list

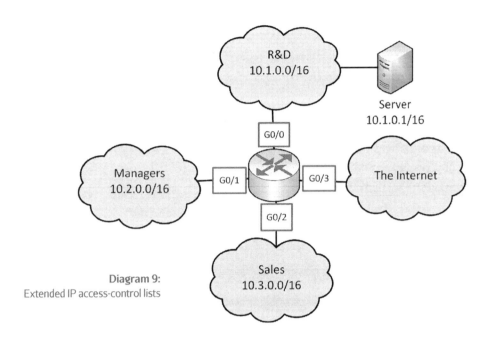

Diagram 9:
Extended IP access-control lists

Solution

Start by creating the access-control list to block Telnet traffic from the Sales LAN.

- router(config)#*access-list 101 deny ip 10.3.0.0 0.0.255.255 host 10.1.0.1 eq 23*

- router01(config)#*access-list 101 permit ip any any*

In the above example, I created a list numbered 101. That tells the router that it's an extended list. Next, I specify that I want to deny a type of traffic. Then, I specify that it's IP traffic from the source 10.3.0.0 with wildcard bits of 0.0.255.255 going to the destination which is an individual host at 10.1.0.1. Finally, I specify port 23 (Telnet) traffic that I wish to block. In the next line, I permit all IP traffic from any source to any destination, so any traffic flow that doesn't match the first line will be permitted.

Next, I have to apply it to an interface. Stop for a moment and consider where to place the list and in which direction it should be placed. There are two possible solutions to the exercise, both of which will work equally well in accomplishing the objectives of the exercise. One of the solutions, however, is a far better solution for reasons not related to the objectives of the exercise. What do you think is the best solution?

One possibility is to place the list on interface g0/0 outbound. That would certainly accomplish the objective to prevent Sales LAN users from gaining Telnet access to the R&D server, while allowing all other access. Here's what it would look like:

- router01(config)#*int g0/0*

- router01(config-if)#*ip access-group 101 out*

A better solution is to place the list on interface g0/2 inbound, like this:

- router01(config)#*int g0/2*

- router01(config-if)#*ip access-group 101 in*

Why do you think the second solution is better than the first? The reason is because in the first solution, the router must process the packets on both the inbound and the outbound interfaces, thus increasing processor utilization on the router. In the second solution, the router stops the affected packets at the inbound interface before they ever get in to the router, thus preventing the router from having to process the packets beyond the inbound interface.

How does a router process an extended Access Control List?

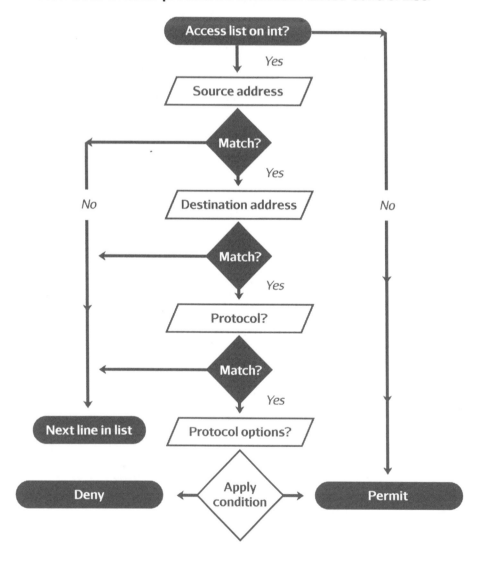

Viewing Access Control Lists on a Router

You can view lists configured on a router with the "show access-lists" command:

```
testrouter#show access-lists
Standard IP access list 10
    10 deny   192.168.1.32, wildcard bits 0.0.0.31
    20 permit any
Standard IP access list BlockSales
    10 deny   10.16.0.0, wildcard bits 0.0.255.255
    15 deny   10.32.0.0, wildcard bits 0.0.255.255
    20 permit any
Extended IP access list 100
    10 permit tcp any host 10.16.0.1 eq 22
    20 permit tcp any host 10.16.0.1 eq telnet
Extended IP access list 101
    10 deny tcp 192.168.100.0 0.0.0.255 any eq www
    20 deny tcp 192.168.100.0 0.0.0.255 any eq 443
    30 permit ip any any
testrouter#
```

Figure 215: The output of the "show access-lists" command on a router
with four different lists configured

Summary

Access-control lists are a very powerful way of managing traffic on and through a Cisco router. They are, however, based primarily on IP addresses. IP addresses can be spoofed fairly easily, so you should not rely on ACLs as your sole layer of security.

Additionally, ACLs can be tricky when you are attempting to troubleshoot connectivity. Remember to build them in a text editor and review them line-by-line before applying them to a router interface or function. As you review them, ensure that you understand the impact of each entry in the list.

Remember the importance of order in the list. Always order your entries from most specific to most general.

Finally, always remember the implicit *deny any* at the end of every ACL. Anything that is not explicitly permitted is implicitly denied. If a packet doesn't match any of the lines in the list, it will be discarded.

CHAPTER 12:
Virtual Private Networks

Chapter Introduction

Learning about VPNs is also one of the most common reasons people seem to attend my classes or view my videos. On the surface, it looks like there is a lot of complexity to configuring VPNs. Indeed, there are lots of options associated with VPNs. Here's the key to understanding them: Break the configuration down into sections. That's what I'm going to do in this chapter. You and I will go through the process of understanding what phase one is, what phase two is, the objective of the access-control lists, and who our peers are. As we do that, I think you'll start to grasp how a VPN works and you'll start to make some sense out of the configurations. Take small bites, digest them completely, and eventually you'll finish consuming the entire buffet of protocols and when you're done, you'll get it!

Chapter Objectives

- Gain a fundamental understanding of VPN protocols and terminology

- Connect two local area networks securely through a VPN on two routers

Online Companion Resources

Videos: Watch the companion videos for this chapter. They're available at
www.soundtraining.net/videos/cisco-router-training-videos

Web Page: There is a supporting web page with live links and other resources for this book
at www.soundtraining.net/cisco-router-book

Facebook: www.soundtraining.net/facebook

Twitter: www.soundtraining.net/twitter

Blog: www.soundtraining.net/blog

Chapter Twelve Network Diagram

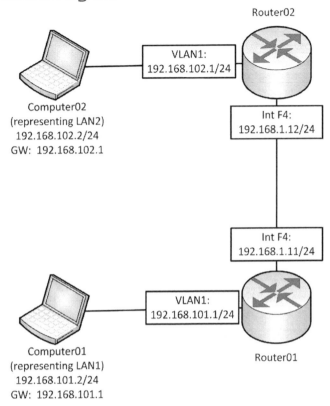

Diagram 10: Site-to-Site VPN

Configuring a Site-to-Site VPN between Two Cisco Routers

A site-to-site virtual private network (VPN) allows you to maintain a secure "always-on" connection between two physically separate sites using an existing non-secure network such as the public Internet. Traffic between the two sites is transmitted over an encrypted tunnel to prevent snooping or other types of data attacks.

There are several protocols used in creating the VPN including protocols used for a key exchange between the peers, those used to encrypt the tunnel, and hashing technologies which produce message digests.

VPN Protocols

IPSec: Internet Protocol Security (IPSec) is a suite of protocols that are used to secure IP communications. IPSec involves both key exchanges and tunnel encryption. You can think of IPSec as a framework for implementing security. When creating an IPSec VPN, you can choose from a variety of security technologies to implement the tunnel.

- ISAKMP (IKE): Internet Security Association and Key Management Protocol (ISAKMP) provides a means for authenticating the peers in a secure communication. It typically uses Internet Key Exchange (IKE), but other technologies can also be used. Public keys or a pre-shared key are used to authenticate the parties to the communication.

- MD5: Message-Digest algorithm 5 (MD5) is an often used, but partially insecure cryptographic hash function with a 128-bit hash value. A cryptographic hash function is a way of taking an arbitrary block of data and returning a fixed-size bit string, the hash value based on the original block of data. The hashing process is designed so that a change to the data will also change the hash value. The hash value is also called the message digest.

- SHA: Secure Hash Algorithm (SHA) is a set of cryptographic hash functions designed by the National Security Agency (NSA). The three SHA algorithms are structured differently and are distinguished as SHA-0,SHA-1, and SHA-2. SHA-1 is a commonly used hashing algorithm with a standard key length of 160 bits.

- ESP: Encapsulating Security Payload (ESP) is a member of the IPsec protocol suite that provides origin authenticity, integrity, and confidentiality protection of packets. ESP also supports encryption-only and authentication-only configurations, but using encryption without authentication is strongly discouraged because it is insecure. Unlike the other IPsec protocol, Authentication Header (AH), ESP does not protect the IP packet header. This difference makes ESP preferred for use in a Network Address Translation configuration. ESP operates directly on top of IP, using IP protocol number 50.

- DES: The Data Encryption Standard (DES) provides 56-bit encryption. It is no longer considered a secure protocol because its short key-length makes it vulnerable to brute-force attacks.

- 3DES: Three DES was designed to overcome the limitations and weaknesses of DES by using three different 56-bit keys in a encrypting, decrypting, and re-encrypting operation. 3DES keys are 168 bits in length. When using 3DES, the data is first encrypted with one 56-bit key, then decrypted with a different 56-bit key, the output of which is then re-encrypted with a third 56-bit key.

- AES: The Advanced Encryption Standard (AES) was designed as a replacement for DES and 3DES. It is available in varying key lengths and is generally considered to be about six times faster than 3DES.

- HMAC: The Hashing Message Authentication Code (HMAC) is a type of message authentication code (MAC). HMAC is calculated using a specific algorithm involving a cryptographic hash function in combination with a secret key.

Requirements

In order to use the following commands, you must have a security feature set associated with your router's license. This chapter was written with two Cisco 871 routers running c870-advipservicesk9-mz.124-15.T6.bin. Use the *show version* command to determine whether your router has the security feature set installed. Toward the bottom of the output, you should see something similar to this on a 1900/2900/3900 router:

```
Technology Package License Information for Module:'c1900'

-----------------------------------------------------------------
Technology    Technology-package          Technology-package
              Current      Type           Next reboot
-----------------------------------------------------------------
ipbase        ipbasek9     Permanent      ipbasek9
security      securityk9   Permanent      securityk9
data          None         None           None

Configuration register is 0x2102
```

Figure 216:
The output of the "show version" command on a Cisco 1941 router with the security feature set installed

On routers running earlier software versions, look for something in the system image file name indicating that you're running an advanced IP services feature set, similar to this:

```
router03 uptime is 5 weeks, 2 days, 2 hours, 8 minutes
System returned to ROM by power-on
System image file is "flash:c870-advipservicesk9-mz.124-15.T6.bin"
```

Figure 217:
The output of the "show version" command on a Cisco 871 router with the Advanced IP Services f eature set installed

The commands should work with other routers, as long as they have the necessary software installed. Obviously, you'll need to change the interface names to match those on your routers.

Configuring a Site-to-Site VPN

The process of configuring a site-to-site VPN involves several steps.

1. Phase One—The key exchange

2. Phase Two—Encrypting the tunnel

3. Applying the crypto map to the outside interface

4. Creating an access list to identify the traffic flow

Phase One configuration involves configuring the key exchange. This process uses ISAKMP (Internet Security Association Key Management Protocol) to identify the hashing algorithm and authentication method. It is also one of two places where you must identify the peer at the opposite end of the tunnel. In the following example, I chose SHA as the hashing algorithm due to its more robust nature, including its 160-bit key. The key "vpnkey" must be identical on both ends of the tunnel. The address "192.168.1.12" is the outside interface of the router at the opposite end of the tunnel.

The following screen captures are from router01 in the preceding diagram.

```
router01#conf t
Enter configuration commands, one per line.  End with CNTL/Z.
router01(config)#crypto isakmp policy 10
router01(config-isakmp)#hash sha
router01(config-isakmp)#authentication pre-share
router01(config-isakmp)#crypto isakmp key vpnkey address 192.168.1.12
router01(config)#
```

Figure 218: VPN Phase One configuration

Phase Two configuration involves configuring the encrypted tunnel. In Phase Two configuration, you create and name a transform set which identifies the encrypting protocols used to create the secure tunnel. You must also create a crypto map in which you identify the peer at the opposite end of the tunnel, specify the transform-set to be used, and specify which access control list will identify permitted traffic flows. In this example, as above, I chose AES due to its heightened security and enhanced performance. The statement "set peer 192.168.1.12" identifies the outside interface of the router at the opposite end of the tunnel. The statement "set transform-set vpnset" tells the router to use the parameters specified in the transform-set vpnset in this tunnel. The "match address 100" statement is used to associate the tunnel with access-list 100 which will be defined later.

```
router01(config)#crypto ipsec transform-set vpnset esp-aes esp-sha-hmac
router01(cfg-crypto-trans)#crypto map vpnset 10 ipsec-isakmp
% NOTE: This new crypto map will remain disabled until a peer
        and a valid access list have been configured.
router01(config-crypto-map)#set peer 192.168.1.12
router01(config-crypto-map)#set transform-set vpnset
router01(config-crypto-map)#match address 100
router01(config-crypto-map)#
```

Figure 219:
VPN Phase Two configuration

The crypto map must be applied to your outside interface (in this example, interface FastEthernet 4).

```
router01(config)#interface f4
router01(config-if)#crypto map vpnset
router01(config-if)#
```

Figure 220:
Applying the crypto map to
the outside interface

You must create an access control list to explicitly allow certain traffic across the tunnel.

```
router01(config)#access-list 100 permit ip 192.168.101.0 0.0.0.255 192.168.102.0 0.0.0.255
router01(config)#
```

Figure 221: You must creae an access-control list to identify and permit traffic
to flow from one inside network to the other inside network.

You must also create a default gateway (also known as the "gateway of last resort").

```
router01(config)#
router01(config)#ip route 0.0.0.0 0.0.0.0 192.168.1.1
router01(config)#
```

Figure 222: Configuring a default gateway on the router

Verifying VPN Connections

The following two commands can be used to verify VPN connections:

– Router#**show crypto ipsec sa** displays the settings used by the current Security Associations (SAs)

```
router01#show crypto isakmp sa
IPv4 Crypto ISAKMP SA
dst             src             state        conn-id slot status
192.168.1.11    192.168.1.12    QM_IDLE         1001    0 ACTIVE

IPv6 Crypto ISAKMP SA

router01#
```

Figure 223: Verifying a VPN Phase One connection
with the command "show crypto isakmp sa"

Notice in the above screen capture that the output shows a security association between 192.168.1.11 (the destination) and 192.168.1.12 (the source).

– Router#**show crypto isakmp sa** displays current IKE Security Associations.

```
router01#show crypto ipsec sa

interface: FastEthernet4
    Crypto map tag: vpnset, local addr 192.168.1.11

   protected vrf: (none)
   local  ident (addr/mask/prot/port): (192.168.101.0/255.255.255.0/0/0)
   remote ident (addr/mask/prot/port): (192.168.102.0/255.255.255.0/0/0)
   current_peer 192.168.1.12 port 500
     PERMIT, flags={origin_is_acl,}
    #pkts encaps: 36, #pkts encrypt: 36, #pkts digest: 36
    #pkts decaps: 88, #pkts decrypt: 88, #pkts verify: 88
    #pkts compressed: 0, #pkts decompressed: 0
    #pkts not compressed: 0, #pkts compr. failed: 0
    #pkts not decompressed: 0, #pkts decompress failed: 0
    #send errors 0, #recv errors 0

     local crypto endpt.: 192.168.1.11, remote crypto endpt.: 192.168.1.12
     path mtu 1500, ip mtu 1500
     current outbound spi: 0xCEA4445E(3466871902)

     inbound esp sas:
      spi: 0x9924DC0A(2569329674)
        transform: esp-aes esp-sha-hmac ,
        in use settings ={Tunnel, }
        conn id: 1, flow_id: C87X_MBRD:1, crypto map: vpnset
        sa timing: remaining key lifetime (k/sec): (4503932/3203)
        IV size: 16 bytes
        replay detection support: Y
        Status: ACTIVE

     inbound ah sas:

     inbound pcp sas:

     outbound esp sas:
      spi: 0xCEA4445E(3466871902)
        transform: esp-aes esp-sha-hmac ,
        in use settings ={Tunnel, }
        conn id: 2, flow_id: C87X_MBRD:2, crypto map: vpnset
```

Figure 224:
Verifying a VPN Phase Two
connection with the command
"show crypto ipsec sa"

There is a lot of material contained in the output of the *show crypto ipsec sa* command. Some things to look for:

- Look at the local and remote identifications. Are they what you expect?

- Same thing for local and remote crypto endpoints.

- Check for the current peer. It should be the other router's outside interface.

Troubleshooting VPN Connections

Use the following checklist to troubleshoot VPN connections:

1. Check all cables and connectors.

2. Verify all IP addresses, including router outside and inside interfaces, plus the address on each of the computers.

3. Check default gateways.

4. Ensure that only one network connection is enabled on each PC.

5. Confirm that the access-control list is configured to allow traffic to flow from the local inside network to the remote inside network.

6. Verify that each router's peer is configured as the remote router's outside interface address.

7. Confirm that the same keys and protocols are in use on each end of the connection. The two router configurations should mirror each other except, obviously, for IP addresses.

8. Confirm the ISAKMP security association. If it doesn't exist, the IPSEC connection cannot be made.

Use debugging to analyze VPN connection difficulties:

- Router#*debug crypto isakmp* allows you to observe Phase 1 ISAKMP negotiations.

- Router#*debug crypto ipsec* allows you to observe Phase 2 IPSec negotiations.

Interactive Exercise 12.1:
Configuring a Site-to-Site VPN

Objectives:

- Configure a site-to-site VPN between two Cisco routers

- Confirm connectivity between two separate LANs through a secure IPSEC tunnel

Steps:

This exercise requires that you work with a pair of routers, configured according to the diagram at the beginning of the chapter.

1. Open a command window on your management workstation and start a continuous ping to your partner's PC address with the following command:

- **On computer 01:** c:\>*ping –t 192.168.102.2*

- **On computer 02:** c:\>*ping –t 192.168.101.2*

2. Move the PC command window so it's out of the way, but still visible.

3. In your router's command line interface, perform Phase One configuration with the following steps:

    – router#*conf t*

    – router(config)#*crypto isakmp policy 10*

    – router(config-isakmp)#*hash sha*

    – router(config-isakmp)#*authentication pre-share*

    For router01:

    • router01(config-isakmp)#*crypto isakmp key vpnkey address 192.168.1.12*

    For router02:

    • router02(config-isakmp)#*crypto isakmp key vpnkey address 192.168.1.11*

```
router01#conf t
Enter configuration commands, one per line.  End with CNTL/Z.
router01(config)#crypto isakmp policy 10
router01(config-isakmp)#hash sha
router01(config-isakmp)#authentication pre-share
router01(config-isakmp)#crypto isakmp key vpnkey address 192.168.1.12
router01(config)#
```

Figure 225: Phase one ISAKMP configuration on router01

4. Perform Phase Two configuration with the following steps:

    – router(config)#*crypto ipsec transform-set vpnset esp-aes esp-sha-hmac*

    – router(cfg-crypto-trans)#*exit*

    – router(config)#*crypto map vpnset 10 ipsec-isakmp*

    – router(config-crypto-map)#*set transform-set vpnset*

    – router(config-crypto-map)#*match address 100*

    For router01:

    • router01(config-crypto-map)#*set peer 192.168.1.12*

    For router02:

    • router02(config-crypto-map)#*set peer 192.168.1.11*

```
router01(config)#crypto ipsec transform-set vpnset esp-aes esp-sha-hmac
router01(cfg-crypto-trans)#crypto map vpnset 10 ipsec-isakmp
% NOTE: This new crypto map will remain disabled until a peer
        and a valid access list have been configured.
router01(config-crypto-map)#set peer 192.168.1.12
router01(config-crypto-map)#set transform-set vpnset
router01(config-crypto-map)#match address 100
router01(config-crypto-map)#
```

Figure 226:
Phase two IPSEC configuration
on router01

5. Apply the crypto map to the router's outside interface (f4):

   – router(config)#*int f4*

   – router(config-if)#*crypto map vpnset*

```
router01(config)#interface f4
router01(config-if)#crypto map vpnset
router01(config-if)#
```

Figure 227:
Applying the crypto map to
router01's F4 interface

6. In global configuration mode, create an access-control list to identify the traffic flows permitted across the tunnel:

   For router01:

   • router01(config)#*access-list 100 permit ip 192.168.101.0 0.0.0.255 192.168.102.0 0.0.0.255*

   For router02:

   • router02(config)#*access-list 100 permit ip 192.168.102.0 0.0.0.255 192.168.101.0 0.0.0.255*

```
router01(config)#access-list 100 permit ip 192.168.101.0 0.0.0.255 192.168.102.0 0.0.0.255
router01(config)#
```

Figure 228: An access-control list identifying the traffic flow between router01's LAN and router02's LAN

7. If a default gateway doesn't already exist, you must create one with the following command:
   router(config)#*ip route 0.0.0.0 0.0.0.0 192.168.1.1*

```
router01(config)#
router01(config)#ip route 0.0.0.0 0.0.0.0 192.168.1.1
router01(config)#
```

Figure 229: A default gateway configuration

8. At this point, the ping between the PCs should be successful. If it's not, review your configuration for typographical errors or missing steps.

9. View the security associations with the following commands:

- router#*show crypto isakmp sa*

```
router01#show crypto isakmp sa
IPv4 Crypto ISAKMP SA
dst              src             state         conn-id slot status
192.168.1.11     192.168.1.12    QM_IDLE          1001    0 ACTIVE

IPv6 Crypto ISAKMP SA

router01#
```

Figure 230:
An ISAKMP security association has been established between router01 and rotuer02

- router#*show crypto ipsec sa*

```
router01#show crypto ipsec sa

interface: FastEthernet4
    Crypto map tag: vpnset, local addr 192.168.1.11

   protected vrf: (none)
   local  ident (addr/mask/prot/port): (192.168.101.0/255.255.255.0/0/0)
   remote ident (addr/mask/prot/port): (192.168.102.0/255.255.255.0/0/0)
   current_peer 192.168.1.12 port 500
     PERMIT, flags={origin_is_acl,}
    #pkts encaps: 36, #pkts encrypt: 36, #pkts digest: 36
    #pkts decaps: 88, #pkts decrypt: 88, #pkts verify: 88
    #pkts compressed: 0, #pkts decompressed: 0
    #pkts not compressed: 0, #pkts compr. failed: 0
    #pkts not decompressed: 0, #pkts decompress failed: 0
    #send errors 0, #recv errors 0

     local crypto endpt.: 192.168.1.11, remote crypto endpt.: 192.168.1.12
     path mtu 1500, ip mtu 1500
     current outbound spi: 0xCEA4445E(3466871902)

     inbound esp sas:
      spi: 0x9924DC0A(2569329674)
        transform: esp-aes esp-sha-hmac ,
        in use settings ={Tunnel, }
        conn id: 1, flow_id: C87X_MBRD:1, crypto map: vpnset
        sa timing: remaining key lifetime (k/sec): (4503932/3203)
        IV size: 16 bytes
        replay detection support: Y
        Status: ACTIVE

     inbound ah sas:

     inbound pcp sas:

     outbound esp sas:
      spi: 0xCEA4445E(3466871902)
        transform: esp-aes esp-sha-hmac ,
        in use settings ={Tunnel, }
        conn id: 2, flow_id: C87X_MBRD:2, crypto map: vpnset
```

Figure 231:
An IPSEC security association has been established between router01 and router02

258

Summary

As you can see from this chapter, setting up a site-to-site VPN involves quite a few steps, but is not terribly difficult. As time goes by, you may want to increase key lengths. The above configuration will allow you to do that.

The most important thing to remember, when setting up a VPN, is that the router configurations on each end of the connection should mirror each other. Obviously, IP addresses will have to be different, but ensure that protocols, encryption algorithms, key lengths, passwords (keys), key lifetimes, and every other aspect of the two configurations is identical.

CHAPTER 13:
Managing Cisco IOS Passwords

Chapter Introduction

I'm going to go over several points related to passwords in this chapter, but I know that the thing you probably want from the chapter is how to get in to a router when you don't know the password. Cisco calls the process *password recovery*, but you don't really recover the password. Instead, you reset it to a known value. The administrator-level password, known as the *enable secret*, uses MD5 encryption and, as of this writing, it is not believed to be reversible.

I'll touch on the different types of passwords, how to provide weak encryption on user-level passwords to protect against shoulder-surfing, and how to reset the enable secret … just in case.

Chapter Objectives

- Understand the types of passwords used on a Cisco router

- Learn how to apply encryption to all passwords

- Perform password recovery procedures in the event of an unknown password

Online Companion Resources

Videos: Watch the companion videos for this chapter. They're available at
www.soundtraining.net/videos/cisco-router-training-videos

Web Page: There is a supporting web page with live links and other resources for this book
at www.soundtraining.net/cisco-router-book

Facebook: www.soundtraining.net/facebook

Twitter: www.soundtraining.net/twitter

Blog: www.soundtraining.net/blog

Types of Passwords

Cisco Routers can use many passwords, including:

- Two for the privileged mode (one that is encrypted by default and one that is not encrypted by default)

- One for user mode

- Console port

- Auxiliary port

- Telnet

In a normal configuration, only the enable secret is encrypted. It's possible, however, to encrypt all passwords. To do so, user the *service password-encryption* command in global configuration mode. After issuing the "service password-encryption" command, issue the privileged EXEC command "show run" which will encrypt the passwords.

```
testrouter(config)#do show run | include enable
enable secret 5 $1$7El/$KusRNhno0u00sK2HtWSRN0
enable password p@ssw0rD
```

Figure 232:
The enable secret is the privileged mode password. It is encrypted by default. The enable password is included for legacy support, but is not normally used. It is not encrypted.

```
testrouter(config)#service password-encryption
testrouter(config)#do show run | include enable
enable secret 5 $1$7El/$KusRNhno0u00sK2HtWSRN0
enable password 7 12092504011C5C160E
```

Figure 233:
By using the "service password-encryption" command, you can apply encryption to all passwords in the router's configuration

The same thing happens to the line console and line vty passwords. They are not encrypted by default. When you issue the *service password-encryption* command, however, they are encrypted in the configuration file, as you can in the following screen captures.

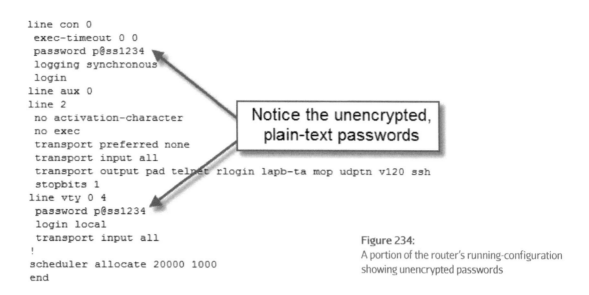

Figure 234:
A portion of the router's running-configuration
showing unencrypted passwords

After issuing the *service password-encryption* command, however, they are encrypted.

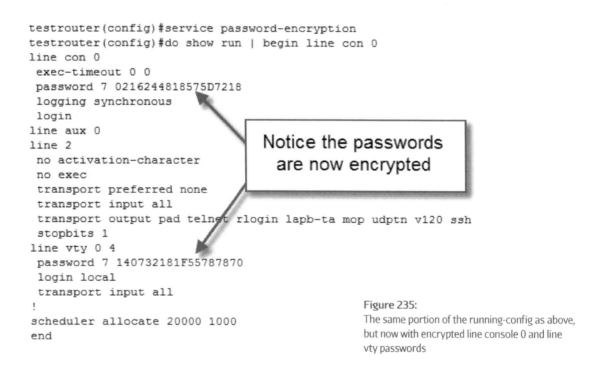

Figure 235:
The same portion of the running-config as above,
but now with encrypted line console 0 and line
vty passwords

Password Recovery

Password recovery is the process used to reset the privileged mode password when it is not known, such as when a previous administrator failed to document passwords. Password recovery on a Cisco router requires physical access to the device. It cannot be accomplished over a network.

In order to recover a password, the configuration source is changed to prevent reading the startup-configuration file in NVRAM on boot. Since the NVRAM is ignored, no password is required for privileged EXEC mode. Once in privileged EXEC mode, the saved configuration is copied to the running configuration. The enable secret is changed, configuration is saved, boot source is changed back to NVRAM, and the router is restarted.

The following interactive exercise provides step-by-step procedures for recovering passwords on most current model routers. For password recovery procedures for other routers and switches, visit www.cisco.com and search on the term "password recovery."

Interactive Exercise 14.1: Password Recovery

Objectives:

- Establish a console connection to the Cisco router using PuTTY or other terminal emulation software

- Change the Privileged Mode password to a known password

- Remove the User Mode password

This lab teaches you how to reset passwords on modern Cisco routers when you don't know the Privileged EXEC password. Procedures for older routers (such as 2500-series) are similar, but not identical.

Soundthinking Point: Non-Secure Password Encryption

The level of encryption applied when using the command "service password-encryption" is not considered secure. The main benefit is protection from "shoulder-surfers" (people looking over your shoulder while you're working).

Soundthinking Point: The Configuration Register

When you perform password recovery on a Cisco router, one of the steps involves changing the router's configuration register. The configuration register is a software value that tells the router how to boot. The default for most modern routers is 0x2102, which tells the router to ignore break, boots the router into ROM if initial boot fails, and sets the console baud rate to 9600 (the default value for most platforms). In password recovery, you set the configuration register to 0x2142, which tells the router to boot normally except that it bypasses NVRAM, thus ignoring the router's saved configuration. For an explanation of each of the configuration register values, visit *www.cisco.com* and search on the term "configuration register."

Steps:

Using Windows to Configure and Manage a Cisco Device

Create a PuTTY serial session to connect to the router.

1. Power-cycle the router by using the power switch on the back to turn it off, then turn it on.

2. Wait about 30 seconds and press *Ctrl-Break* (in TeraTerm, press Alt-B) on the computer keyboard to put the router into ROMMON mode. (Don't issue the break sequence immediately after power-up…wait a few seconds.) You should see the "rommon 1" prompt immediately after issuing the break sequence.

3. Type *confreg 0x2142 <Enter>* at the **rommon 1 >** prompt to tell the router to boot from Flash without loading the configuration from NVRAM.

4. Type *reset* at the **rommon 2 >** prompt and press Enter.

```
rommon 1 > confreg 0x2142


You must reset or power cycle for new config to take effect
rommon 2 > reset
```

Figure 236: Changing the router's configuration register in ROM monitor mode

5. The router reboots, but ignores its startup configuration.

6. Press *Ctrl-C* to skip the initial setup dialog. Several lines of text will fly by. When the text stops, press the Enter key.

7. Type *en* at the Router> prompt

8. You'll be in Privileged EXEC mode (without being prompted for the enable secret) and see the **Router#** prompt.

9. *Important*: Type *copy start running* to copy the contents of the startup-config file in nonvolatile RAM (NVRAM) configuration file into the running-config in DRAM.

10. Accept the default destination filename of "running-config" by simply pressing the Enter key.

```
Router>enable
Router#copy startup-config running-config
Destination filename [running-config]?
2907 bytes copied in 0.212 secs (13712 bytes/sec)

testrouter#
```

Figure 237: Notice how the prompt changes after the startup-config
is copied into the router's running-config

11. Type *show running | begin interface* to view the router's current interface configuration in which you see that all interfaces are shutdown. You can also view the passwords either in encrypted or unencrypted format.

```
interface GigabitEthernet0/0
 ip address 192.168.101.1 255.255.255.0
 shutdown
 duplex auto
 speed auto
 ipv6 address autoconfig default
 no mop enabled
!
interface GigabitEthernet0/1
 ip address dhcp
 shutdown
 duplex auto
 speed auto
 no cdp enable
!
```

Figure 238:
The default state of interfaces is shutdown

12. Type *conf t*

13. The prompt is now **Router(config)**#.

14. Type *enable secret p@ss5678 <Enter>* (This command sets your privileged mode password to "p@ss5678.")

```
testrouter#
testrouter#conf t
Enter configuration commands, one per line.  End with CNTL/Z.
testrouter(config)#enable secret p@ss5678
testrouter(config)#
```

Figure 239:
Modifying the enable secret on a router

15. Activate each of your router's interfaces with the following commands:

    – router(config)#*int g0/0*

    – router(config-if)#*no shutdown*

    – router(config-if)#*int g0/1*

    – router(config-if)#*no shutdown*

```
testrouter(config)#
testrouter(config)#int g0/0
testrouter(config-if)#no shut
testrouter(config-if)#int g0/1
testrouter(config-if)#no shut
testrouter(config-if)#
```

Figure 240:
Turning interfaces on with the "no shutdown" command (abbreivated to "no shut")

16. View your router's interfaces with the following command:

    – router(config-if)#*do show ip interface brief*

```
testrouter#show ip interface brief
Interface                  IP-Address      OK? Method Status                 Protocol
Embedded-Service-Engine0/0 unassigned      YES unset  administratively down down
GigabitEthernet0/0         192.168.101.1   YES TFTP   up                     up
GigabitEthernet0/1         192.168.1.90    YES DHCP   up                     up
```

Figure 241: Viewing the state of interfaces on the router.
Note that the embedded-service-engine is not used on this
particular router, thus its state is administratively down.

All connected interfaces should be up.

Remove the user mode password from your router, set the configuration register value back to the default and save the configuration to NVRAM with the following commands (use the screen capture to the right as an example):

– Type *line console 0 <Enter>*

– Type *no login <Enter>*

– Type *no password* **<Enter>**

– Type *config-register 0x2102*

17. Press *exit* to leave the configuration mode and return to privileged mode.

```
testrouter#
testrouter#conf t
Enter configuration commands, one per line.  End with CNTL/Z.
testrouter(config)#line con 0
testrouter(config-line)#no login
testrouter(config-line)#no password
testrouter(config-line)#config-register 0x2102
testrouter(config)#exit
testrouter#
```

Figure 242: Removing the line console 0 password so that
authentication is not required for user mode

18. Type *wr* (write memory) in privileged mode to save the changes:

    – router#*wr*

19. Reload your router:

    – router#*reload*

```
testrouter#
testrouter#wr
Building configuration...
[OK]
testrouter#reload
Proceed with reload? [confirm]

Aug 13 18:18:13.799: %SYS-5-RELOAD: Reload requested by console. Reload Reason: Reload Command.
```

Figure 243: Saving the router's running-config to NVRAM
with the "wr" command (short for "write memory")

20. When the router finishes rebooting, you can log in to user mode with no password and into privileged mode with the password you configured above.

The above procedure is for Cisco 1941 routers. The password recovery procedure is similar for other router models, but not identical. You can find the password recovery procedures for all Cisco network devices by going to www.cisco.com and searching on the term "password recovery."

Summary

Password recovery is often one of the big mysteries for new Cisco admins. As you can see from the steps outlined in this chapter, it's pretty easy. When you think through the steps, they're quite logical. I hope you don't have to do this often, but it's sure good to have the capability when you need it.

CHAPTER 14:
Understanding and Configuring Internet Protocol Version 6 (IPv6)

Chapter Introduction

IPv6 has been growing as the hot buzzword in IT circles since it was originally conceived and created. Is it just a buzzword? No, definitely not! Do you really need to think about it as an option for your network? The answer is, "probably." The reason I say "probably" is because nothing is certain, but the adoption of IPv6 seems about as certain as anything.

In the late 90s and early 2000s, I heard Novell Netware admins say that they would *never* quit using IPX/SPX. There were even DECNet admins who said the same thing about DECNet. There are very few networks today that run either IPX/SPX or DECNet. It's not that they weren't good protocols. It's simply that we have become a world based on IP and it sure looks like we're going to become a world based on IPv6. I'm certainly not suggesting that you should immediately drop everything and switch to IPv6. I am suggesting, however, that IPv6 will probably arrive on your doorstep sooner than you think (and maybe sooner than you'd like). The sooner you get familiar with it and the sooner you start testing it, the sooner you will be ready for its arrival.

Chapter Objectives

- Understanding the new addressing scheme

- The creation of IPv6

- Types of IPv6 addresses

- Preparing for your transition to IPv6

- Configure IPv6 on a Cisco router, including routing and access-control lists

Online Companion Resources

Videos: Watch the companion videos for this chapter. They're available at
www.soundtraining.net/videos/cisco-router-training-videos

Web Page: There is a supporting web page with live links and other resources for this book
at www.soundtraining.net/cisco-router-book

Facebook: www.soundtraining.net/facebook

Twitter: www.soundtraining.net/twitter

Blog: www.soundtraining.net/blog

Chapter Network Diagram

Examples and exercises in this chapter are based on the following network diagram. I intentionally used generic names to describe the interfaces, since you might be using any of a number of different types of routers with different interface names.

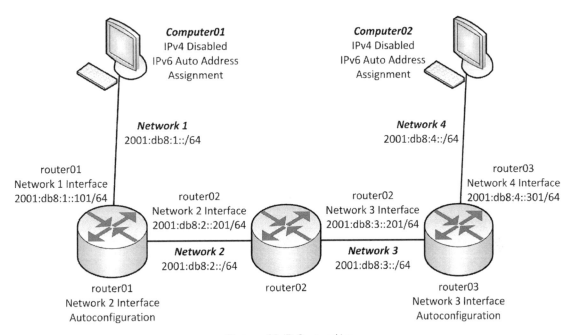

Diagram 11: IPv6 networking

Understanding the IPv6 protocol

IPv4's 32-bit address space provide approximately 4.3 billion IP addresses mathematically. Because of the manner in which the IPv4 address space was originally designed, a maximum of about 3.7 billion addresses are actually usable and, realistically, the actual number is even less than that. The growth of the public Internet, combined with new technologies has put tremendous pressure on the IPv4 address space. Technologies such as CIDR and NAT have extended the life of the IPv4 address space, but a longer term solution is required in order to maintain the viability of the Internet. A new layer three protocol called Internet Protocol version 6 (IPv6) has been created and is being implemented to relieve the pressure on the IPv4 address space.

The Creation of IPv6

IPv6 was created out of work done by many people including Steve Deering and Craig Mudge at Xerox PARC and Robert Hinden at Ipsilon Networks. RFC 1883, written by Deering and Hinden, specifying the new Internet standard protocol was published in December of 1995. RFC 1883 was obsoleted by

RFC 2460, which was updated by RFC 5871. (If you're wondering about IPv5, it is an experimental streaming protocol designed to support audio and video.) IPv6 evolved as a set of specifications, starting with RFC 1752 in January of 1995, to improve upon the limitations of IPv4. IPv6 was also known as "IPng" (IP Next Generation). The "6" refers to version number.

The United States government required all federal agencies to pass IPv6 traffic on their backbone networks by the summer of 2008. This created a catalyst for other agencies, government contractors, hardware and software vendors to follow, potentially causing this new IP protocol to be much more rapidly adopted and implemented.

IPv6 addresses are increased from 32 bits to a whopping 128 bits. This is a considerable increase from IPv4. This creates enough IP addresses for every device and PC needing an IP address.

In many cases, IPv6 can be installed as a software application upgrade for IP devices and can run in dual-stack mode with IPv4.

Here is an example of an IPv6 address: **fe80::702c:f196:c87c:b2b** which is a shorthand version of the following address: **fe80:0000:0000:0000:702c:f196:c87c:0b2b**

Benefits of IPv6

- **Ease of design and routing efficiency**—by increasing the IP address size to 128 bits.

- **New address called "anycast" address**—used to identify sets of nodes where a packet sent to an "anycast" address is delivered to one of the nodes. An anycast address, for example, could be assigned to every DNS server within a traffic domain and traffic would be routed to the closest one.

- **Fixed-Length Basic Header with Extension Header Options Capability**

- **Header format simplification**—there were many in an IPv4 header that weren't use, but which added to processor utilization. Fields in an IPv6 header are made optional to reduce processing time and bandwidth utilization.

- **Improved options**—IP header options are encoded to allow more efficient forwarding, less stringent limits on the length of options, and greater flexibility for introducing any future options.

- **Quality of service**—labeling of packets that belong to particular traffic "flows." This is one of the future benefits of IPv6 that is still under development.

- **Authentication & Privacy**—extensions are defined and provide support for authentication, data integrity, and confidentiality.

- **Autoconfiguration**—Stateless Local Address Autoconfiguration (SLAAC) allows a host to come online, get its network address from the router, and automatically generate its unique node ID to simplify administration.

Types of IPv6 Addresses

IPv6 has three types of addresses. These three types of addresses can be categorized by both type and scope:

- Unicast addresses. A packet is delivered to one interface

- Multicast addresses. A packet is delivered to multiple interfaces

- Anycast addresses. A packet is delivered to the nearest (as defined by routing distance) of multiple interfaces, typically on multiple nodes

Broadcast messages are not used in IPv6.

Additionally, within the unicast and anycast types of addresses are three scopes of addresses:

- Link-local: The scope is the local link (nodes on the same subnet)

- Unique local addresses: The scope is the organization (private site addressing)

- Global: The scope is global (IPv6 Internet addresses).

Unicast Global Addresses

Unicast global addresses are similar to IPv4 public addresses. They are globally routable on the public internet. Unicast global addresses have a prefix of 2000::/3.

Unicast Global Address Packet					
001	TLA ID	Reserved	NLA ID	SLA ID	Interface ID
3 bits	13 bits	8 bits	24 bits	16 bits	64 bits
Public Topology (48 bits total)				Site Topology	A node interface on a specific subnet

Understanding the Fields of a Unicast Global Address

Field	Function
001	Identifies it as an IPv6 unicast global address
TLA ID (Top Level Aggregation Identifier)	The highest level in the routing hierarchy. Administered by IANA and ultimately allocated to a global ISP
Reserved	Reserved for future use
NLA ID (Next Level Aggregation Identifier)	Used to identify a specific customer site.
SLA ID (Site Level Aggregation Identifier)	Supports up to 65,536 subnets within the site of an individual organization. An SLA ID cannot be changed by an ISP; it is assigned within the site.
Interface ID	Identifies an interface of a particular node on a specific subnet

Unique Local Addresses

Unique local addresses, specified in RFC 4193, are the IPv6 equivalent of IPv4 private addresses as specified in RFC 1918. They have replaced the former unicast site-local addresses. Unique local addresses use the address block fc00::/7. Unique local addresses are not routable on the IPv6 global Internet. For more information about unique local addresses, read RFC 4193.

Note: Even though Unique Local Addresses are not globally routable, a router will forward them to the global Internet. Best practice, therefore, is to filter them at the network edge.

Unique Local Address Packet				
Prefix	**L**	**Global ID**	**Subnet ID**	**Interface ID**
7 bits	1	40 bits	16 bits	64 bits

Explanation	
Prefix	Local IPv6 unicast addresses are identified by a prefix of FC00::/7
L	If the prefix is locally assigned, this is set to 1. A setting of 0 may be defined in the future.
Global ID	This is a 40-bit global identifier which is used to create a globally unique prefix.
Subnet ID	This is a 16-bit subnet ID, which is an identifier of a subnet contained within the site.
Interface ID	What the name implies.

Unicast Site-Local Addresses are now Deprecated

You may read elsewhere about Unicast Site-Local addresses. Unicast site-local addresses are similar to IPv4 private addresses. They would be typically used within an organization's site internetwork. It is possible to use both unicast site-local addresses and unicast global addresses within the same internetwork. Site-local addresses have a prefix of FEC0::/48. Site-local addressing has been deprecated, and has been replaced by *unique local addressing*.

Unicast Site-Local Address Packet			
1111 1110 11	000…000	Subnet ID	Interface ID
10 bits	38 bits	16 bits	64 bits

Unicast Link-Local Addresses

Unicast link-local addresses are similar to IPv4 APIPA addresses. They are configured by stateless address autoconfiguration (SLAAC). Link-local addresses are required for neighbor discovery. Even in the absence of other unicast addresses, a link-local address is always automatically configured. They have a prefix of FE80::/64. (It's actually FE80::/10, but the next 54 bits are filled in with zeros.)

The lower 64 bits of a link-local address include a 64-bit interface identifier that is usually shared by all automatically configured addresses on that interface.

Link-local addresses are never forwarded by an IPv6 router.

Unicast Link-Local Address Packet		
1111 1110 10	000…000	Interface ID
10 bits	54 bits	64 bits

Other Types of IPv6 Addresses

Anycast IPv6 Addresses

Anycast addresses are used by IPv6 to identify multiple interfaces. When packets are addressed to an anycast address, they are delivered to the nearest interface identified by the address. Think of an anycast address as being a one to one-of-many. An anycast address is syntactically indistinguishable from a unicast address. As mentioned previously, an example of the use of an anycast address would be when all DNS servers in a domain are given the same anycast address. DNS resolver requests are then forwarded to the nearest interface.

Multicast IPv6 Addresses

Similar to an IPv4 multicast address, IPv6 packets addressed to a multicast address are delivered to all interfaces identified by the address. As you can see in the following diagram of an IPv6 multicast packet header, the leading bit pattern is four ones, thus a multicast address always begins with FF. For example, the multicast address used by RIP routers is ff02::9, reminiscent of the IPv4 multicast address used by RIP routers of 224.0.0.9.

IPv6 Multicast Packet			
1111 1111	Flags	Scope	Group ID
8 bits	4 bits	4 bits	112 bits

Understanding the Fields of a Multicast Address

Field	Function
1111 1111	Identifies it as an IPv6 multicast address
TLA ID (Top Level Aggregation Identifier)	The highest level in the routing hierarchy. Administered by IANA and ultimately allocated to a global ISP
Flags	Identifies types of address (e.g. permanent or transient)
Scope	Identifies the multicast traffic scope, e.g. global, organization-local, site-local, linke-local, or interface-local
Group ID	Multicast group identifier

Unicast 6to4 Addresses

6to4 addresses are used when it is necessary to communicate between two IPv6/IPv4 nodes over the existing IPv4 public internet. A 6to4 address uses a 48 bit prefix made up of the assigned 2002::/16 prefix combined with the 32 bits of the node's public IPv4 address. The resulting 48-bit prefix looks like this: 2002:WWXX:YYZZ::/48 (where WWXX:YYZZ represents the four octets of the IPv4 address). An IPv4 address of 64.49.254.57 would convert to a 6to4 address of 2002:4031:FE39::/48. (Use a calculator to convert 64, 49, 254, and 57 to hexadecimal notation to understand how the conversion works.)

Unicast 6to4 Packet			
0010 0000 0000 0020	WWXX:YYZZ	SLA ID	Interface ID
16 bits	32 bits	16 bits	64 bits

Unicast ISATAP Addresses

ISATAP (Intra-Site Automatic Tunnel Addressing Protocol) is a mechanism designed to aid in transition to IPv6. It provides a means to transmit IPv6 packets between dual-stack nodes on top of an IPv4 network.

ISATAP addresses can incorporate either public or private IPv4 addresses, unlike 6to4 addresses which can incorporate only public IPv4 addresses. Additionally, ISATAP addresses incorporate the IPv4 address at the end of the ISATAP address and IPv4 addresses can be written in either dotted-decimal or hexadecimal notation.

Using the previous IPv4 example of 64.49.254.57, the ISATAP equivalent address using dotted-decimal notation would be FE80::5EFE: 64.49.254.57 or in hexadecimal notation, FE80::5EFE: 4031:FE39.

Unicast ISATAP Addresses		
Subnet prefix (link-local, site-local, or global prefix)	0000:5EFE	WWXX:YYZZ
64 bits	32 bits	32 bits

Unicast Loopback Address

Equivalent to the IPv4 loopback address of 127.0.0.1, the IPv6 loopback address is 0:0:0:0:0:0:0:1/128, which can also be represented by ::1/128.

Unicast Unspecified Address

Equivalent to the IPv4 unspecified address of 0.0.0.0, the IPv6 unspecified address is 0:0:0:0:0:0:0:0 which can also be represented by a double colon (::).

Similarly, the default route in IPv6 is ::/0, similar to 0.0.0.0/0 in IPv4.

For More Information on the IPv6 Address Space

For more information about the IPv6 address space, visit the following link:

http://www.iana.org/assignments/ipv6-address-space/ipv6-address-space.xml

Preparing to Transition to IPv6

Most network users refer to a host or domain name instead of an IP address. For a successful migration, an upgrade to your DNS will have to occur. This includes populating DNS servers with records to support IPv6 names-to-addresses and address-to-name resolution. The sending hosts will obtain IP addresses using a DNS name query, then the node must select which IP address to use for communication.

Soundthinking Point: Addresses for Documentation

Have you noticed that I use the unicast global address prefix of 2001:db8::/64 in much of this book? The reason is because the 2001:db8::/32 address space is set aside for documentation. Addresses in that space will never be assigned to global Internet hosts, thus avoiding potential address conflicts. Why /64 instead of /32? That was really just an arbitrary decision on my part to limit the address space available for hosts. Frankly, if I had it all to do over again, I probably would have limited it even more just to make things simpler for me to write and for you read.

For more information, see RFC 3849.

Address records in the DNS infrastructure must contain resource records populated manually or dynamically for name resolution of domain names to IPv6 addresses.

- "A" Records for IPv4 only and IPv6/IPv4 node

- "AAAA" records for IPv6 only and IPv6/IPv4 nodes (RFC3596)

Increased security is a feature of IPv6 due to the many standardized requirements and features. This makes it convenient so that applications do not need updating or changing. One feature, packet signing, handles authentication. Another benefit is data confidentiality through encryption. IPv6 includes an end-to-end security model that is specifically designed to protect DHCP, DNS, and IPv6 mobility.

Another benefit discussed earlier is that IPv6 routing uses much less overhead resulting in faster route computation and aggregation.

Transitioning to IPv6 is not without challenges. Successful migration to IPv6 requires IPv4 nodes to communicate to IPv6 nodes and vice versa during the migration period. Techniques to assist a variety of topologies to be able to do this are:

- Dual stack

- Tunneling

- ISATAP

- 6to4

Dual stack

Routers use this technique to handle IPv4 and IPv6 protocols. With routers handling this protocol, network segments can have both IPv4 and IPv6 hosts. Unfortunately, this requires IPv4 IP addresses. This is useful as a short-term solution, though not recommended for long term implementation. *Dual Stack Transition Mechanism* (DSTM) assists with this process by giving an IPv4 IP address temporarily to reduce the burden on the available IPv4 address pool. DSTM allows IPv4 allows applications to run over IPv6 networks.

Tunneling

Another method used to handle the IPv6 migration is IPv6 over IPv4 tunneling. Tunneling takes an IPv6 packet and encapsulates it in an IPv4 packet to allow the IPv4 infrastructure to handle it. Tunneling allows IPv6 hosts to communicate over IPv4 infrastructures. It also supports router-to-router, host-to-router, and host-to-host communication.

ISATAP

ISATAP (Intra-Site Automatic Tunnel Addressing Protocol) is a mechanism designed to aid in transition to IPv6. It provides a means to transmit IPv6 packets between dual-stack nodes on top of an IPv4 network.

Unlike *6to4*, discussed in the next section, ISATAP uses IPv4 as a virtual nonbroadcast multiple-access network (NBMA) data link layer. It, therefore, does not require the underlying IPv4 network infrastructure to support multicast.

The ISATAP protocol specifies the IPv6 connections of hosts and routers within an IPv4 infrastructure. ISATAP allows for incremental migration from IPv4 to IPv6. The benefit is that implementation of this configuration does not require manual configuration. It uses the following format: "::0:5EFE:w.x.y.z." A type that indicates an embedded IPv4 address (FE) is combined with an organizational unit identifier (00-00-5E) to form the portion that is "0:5EFE." The w.x.y.z portion is the IPv4 address.

6to4

The 6to4 configuration allows for IPv6 domains to communicate with other IPv6 domains. Even when an IPv6 provider is unavailable for connection, a special prefix is used to designate a 6to4 address, by encapsulating it in an IPv4 packet. When an IPv4 packet arrives at the destination 6to4 router, it is recognized as an IPv6 packet. Then the IPv4 header is removed and the original IPv6 packet is forwarded locally.

General steps for an organization to migrate to IPv6

Transition to IPv6 should be well planned and carried out incrementally. An abrupt transition carries the high potential for failure and the resulting costly downtime. The multiple methods of transition provide a flexible path for different organizations. The specific method used depends on the particular needs of the organization. Often, migrations to IPv6 will make use of a mixture of different techniques.

Here are some best practices to follow for IPv6 migration:

- Upgrade applications to support IPv6.

- Update the DNS infrastructure to handle IPv6.

- Upgrade and implement IPv6 capable routing infrastructure

- Upgrade hosts to IPv4/IPv6 compatible hosts/nodes

- Upgrade the routing infrastructure to native IPv6 routing structure

- Convert all nodes to IPv6 through a gradual rolling/testing process

Configuring IPv6 on a Cisco Router

Does Your Router Support IPv6?

Cisco began providing limited support for IPv6 on the high-end 12000 series router with version 12.0S. Gradually, over the next few versions, full support for IPv6 was implemented in many IOS editions. IOS versions 12.4 and 12.4T provide full support in many editions and are suitable for production use (after testing, of course).

You can check your router for IPv6 support by using the privileged mode command *show ipv6 ?*. If your router supports IPv6, you'll see a list of options to complete the command.

```
router02#show ipv6 ?
  access-list      Summary of access lists
  cef              Cisco Express Forwarding for IPv6
  dhcp             IPv6 DHCP
  eigrp            Show IPv6 EIGRP
  features         IPV6 features
  general-prefix   IPv6 general prefixes
  interface        IPv6 interface status and configuration
  lisp             Locator/ID Separation Protocol
  local            IPv6 local options
  mfib             IP multicast forwarding information base
  mld              Multicast group membership information
  mrib             Multicast Routing Information Base
  mroute           IPv6 multicast routing table
  mtu              MTU per destination cache
  neighbors        Show IPv6 neighbor cache entries
  ospf             OSPF information
  pim              PIM information
  policy           Policy routing
  prefix-list      List IPv6 prefix lists
  protocols        IPv6 Routing Protocols
  rip              RIP routing protocol status
  route            Show IPv6 route table entries
  routers          Show local IPv6 routers
  rpf              Multicast RPF information
  spd              IPv6 Selective Packet Discard
  static           IPv6 static routes
  traffic          IPv6 traffic statistics

router02#show ipv6
```

Figure 244:
Testing for IPv6 capability
on a router

Otherwise, your router will return an *Unrecognized command* error.

Stateless Address Autoconfiguration (SLAAC)

SLAAC is one of the most compelling aspects of IPv6. Think of SLAAC as DHCP with minimal configuration. Fundamentally, all you have to do is enable IPv6 on a router and assign an interface address. SLAAC does the rest of the work for you, even including duplicate address detection to ensure the uniqueness of the autoconfigured address. IPv6 routers send Router Advertisements (RAs) every 200 seconds or upon request. RAs include the IPv6 network identifier. As an alternative to waiting 200 seconds (slightly more than three minutes), when an IPv6 host comes online, it sends a Router Solicitation (RS) multicast requesting its configuration parameters.

SLAAC works with both routers and hosts. A host, such as Windows 7, that is configured to obtain an IP address automatically, will query its network for a DHCP server. If no DHCP server is available, but a neighboring router is running IPv6, the router can provide a network address to the host. The host will then generate a unique identifier to combine with the network address for its IPv6 address.

For more information about SLAAC, read RFC 4862.

Assigning Addresses to an Interface

Static assignment

As with IPv4, addresses can be assigned statically on an interface-by-interface basis. Unless you've gotten an address space from your provider, use *unique local addresses* from the fc00::/7 address block. Use the syntax *ipv6 address [x:x:x:x:x:x:x:x/mask]*, as shown in the following screen capture.

```
router02(config)#int g0/0
router02(config-if)#ipv6 address fc00:201::1/64
router02(config-if)#int g0/1
router02(config-if)#ipv6 address fc00:301::1/64
router02(config-if)#
```

Figure 245:
Assigning a static IPv6 address to two interfaces on a router

In the preceding screen capture, I assigned two similar, but unique, addresses to the two interfaces on router02. By using a /64 mask, I effectively split the 128-bit address in half, using the first half for the network (or subnet) and the last half to uniquely identify the host. Notice that interface g0/0 was given an address on the fc00:201::/64 network, while interface g0/1 was given an address on the fc00:301::/64 network.

Autoconfiguration

If your router has an interface connected to another router, you may wish to enable SLAAC on it with the command *ipv6 address autoconfig*.

```
router02(config)#int g0/0
router02(config-if)#ipv6 address autoconfig
router02(config-if)#
```

Figure 246:
Using the autoconfiguration feature of SLAAC to assign an IPv6 address to an interface

DHCP

Similarly to autoconfiguration, you can configure an interface on a router to obtain its address from a DHCP server. The difference between autoconfig and DHCP is that, with autoconfig, the router will obtain its network information from the neighboring router and will generate its own host identifier. There is no bindings database with a record of which address was assigned to which host. With DHCP, all address parameters are provided by the DHCP server and a database is maintained with records of which node has which address.

Use the interface configuration mode command *ip address dhcp* to configure the interface as a DHCP client.

```
router02(config)#int g0/0
router02(config-if)#ipv6 address dhcp
router02(config-if)#
```

Figure 247:
Configuring an interface to obtain an IPv6 address from a DHCP server

Verifying Address Assignment

After you configure the address(es), you can verify your configuration with the command *show ipv6 interface brief.*

```
router02(config-if)#do show ipv6 interface brief
Embedded-Service-Engine0/0 [administratively down/down]
    unassigned
GigabitEthernet0/0          [up/up]
    FE80::7281:5FF:FE70:8500
    2001:3::201
GigabitEthernet0/1          [up/up]
    FE80::7281:5FF:FE70:8501
    2001:2::201
Tunnel0                     [up/up]
    FE80::7281:5FF:FE70:8500
    unnumbered (GigabitEthernet0/1)
router02(config-if)#
```

Figure 248:
Using the "show ipv6 interface brief" command to view address configuration

Soundthinking Point: Manually Remove Unneeded Addresses

One change from IPv4 that's pretty significant: Adding a new address to an interface does not automatically overwrite or remove existing addresses. As I was first learning about IPv6, I once found my router with many addresses on an interface. That made for an interesting autoconfiguration on a neighboring router!

Configuring Names Resolution through Host Files

Configuring IPv6 host files is a way of enabling names resolution when you don't have access to an IPv6-enabled DNS server. The procedure is much the same as building an IPv4 host file. Use the command *ipv6 host [hostname] [ipv6 address]* as you can see in the following screen capture.

```
router02(config)#
router02(config)#ipv6 host router01 2001:db8:2::21a:e2ff:fe19:aad
router02(config)#ipv6 host router03 2001:db8:3::222:55ff:fee2:300
router02(config)#do ping router01
Type escape sequence to abort.
Sending 5, 100-byte ICMP Echos to 2001:DB8:2:0:21A:E2FF:FE19:AAD, timeout is 2 s
econds:
!!!!!
Success rate is 100 percent (5/5), round-trip min/avg/max = 0/0/0 ms
router02(config)#do ping router03
Type escape sequence to abort.
Sending 5, 100-byte ICMP Echos to 2001:DB8:3:0:222:55FF:FEE2:300, timeout is 2 s
econds:
!!!!!
Success rate is 100 percent (5/5), round-trip min/avg/max = 0/0/4 ms
router02(config)#
```

Figure 249: Configuring static host name to IPv6 address translation

Notice in the preceding screen capture that after configuring the host file, I was able to ping both router01 and router03 by name instead of IPv6 address. After you configure the host file, you can view it with the command *show hosts*:

```
router02#show hosts
Default domain is not set
Name/address lookup uses static mappings

Codes: UN - unknown, EX - expired, OK - OK, ?? - revalidate
       temp - temporary, perm - permanent
       NA - Not Applicable None - Not defined

Host                     Port  Flags       Age Type  Address(es)
router01                 None  (perm, OK)   0  IPv6  2001:DB8:2:0:21A:E2FF:FE19:AAD
router03                 None  (perm, OK)   0  IPv6  2001:DB8:3:0:222:55FF:FEE2:300
router02#
```

Figure 250: Viewing the IPv6 hosts file on a router

Configuring Routing

As with IPv4 routing, you can either enable static routing or dynamic routing. The reasons you would choose one or the other in IPv6 are the same as with IPv4.

Unlike IPv4 routing, which is enable by default on a router, you must explicitly enable IPv6 unicast-routing with the global configuration mode command *ipv6 unicast-routing*.

```
router02(config)#ipv6 unicast-routing
```

Figure 251: The first step to enable routing

Once routing is enabled, you can proceed to configure routing, either through manual static configuration or by enabling and configuring a routing protocol.

IPv6 Static routing

Again, you'll notice similarities between IPv4 and IPv6 commands when configuring IPv6 static routing. Use the command *ipv6 route [target network/mask] [next hop router or outbound interface]*.

```
router02#
router02#conf t                    Target Network and Mask      Next Hop (Neighboring) Router
Enter configuration commands, one per line.  End with CTL/Z.
router02(config)#ipv6 route 2001:db8:4::/64 2001:db8:3::222:55ff:fee2:300
router02(config)#ipv6 route 2001:db8:1::/64 g0/1
router02(config)#
                                   Interface from which to send packets
```

Figure 252: Configuring two static IPv6 routes

Verify the configuration of the routes with the *show ipv6 route* command.

Interactive Exercise 14.1:
Configuring IPv6 Static Routes

Use the diagram at the beginning of the chapter to configure static routes. When you're finished, you should be able to ping any interface on any of the three routers, plus either of the two PCs from any location in the network.

1. On each router, in global configuration mode, enter the command *ipv6 unicast-routing*.

```
router02(config)#ipv6 unicast-routing
```

Figure 253: Enabling IPv6 unicast routing

2. On each router, in global configuration mode, enter the command *ipv6 route [destination network/mask] [next hop router's address]*. As you build the configurations, remember that you're using network addresses as the destination, not individual nodes. Also, remember that the next hop router's address must be an address already known to the router you're configuring. Use the command *show ipv6 route* to determine what the router already knows. Try to successfully complete the configuration without looking at the examples below.

   Router01 and router03 are pretty straightforward, because you can see the IP addresses of the next hop router (router02) on the diagram.

```
router01#conf t
Enter configuration commands, one per line.  End with CNTL/Z.
router01(config)#ipv6 route 2001:db8:3::/64 2001:db8:2::201
router01(config)#ipv6 route 2001:db8:4::/64 2001:db8:2::201
router01(config)#
```

Figure 254: The static route configuration on router01 from the diagram

The configuration for router02, however, is not so straight forward. Since both of router02's neighbors are configured to obtain an IP address through autoconfiguration, you have to determine what their IP addresses are. One option, of course, if to move to the console for each of the other two routers, either by physically going to the router and opening a serial console session, or by using a remote login protocol such as Telnet or SSH to log in to the router. Another option, shown below, is to use the command *show cdp neighbor detail | include IPv6* to display the IPv6 address configuration on each of the neighboring routers. (Recall how the use of filtering can limit what you see in the output of *show* commands, thus the use of | *include IPv6* limits the output to lines from the configuration including "IPv6.") You can then copy and paste their IP addresses into the *ipv6 route* command to complete the configuration.

```
router02#show cdp neighbor g0/1 detail | include IPv6
  IPv6 address: FE80::21A:E2FF:FE19:AAD  (link-local)
  IPv6 address: 2001:DB8:2:0:21A:E2FF:FE19:AAD  (global unicast)
router02#conf t
Enter configuration commands, one per line.  End with CNTL/Z.
router02(config)#ipv6 route 2001:db8:1::/64 2001:DB8:2:0:21A:E2FF:FE19:AAD
router02(config)#do show cdp neighbor g0/0 detail | include IPv6
  IPv6 address: FE80::222:55FF:FEE2:300  (link-local)
  IPv6 address: 2001:DB8:3:0:222:55FF:FEE2:300  (global unicast)
router02(config)#ipv6 route 2001:db8:4::/64 2001:DB8:3:0:222:55FF:FEE2:300
router02(config)#
```

Figure 255:
The static route
configuration
for router02 in
the diagram

```
router03#conf t
Enter configuration commands, one per line.  End with CNTL/Z.
router03(config)#ipv6 route 2001:db8:1::/64 2001:db8:3::201
router03(config)#ipv6 route 2001:db8:2::/64 2001:db8:3::201
router03(config)#
```

Figure 256:
IPv6 static route
configuration on router03
from the chapter diagram

3. When you've completed the configuration, use the *show ipv6 route* command to verify that you've configured the routes properly.

```
router02#
router02#show ipv6 route
IPv6 Routing Table - default - 8 entries
Codes: C - Connected, L - Local, S - Static, U - Per-user Static route
       B - BGP, R - RIP, I1 - ISIS L1, I2 - ISIS L2
       IA - ISIS interarea, IS - ISIS summary, D - EIGRP, EX - EIGRP external
       ND - Neighbor Discovery, l - LISP
       O - OSPF Intra, OI - OSPF Inter, OE1 - OSPF ext 1, OE2 - OSPF ext 2
       ON1 - OSPF NSSA ext 1, ON2 - OSPF NSSA ext 2
S   ::/0 [2/0]
     via FE80::222:55FF:FEE2:300, GigabitEthernet0/0
S   2001:DB8:1::/64 [1/0]
     via 2001:DB8:2:0:21A:E2FF:FE19:AAD
C   2001:DB8:2::/64 [0/0]
     via GigabitEthernet0/1, directly connected
L   2001:DB8:2::201/128 [0/0]
     via GigabitEthernet0/1, receive
C   2001:DB8:3::/64 [0/0]
     via GigabitEthernet0/0, directly connected
L   2001:DB8:3::201/128 [0/0]
     via GigabitEthernet0/0, receive
S   2001:DB8:4::/64 [1/0]
     via 2001:DB8:3:0:222:55FF:FEE2:300
L   FF00::/8 [0/0]
     via Null0, receive
router02#
```

Figure 257:
Viewing the just-configured
IPv6 static routes

Bear in mind that, just as with any routing environment, when you configure static routes, you must also configure routes on neighboring routers in order for routing to take place.

IPv6 RIP routing

IPv6 RIP is very similar in configuration and operation to IPv4 RIP, especially IPv4 RIP version 2. IPv6 RIP sends its updates to the IPv6 multicast address of FF02::9. Unlike IPv4 RIP, multiple instances of IPv6 RIP can run as separate processes on the same router. Each process maintains its own local routing table, known as *Routing Information Database* (RIB).

Like IPv4 RIP, IPv6 RIP is a distance-vector routing protocol that uses hop count to determine its metric. Routes with a lower hop count are considered more desirable than routes with a higher hop count, regardless of bandwidth or load. IPv6 RIP has a maximum hop count of 15, thus making is undesirable for large networks.

Interactive Exercise 14.2:
Configuring IPv6 RIP

The following exercise assumes that IPv6 has already been enabled on all affected interfaces and that the interfaces are configured as indicated on the network diagram at the beginning of the chapter.

Configuring IPv6 RIP is, in many ways, much simpler than configuring IPv4 RIP. The following steps must be performed on each router in your network. If you're using the diagram at the beginning of this chapter, you must perform these steps on all three routers. The screen captures are from a Cisco 1941 router. The names of the interfaces on your router may be different. The rest of the commands will be the same.

1. Enable IPv6 unicast-routing on the router with the global configuration mode command *ipv6 unicast-routing*.

2. Enable IPv6 RIP on each interface you want to participate in the RIP routing process with the interface configuration mode command *ipv6 rip [process name] enable.*

```
router02(config)#
router02(config)#ipv6 unicast-routing
router02(config)#int g0/0
router02(config-if)#ipv6 rip process_01 enable
router02(config-if)#int g0/1
router02(config-if)#ipv6 rip process_01 enable
router02(config-if)#
```

Figure 258:
Configuring IPv6 RIP on a router

Soundthinking Point: The Routing Protocol Must Be Configured on Each Router

As with static routing, when you configure dynamic routing, whether with RIP, OSPF, or EIGRP, you must build a configuration on each router in the network. Otherwise, the routers will not exchange routing updates.

3. Verify that RIP is enabled on the desired interfaces with the privileged mode command *show ipv6 protocols*.

```
router02(config-if)#
router02(config-if)#do show ipv6 protocols
IPv6 Routing Protocol is "connected"
IPv6 Routing Protocol is "ND"
IPv6 Routing Protocol is "static"
IPv6 Routing Protocol is "rip process_01"
  Interfaces:
    GigabitEthernet0/1
    GigabitEthernet0/0
  Redistribution:
    None
router02(config-if)#
```

Figure 259:
Using the "show ipv6 protocols" command to verify proper configuration of the routing protocol

4. Display the IPv6 routing table with the privileged mode command *show ipv6 route*.

```
router02#show ipv6 route
IPv6 Routing Table - default - 8 entries
Codes: C - Connected, L - Local, S - Static, U - Per-user Static route
       B - BGP, R - RIP, I1 - ISIS L1, I2 - ISIS L2
       IA - ISIS interarea, IS - ISIS summary, D - EIGRP, EX - EIGRP external
       ND - Neighbor Discovery, l - LISP
       O - OSPF Intra, OI - OSPF Inter, OE1 - OSPF ext 1, OE2 - OSPF ext 2
       ON1 - OSPF NSSA ext 1, ON2 - OSPF NSSA ext 2
S    ::/0 [2/0]
     via FE80::222:55FF:FEE2:300, GigabitEthernet0/0
R    2001:DB8:1::/64 [120/2]
     via FE80::21A:E2FF:FE19:AAD, GigabitEthernet0/1
C    2001:DB8:2::/64 [0/0]
     via GigabitEthernet0/1, directly connected
L    2001:DB8:2::201/128 [0/0]
     via GigabitEthernet0/1, receive
C    2001:DB8:3::/64 [0/0]
     via GigabitEthernet0/0, directly connected
L    2001:DB8:3::201/128 [0/0]
     via GigabitEthernet0/0, receive
R    2001:DB8:4::/64 [120/2]
     via FE80::222:55FF:FEE2:300, GigabitEthernet0/0
L    FF00::/8 [0/0]
     via Null0, receive
router02#
```

Figure 260:
Viewing RIP discovered routes with the "show ipv6 route" command

Notice in the output of *show ipv6 route* above that there are two RIP routes in addition to the local, directly connected, and static routes.

Other IPv6 RIP Commands

- *show ipv6 rip* displays information about all current IPv6 RIP processes.

- *debug ipv6 rip* shows IPv6 RIP routing transaction debugging messages. Using this tool you can see the source of routing updates and route metrics.

- *show ipv6 rip [process name] database* displays information about the specified IPv6 RIP process database including metrics and timer information.

- *show ipv6 route [process name] next-hops* shows what the name implies.

- *show ipv6 rip next-hops* also shows what the name implies.

There are quite a few IPv6 RIP debugging options, as you can see by using the question mark with the command *debug ipv6 rip*.

```
router02#debug ipv6 rip ?
  Async                     Async interface
  Auto-Template             Auto-Template interface
  BVI                       Bridge-Group Virtual Interface
  CDMA-Ix                   CDMA Ix interface
  CTunnel                   CTunnel interface
  Dialer                    Dialer interface
  Embedded-Service-Engine   cisco embedded service engine module
  GigabitEthernet           GigabitEthernet IEEE 802.3z
  LISP                      Locator/ID Separation Protocol Virtual Interface
  Lex                       Lex interface
  LongReachEthernet         Long-Reach Ethernet interface
  Loopback                  Loopback interface
  MFR                       Multilink Frame Relay bundle interface
  Multilink                 Multilink-group interface
  Null                      Null interface
  Port-channel              Ethernet Channel of interfaces
  Tunnel                    Tunnel interface
  Vif                       PGM Multicast Host interface
  Virtual-PPP               Virtual PPP interface
  Virtual-Template          Virtual Template interface
  Virtual-TokenRing         Virtual TokenRing
  events                    RIPng Events
  vmi                       Virtual Multipoint Interface
  <cr>

router02#debug ipv6 rip
```

Figure 261:
IPv6 RIP debugging options

IPv6 OSPF routing

OSPF version 2 is heavily dependent on IPv4 addressing for most aspects of its operation. OSPF version 3 was developed to allow OSPF to integrate more seamlessly with IPv6 and to route IPv6 packets.

OSPF is often known as a difficult and complex routing protocol to configure and manage. While that certainly can be true, especially in large, multi-area networks, OSPF in a single area is not much more difficult to configure and manage than RIP. Frankly, OSPF for IPv6 is simpler than OSPF for IPv4.

Interactive Exercise 14.3:
Configuring Single-Area IPv6 OSPFv3

The following exercise assumes that IPv6 has already been enabled on all affected interfaces and that the interfaces are configured as indicated on the network diagram at the beginning of the chapter.

In order to enable OSPFv3 for IPv6, perform the following steps on each router in the network:

1. Enable IPv6 unicast-routing with the global configuration mode command *ipv6 unicast-routing*.

```
router02(config)#ipv6 unicast-routing
```

Figure 262: Enabling IPv6 unicast-routing

2. If you are not running IPv4 on the router, you must configure a router ID with the router configuration mode command *router-id [router ID]*. The router is expressed in IPv4 dotted decimal notation. I usually try to tie it to the router's name, so router03 would have a router ID of 3.3.3.3. Alternatively, you could tie it to an IP address on one of the router's interfaces. (If no router ID exists on the router, it will complain when you go into router configuration mode that it doesn't have an ID.)

```
router02(config)#
router02(config)#ipv6 router ospf 10
router02(config-rtr)#router-id 2.2.2.2
router02(config-rtr)#
```

Figure 263: Assigning a router-ID for OSPFv3

3. Enable OSPF routing on each interface that is to participate in OSPF routing with the interface configuration mode command *ipv6 ospf [process ID] area [area ID]*. The process ID is local to the router and is any number between 1 and 65,535. You can run multiple OSPF processes on a router, but doing so consumes additional processor resources, thus potentially having a negative effect on performance. The area ID is either a number within the range of 0 to 4294967295 or it can be expressed in an IP address format (w.x.y.z). The area ID is shared among all routers that are to exchange route updates. In single-area OSPF, it must be the same on all routers. Notice in the screen capture below how, as you enable OSPF on each interface, it forms an adjacency with its neighboring router.

```
router02(config)#
router02(config)#int g0/0
router02(config-if)#ipv6 ospf 10 area 0
router02(config-if)#int g0/1
router02(config-if)#ipv6 ospf 10 area 0
router02(config-if)#
Aug 21 22:19:38.804: %OSPFv3-5-ADJCHG: Process 10, Nbr 1.1.1.1 on GigabitEthe
rnet0/1 from LOADING to FULL, Loading Done
```

Figure 264:
Configuring IPv6 OSPF on each
of the router's interfaces

If other routers in the same area are already configured for OSPF, you will probably see the console message indicating the process has changed from LOADING to FULL, similar to what you see above.

The following screen capture shows the entire process of configuring OSPFv3 for IPv6 on a Cisco 1941 router with two interfaces.

```
router02#conf t
Enter configuration commands, one per line.  End with CNTL/Z.
router02(config)#ipv6 unicast-routing
router02(config)#ipv6 router ospf 10
router02(config-rtr)#router-id 2.2.2.2
router02(config-rtr)#int g0/0
router02(config-if)#ipv6 ospf 10 area 0
router02(config-if)#int g0/1
router02(config-if)#ipv6 ospf 10 area 0
router02(config-if)#
```

Figure 265:
The entire process of configuring IPv6
OSPF on a router with two interfaces

Bear in mind that your router may complain about not having a router ID, but the above configuration will take care of that. You may also see console messages saying the process is going from LOADING to FULL, depending on how neighbor routers are configured.

Verify your configuration with the command *show ipv6 protocols*.

```
router02(config-if)#do show ipv6 protocols
IPv6 Routing Protocol is "connected"
IPv6 Routing Protocol is "ND"
IPv6 Routing Protocol is "static"
IPv6 Routing Protocol is "ospf 10"
  Interfaces (Area 0):
    GigabitEthernet0/1
    GigabitEthernet0/0
  Redistribution:
    None
router02(config-if)#
```

Figure 266:
Using the "show ipv6 protocols"
command to verify proper configuration
of the routing protocol

Verify that the routers are exchanging information and populating each other's routing table with the command *show ipv6 route*.

293

```
router02(config-if)#do show ipv6 route
IPv6 Routing Table - default - 8 entries
Codes: C - Connected, L - Local, S - Static, U - Per-user Static route
       B - BGP, R - RIP, I1 - ISIS L1, I2 - ISIS L2
       IA - ISIS interarea, IS - ISIS summary, D - EIGRP, EX - EIGRP external
       ND - Neighbor Discovery, l - LISP
       O - OSPF Intra, OI - OSPF Inter, OE1 - OSPF ext 1, OE2 - OSPF ext 2
       ON1 - OSPF NSSA ext 1, ON2 - OSPF NSSA ext 2
S   ::/0 [2/0]
     via FE80::222:55FF:FEE2:300, GigabitEthernet0/0
O   2001:DB8:1::/64 [110/2]
     via FE80::21A:E2FF:FE19:AAD, GigabitEthernet0/1
C   2001:DB8:2::/64 [0/0]
     via GigabitEthernet0/1, directly connected
L   2001:DB8:2::201/128 [0/0]
     via GigabitEthernet0/1, receive
C   2001:DB8:3::/64 [0/0]
     via GigabitEthernet0/0, directly connected
L   2001:DB8:3::201/128 [0/0]
     via GigabitEthernet0/0, receive
O   2001:DB8:4::/64 [110/2]
     via FE80::222:55FF:FEE2:300, GigabitEthernet0/0
L   FF00::/8 [0/0]
     via Null0, receive
router02(config-if)#
```

Figure 267:
Viewing the IPv6 OSPF-discovered routes with the "show ipv6 ospf route" command

Other IPv6 OSPFv3 Commands

Use the command *show ipv6 ospf events* to view a summary of logged ospf events.

```
router02#show ipv6 ospf events

            OSPFv3 Router with ID (2.2.2.2) (Process ID 10)

1    Aug 21 23:00:32.224: Timer Exp:  ospfv3_if_ack_delayed  0x30B67E98
2    Aug 21 23:00:29.724: Rcv Unchanged Type-0x2001 LSA, LSID 0.0.0.0, Adv-Rt
r 1.1.1.1, Seq# 8000003C, Age 1, Area 0
3    Aug 21 22:59:54.736: End of SPF, SPF time 0ms, next wait-interval 10000m
s
4    Aug 21 22:59:54.736: Starting External processing in area 0
5    Aug 21 22:59:54.736: Starting External processing
6    Aug 21 22:59:54.736: Starting Inter-Area SPF in area 0
7    Aug 21 22:59:54.736: Generic:  post_spf_intra  0x0
8    Aug 21 22:59:54.736: RIB Update, Prefix 2001:DB8:1::/64, gw FE80::21A:E2
FF:FE19:AAD, via GigabitEthernet0/1, type Intra
9    Aug 21 22:59:54.736: RIB Update, Prefix 2001:DB8:4::/64, gw FE80::222:55
FF:FEE2:300, via GigabitEthernet0/0, type Intra
10   Aug 21 22:59:54.736: RIB Update, Prefix 2001:DB8:3::/64, gw ::, via Giga
bitEthernet0/0, type Intra
11   Aug 21 22:59:54.736: RIB Update, Prefix 2001:DB8:2::/64, gw ::, via Giga
bitEthernet0/1, type Intra
12   Aug 21 22:59:54.736: Starting Intra-Area SPF in Area 0
13   Aug 21 22:59:54.736: Starting SPF, wait-interval 5000ms
14   Aug 21 22:59:52.236: Timer Exp:  ospfv3_if_ack_delayed  0x30B67E98
15   Aug 21 22:59:49.736: Schedule SPF, Area 0, Change in LSA type PLSID 0.0.
0.0, Adv-Rtr 1.1.1.1
 --More--
```

Figure 268:
The "show ipv6 ospf events" command

Use the *show ipv6 ospf [process ID]* to view a summary of information about the specified OSPF process, including the router ID, number and type of areas, and timer information.

```
router02#show ipv6 ospf 10
 Routing Process "ospfv3 10" with ID 2.2.2.2
 Event-log enabled, Maximum number of events: 1000, Mode: cyclic
 Initial SPF schedule delay 5000 msecs
 Minimum hold time between two consecutive SPFs 10000 msecs
 Maximum wait time between two consecutive SPFs 10000 msecs
 Minimum LSA interval 5 secs
 Minimum LSA arrival 1000 msecs
 LSA group pacing timer 240 secs
 Interface flood pacing timer 33 msecs
 Retransmission pacing timer 66 msecs
 Number of external LSA 0. Checksum Sum 0x000000
 Number of areas in this router is 1. 1 normal 0 stub 0 nssa
 Graceful restart helper support enabled
 Reference bandwidth unit is 100 mbps
    Area BACKBONE(0)
        Number of interfaces in this area is 2
        SPF algorithm executed 3 times
        Number of LSA 13. Checksum Sum 0x051CB6
        Number of DCbitless LSA 0
        Number of indication LSA 0
        Number of DoNotAge LSA 0
        Flood list length 0

router02#
```

Figure 269:
The "show ipv6 ospf
[process ID] command

Show ipv6 ospf neighbor displays your OSPF neighbor routers.

```
router02#show ipv6 ospf neighbor

Neighbor ID     Pri   State         Dead Time    Interface ID    Interface
1.1.1.1          1    FULL/BDR      00:00:38     8               GigabitEtherne
t0/1
3.3.3.3          1    FULL/BDR      00:00:37     8               GigabitEtherne
t0/0
router02#
```

Figure 270: The "show ipv6 ospf neighbor" command

Use the command *show ipv6 ospf database* to view information about the routers and interfaces in the area.

```
router02#show ipv6 ospf database

          OSPFv3 Router with ID (2.2.2.2) (Process ID 10)

               Router Link States (Area 0)

ADV Router      Age        Seq#         Fragment ID  Link count  Bits
  1.1.1.1       2          0x80000004   0            1           None
  2.2.2.2       48         0x80000003   0            2           None
  3.3.3.3       41         0x80000004   0            1           None

               Net Link States (Area 0)

ADV Router      Age        Seq#         Link ID   Rtr count
  2.2.2.2       83         0x80000001   3         2
  2.2.2.2       48         0x80000001   4         2

               Link (Type-8) Link States (Area 0)

ADV Router      Age        Seq#         Link ID   Interface
  1.1.1.1       49         0x80000001   8         Gi0/1
  2.2.2.2       140        0x80000001   4         Gi0/1
  2.2.2.2       144        0x80000001   3         Gi0/0
  3.3.3.3       89         0x80000001   8         Gi0/0

               Intra Area Prefix Link States (Area 0)

ADV Router      Age        Seq#         Link ID   Ref-lstype  Ref-LSID
  1.1.1.1       42         0x80000001   0         0x2001      0
  2.2.2.2       83         0x80000001   3072      0x2002      3
  2.2.2.2       48         0x80000001   4096      0x2002      4
  3.3.3.3       75         0x80000003   0         0x2001      0
router02#
```

Figure 271:
The "show ipv6 ospf database" command

As you can imagine, there are several other ospf *show* commands available. Use the question mark to see all of them.

```
router02#show ipv6 ospf ?
  <1-65535>          Process ID number
  border-routers     Border and Boundary Router Information
  database           Database summary
  events             OSPF event information
  flood-list         Link state flood list
  graceful-restart   Graceful restart state information
  interface          Interface information
  neighbor           Neighbor list
  request-list       Link state request list
  retransmission-list Link state retransmission list
  statistic          Various OSPF Statistic
  summary-prefix     Summary-prefix redistribution Information
  timers             OSPF timers information
  traffic            Traffic related statistics
  virtual-links      Virtual link information
  |                  Output modifiers
  <cr>

router02#show ipv6 ospf
```

Figure 272:
Other OSPF show commands

Similarly, there are many IPv6 OSPF debugging options. Use the command ***debug ipv6 ospf*** to view them.

```
router02#debug ipv6 ospf ?
  adj                OSPF adjacency events
  database-timer     OSPF database timer
  events             OSPF events
  flood              OSPF flooding
  graceful-restart   OSPFv3 Graceful Restart processing
  hello              OSPF hello events
  ipsec              OSPF ipsec events
  l2api              OSPF L2/L3 API
  lsa-generation     OSPF lsa generation
  lsdb               OSPF database modifications
  packet             OSPF packets
  retransmission     OSPF retransmission events
  spf                OSPF spf

router02#debug ipv6 ospf
```

Figure 273:
IPv6 OSPF debugging options

IPv6 EIGRP routing

As with RIP for IPv6 and OSPF for IPv6, you'll probably notice some similarities between EIGRP for IPv6 and EIGRP for IPv4. As with RIP, the biggest difference is that we no longer use the *network* command to tell EIGRP what networks and interfaces are participating in the routing process. We now go to interface configuration mode for the interfaces we want participating in EIGRP and enable EIGRP on those interfaces. We still have to identify the EIGRP anonymous system (AS) which is shared among all the routers in the network, somewhat like an OSPF area. EIGRP uses neighbor discovery to dynamically learn of other directly connected routers. Small *hello* packets are periodically sent by EIGRP routers to their neighbors. When hello packets are being received from a neighbor, that neighbor is assumed to be up and functioning normally. With that information, the EIGRP routers exchange routing information and build their routing tables.

Like EIGRP for IPv4, EIGRP for IPv6 is a Cisco proprietary protocol that offers very rapid network convergence (the process of making all routers in the network aware of all possible routes). It does this by maintaining a backup table of all possible routes in the network. When one route fails, EIGRP first refers to its backup topology table to avoid the necessity of re-computing routes.

Considerations for Running EIGRP for IPv6

- EIGRP for IPv6 is now configured on the interfaces where it will run. It is no longer necessary to use the *network* statement to configure EIGRP.

- Like OSPF, EIGRP for IPv6 now requires a router ID in order to run. The EIGRP router ID must be unique on each router.

- EIGRP for IPv6 includes a shutdown command which is enabled by default. EIGRP must be enabled by using the *no shutdown* command before it will run.

- EIGRP is limited to a maximum network width of 224 hops.

Interactive Exercise 14.4:
Configuring EIGRP for IPv6

The following exercise assumes that IPv6 has already been enabled on all affected interfaces and that the interfaces are configured as indicated on the network diagram at the beginning of the chapter.

In order to enable OSPFv3 for IPv6, perform the following steps on each router in the network:

1. Enable IPv6 unicast routing with the global configuration mode command *ipv6 unicast-routing.*

```
router02(config)#ipv6 unicast-routing
```

Figure 274: Enabling ipv6 unicast-routing

2. Enable EIGRP routing for IPv6 on each affected interface with the interface configuration mode command *ipv6 router eigrp [autonomous system number]*, where the AS is any number between 1 and 65,535. All EIGRP routers must share the same AS number in order to exchange routing updates.

```
router02(config)#int g0/0
router02(config-if)#ipv6 eigrp 61
router02(config-if)#int g0/1
router02(config-if)#ipv6 eigrp 61
```

Figure 275: Enabling IPv6 EIGRP on router interfaces

3. Configure an EIGRP router ID in router configuration mode with the command *eigrp router-id [w.x.y.z]*. (Note that, on some routers the command is simply *router-id [w.x.y.z]*. (In the screen capture below, I went directly from interface configuration mode to router configuration mode. You can also get to router configuration mode from global configuration mode.) After you assign a router ID, enable EIGRP on the router with the router configuration mode command *no shutdown.*

Be sure to assign each router a different router ID. I named router01 1.1.1.1, router02 2.2.2.2, and router03 3.3.3.3.

```
router02(config-if)#ipv6 router eigrp 61
router02(config-rtr)#eigrp router-id 2.2.2.2
router02(config-rtr)#no shutdown
```

Figure 276: Assigning an IPv6 EIGRP router ID

As you bring EIGRP routers online, you'll see console messages showing the routers establishing neighborhood and exchanging routing updates.

```
Aug 21 23:17:16.800: %DUAL-5-NBRCHANGE: EIGRP-IPv6 61: Neighbor FE80::21A:E2F
F:FE19:AAD (GigabitEthernet0/1) is up: new adjacency
Aug 21 23:17:16.812: EIGRP-IPv6(61): Processing incoming UPDATE packet
Aug 21 23:17:16.812: EIGRP-IPv6(61): Processing incoming UPDATE packet
Aug 21 23:17:16.816: EIGRP-IPv6(61): 2001:DB8:3::/64 - do advertise out Gigab
itEthernet0/1
Aug 21 23:17:16.816: EIGRP-IPv6(61): Int 2001:DB8:3::/64 metric 28160 - 25600
 2560
Aug 21 23:17:16.816: EIGRP-IPv6(61): 2001:DB8:2::/64 - do
router02(config-if)#advertise out GigabitEthernet0/1
Aug 21 23:17:16.816: EIGRP-IPv6(61): Int 2001:DB8:2::/64 metric 28160 - 25600
 2560
Aug 21 23:17:16.820: EIGRP-IPv6(61): Processing incoming UPDATE packet
Aug 21 23:17:16.820: EIGRP-IPv6(61): Processing incoming UPDATE packet
Aug 21 23:17:16.820: EIGRP-IPv6(61): Int 2001:DB8:2::/64 M 30720 - 25600 5120
 SM 28160 - 25600 2560
```

Figure 277: Routers establishing "neighborhood" and exchanging updates

Verify your configuration with the privileged mode command *show ipv6 protocols.*

```
router02(config-rtr)#do show ipv6 prot
IPv6 Routing Protocol is "connected"
IPv6 Routing Protocol is "ND"
IPv6 Routing Protocol is "static"
IPv6 Routing Protocol is "eigrp 61"
EIGRP-IPv6 Protocol for AS(61)
  Metric weight K1=1, K2=0, K3=1, K4=0, K5=0
  NSF-aware route hold timer is 240
  Router-ID: 2.2.2.2
  Topology : 0 (base)
    Active Timer: 3 min
    Distance: internal 90 external 170
    Maximum path: 16
    Maximum hopcount 100
    Maximum metric variance 1

  Interfaces:
    GigabitEthernet0/0
    GigabitEthernet0/1
  Redistribution:
    None
router02(config-rtr)#
```

Figure 278:
Using the "show ipv6 protocols" command to verify proper configuration of the routing protocol

Verify that EIGRP is functioning properly by displaying the IPv6 routing table with the command *show ipv6 route.*

```
router02(config-if)#do show ipv6 route
IPv6 Routing Table - default - 8 entries
Codes: C - Connected, L - Local, S - Static, U - Per-user Static route
       B - BGP, R - RIP, I1 - ISIS L1, I2 - ISIS L2
       IA - ISIS interarea, IS - ISIS summary, D - EIGRP, EX - EIGRP external
       ND - Neighbor Discovery, l - LISP
       O - OSPF Intra, OI - OSPF Inter, OE1 - OSPF ext 1, OE2 - OSPF ext 2
       ON1 - OSPF NSSA ext 1, ON2 - OSPF NSSA ext 2
S    ::/0 [2/0]
      via FE80::222:55FF:FEE2:300, GigabitEthernet0/0
D    2001:DB8:1::/64 [90/30720]
      via FE80::21A:E2FF:FE19:AAD, GigabitEthernet0/1
C    2001:DB8:2::/64 [0/0]
      via GigabitEthernet0/1, directly connected
L    2001:DB8:2::201/128 [0/0]
      via GigabitEthernet0/1, receive
C    2001:DB8:3::/64 [0/0]
      via GigabitEthernet0/0, directly connected
L    2001:DB8:3::201/128 [0/0]
      via GigabitEthernet0/0, receive
D    2001:DB8:4::/64 [90/30720]
      via FE80::222:55FF:FEE2:300, GigabitEthernet0/0
L    FF00::/8 [0/0]
      via Null0, receive
router02(config-if)#
```

Figure 279:
Viewing the IPv6 EIGRP routes with the "show ipv6 routes" command

Other IPv6 EIGRP Commands

- *Show ipv6 eigrp [process ID] interfaces detail* displays a summary of information about each of the EIGRP-enabled interfaces on the router including timer intervals and types of EIGRP-related traffic on the interfaces.

```
router02#show ipv6 eigrp 61 interfaces detail
EIGRP-IPv6 Interfaces for AS(61)
                          Xmit Queue   Mean    Pacing Time   Multicast    Pending
Interface       Peers   Un/Reliable   SRTT   Un/Reliable   Flow Timer   Routes
Gi0/0              1        0/0         2         0/1           50          0
  Hello-interval is 5, Hold-time is 15
  Split-horizon is enabled
  Next xmit serial <none>
  Un/reliable mcasts: 0/3  Un/reliable ucasts: 3/2
  Mcast exceptions: 0  CR packets: 0  ACKs suppressed: 0
  Retransmissions sent: 1  Out-of-sequence rcvd: 0
  Topology-ids on interface - 0
  Authentication mode is not set
Gi0/1              1        0/0         2         0/1           50          0
  Hello-interval is 5, Hold-time is 15
  Split-horizon is enabled
  Next xmit serial <none>
  Un/reliable mcasts: 0/2  Un/reliable ucasts: 3/1
  Mcast exceptions: 0  CR packets: 0  ACKs suppressed: 0
  Retransmissions sent: 0  Out-of-sequence rcvd: 0
  Topology-ids on interface - 0
  Authentication mode is not set
router02#
```

Figure 280:
The "show ipv6 eigrp interfaces" command

- *clear ipv6 eigrp neighbors* (you can also limit this to a single autonomous system by specifying the AS number between *eigrp* and *neighbors*) deletes the entries from the IPv6 EIGRP routing tables. It's interesting to do this on a test router because you can see how very quickly the routers re-establish neighborhood with each other and re-populate the routing tables.

```
router02#
router02#clear ipv6 eigrp neighbors
router02#
Aug 21 23:23:27.988: %DUAL-5-NBRCHANGE: EIGRP-IPv6 61: Neighbor FE80::222:55F
F:FEE2:300 (GigabitEthernet0/0) is down: manually cleared
Aug 21 23:23:27.988: EIGRP-IPv6(0:61): 2001:DB8:4::/64 deleted FE80::222:55FF
:FEE2:300(FE80::222:55FF:FEE2:300)/GigabitEthernet0/0
Aug 21 23:23:27.988: %DUAL-5-NBRCHANGE: EIGRP-IPv6 61: Neighbor FE80::21A:E2F
F:FE19:AAD (GigabitEthernet0/1) is down: manually cleared
router02#
Aug 21 23:23:27.988: EIGRP-IPv6(0:61): 2001:DB8:1::/64 deleted FE80::21A:E2FF
:FE19:AAD(FE80::21A:E2FF:FE19:AAD)/GigabitEthernet0/1
router02#
Aug 21 23:23:29.632: %DUAL-5-NBRCHANGE: EIGRP-IPv6 61: Neighbor FE80::222:55F
F:FEE2:300 (GigabitEthernet0/0) is up: new adjacency
Aug 21 23:23:29.644: EIGRP-IPv6(61): Processing incoming UPDATE packet
Aug 21 23:23:29.644: EIGRP-IPv6(61): Processing incoming UPDATE packet
Aug 21 23:23:29.648: EIGRP-IPv6(61): 2001:DB8:3::/64 - do advertise out Gigab
itEthernet0/0
Aug 21 23:23:29.648: EIGRP-IPv6(61): Int 2001:DB8:3::/64 metric 28160 - 25600
 2560
```

Figure 281:
The "clear ipv6 eigrp neighbors" command

- You can view EIGRP neighbors with the *show ipv6 eigrp neighbors* command.

```
router02#
router02#show ipv6 eigrp neighbors
EIGRP-IPv6 Neighbors for AS(61)
H   Address                    Interface       Hold Uptime   SRTT   RTO  Q   Seq
                                               (sec)         (ms)       Cnt Num
1   Link-local address:        Gi0/1            13 00:01:48    1    200  0   6
    FE80::21A:E2FF:FE19:AAD
0   Link-local address:        Gi0/0            14 00:01:49    2    200  0   6
    FE80::222:55FF:FEE2:300
router02#
```

Figure 282:
The "show ipv6 eigrp neighbors" command

- Check the configuration of each of the EIGRP interfaces on the router with the command *show ipv6 eigrp interfaces*.

```
router02#show ipv6 eigrp interfaces
EIGRP-IPv6 Interfaces for AS(61)
                      Xmit Queue   Mean  Pacing Time  Multicast    Pending
Interface      Peers  Un/Reliable  SRTT  Un/Reliable  Flow Timer   Routes
Gi0/0           1       0/0         1       0/1          50           0
Gi0/1           1       0/0         1       0/1          50           0
router02#
```

Figure 283: The "show ipv6 eigrp interfaces" command

- The *show ipv6 eigrp traffic* command displays a summary of packets sent and received.

```
router02#show ipv6 eigrp traffic
EIGRP-IPv6 Traffic Statistics for AS(61)
  Hellos sent/received: 6277/6167
  Updates sent/received: 16/14
  Queries sent/received: 0/0
  Replies sent/received: 0/0
  Acks sent/received: 12/7
  SIA-Queries sent/received: 0/0
  SIA-Replies sent/received: 0/0
  Hello Process ID: 127
  PDM Process ID: 29
  Socket Queue: 0/2000/1/0 (current/max/highest/drops)
  Input Queue: 0/2000/1/0 (current/max/highest/drops)

router02#
```

Figure 284:
The "show ipv6 eigrp traffic" command

Debugging is also available for IPv6 EIGRP. Use the command *debug ipv6 eigrp ?* to see the options.

```
router02#debug ipv6 eigrp
EIGRP-IPv6 Route Event debugging is on
router02#debug ipv6 eigrp ?
  <1-65535>             Autonomous System
  X:X:X:X::X/<0-128>   IPv6 prefix
  neighbor              Neighbor debugging
  notifications         Event notifications
  summary               Summary Route Processing
  <cr>

router02#debug ipv6 eigrp
```

Figure 285:
IPv6 EIGRP debugging options

Soundthinking Point: Windows IPv6 Commands

Microsoft has introduced some IPv6-specific commands that you can use with the ipconfig utility. To release just the IPv6 address, use the command *ipconfig /release6*. To renew just the IPv6 address, use the command *ipconfig /renew6*.

IPv6 Access-Control Lists (ACLs)

If you are familiar with IPv4 access-control lists, IPv6 ACLs will seem very familiar to you. IPv6 ACLs do not support numbered lists. Only named lists are supported. The syntax is very similar to that used in IPv4 ACLs. Most of the same concepts apply in IPv6 ACLs as in IPv4 ACLs.

IPv6 ACL Considerations

- Packets are compared against each entry in a list in sequential order until there is a match.

- Once a packet matches an entry, all subsequent entries are ignored.

- There is an implicit *deny any* at the end of every ACL.

- Since IPv6 makes extensive use of neighbor discovery, neighbor discovery is implicitly allowed in IPv6 ACLs. It can be blocked, however, by the use of a *deny ipv6 any any* statement.

In the following example, I created a very simple IPv6 named access-control list to block all IPv6 traffic from router03's FastEthernet4 interface to any destination on router02. Notice how I first created the list with the command ***ipv6 access-list [name of list]***. The router then moved into ACL configuration mode where I created the access-control entries using standard named ACL syntax where the permit or deny condition is followed by the protocol type (ahp, esp, icmp, ipv6, pcp, sctp, tcp, or udp, as well as several other options—use the question mark to see all options), then the source of the traffic, and finally the destination of the traffic.

```
router02(config)#ipv6 access-list BlockRouter03
router02(config-ipv6-acl)#deny ipv6 host FE80::222:55FF:FEE2:300 any
router02(config-ipv6-acl)#deny ipv6 host 2001:DB8:3:0:222:55FF:FEE2:300 any
router02(config-ipv6-acl)#permit ipv6 any any
router02(config-ipv6-acl)#
```

Figure 286: A sample of a fairly general IPv6 access-control list

As with IPv4 ACLs, in order for it to take effect, it must be placed on an interface using the ***ipv6 traffic-filter*** command (similar to the ***ip traffic-filter*** command in IPv4). Note in the following screen capture that the access-control list *BlockRouter03* was placed on interface g0/0 on router02 on inbound traffic. Again, as with IPv4 access-control lists, the commands *in* and *out* refer to traffic from the perspective of the router.

```
router02#
router02#conf t
Enter configuration commands, one per line.  End with CNTL/Z.
router02(config)#int g0/0
router02(config-if)#ipv6 traffic-filter BlockRouter03 in
router02(config-if)#
```

Figure 287: Using the "ipv6 traffic-filter" command to apply an ipv6 access-control list

Here is an example of configuring an access-control list that permits only Telnet (port 23) traffic into a router. Note that, because of the implicit *deny any* at the end of every access-control list, only Telnet traffic from the 2001:db8:1::/64 network will be permitted through this ACL.

```
router02(config)#ipv6 access-list AllowOnlyTelnet
router02(config-ipv6-acl)#permit tcp any 2001:db8:1::/64 eq telnet
router02(config-ipv6-acl)#
```

Figure 288: A more specific IPv6 access-control list that allows only Telnet traffic to pass

For more information about configuring and managing access-control lists on a router, see chapter 11 in this book.

IPv6 Security Considerations

Entire books have been written about how to secure networks and systems, whether using IPv6 or some other protocol. To include a few pointers at the end of a chapter seems woefully inadequate. This is a book for the Accidental Administrator® and the objective is to provide you with a starting point for learning router configuration. With that in mind, here are some tips, based to a large extent on documentation from the United States National Security Agency and my own experience on how to secure an IPv6-enabled router. Please, please, please do not consider these to be all-encompassing recommendations. System and network security is as fluid as the attackers who are constantly trying to bypass the security. You must be ever vigilant and always building your security knowledge base. Subscribe to updates from Cisco (http://www.cisco.com/security) and other sources.

Physical Security

As with every aspect of network and system security, the most fundamental threat is physical. Without physical security, all other security measures are moot. If an attacker can gain physical access to a router he or she can compromise every aspect of the router's operations and, subsequently, the operations of the entire network. All network devices should be placed in locked rooms or, at the very least, locked equipment racks.

> **Soundthinking Point: Treat IPv6 as a Separate, Independent Protocol**
>
> As you consider implementing IPv6 in your network, remember that it is a separate and distinct protocol from IPv4. That means that you must also implement security for IPv6 separately from IPv4. Nothing that you configure for IPv4 will automatically apply to IPv6.

Management Remote Access

As with IPv4, management access must be restricted. One of the things to remember is that IPv6 provides a separate, independent pathway for accessing a router. The same procedures you use in implementing IPv4 security must also be implemented for IPv6 security. Remote management protocols that run over IPv4 can also run over IPv6. Such protocols include HTTP, HTTPS, SSH, SNMP, and Telnet. You must impose the same access controls for these protocols over IPv6 as you do for IPv4. Disable non-secure protocols such as Telnet. If SNMP (Simple Network Management Protocol), run it in read-only mode. If write-mode is required, ensure access-controls are implemented, along with confidentiality and integrity protections.

Disclosure of Router Configuration Information

Consider disabling services such as Cisco Discovery Protocol (CDP) which can divulge information about neighboring devices. Tools such as *traceroute* can be used to determine router transit address, so such addresses should not be used for router services. NSA (National Security Agency) recommends using static addresses tied to loopback interfaces instead.

Create an Obscure Addressing Scheme

The IPv6 address space is so large that it's unrealistic for an attacker to scan the entire space. Avoid using obvious, easily-guessed addresses such as 2001::1.

Prevent Denial of Service

Impose strict timeouts on control protocols and disable all unneeded services.

Limit ICMPv6 Messages

ICMPv6 can used to aid in mapping network topology. Although it is undeniably a helpful troubleshooting tool, it can also be used by an attacked to perform network discovery. Consider disabling ICMP, especially ping responses. This is particularly true on interfaces connected to the global Internet or any publicly accessible network.

Unauthorized Tunnels

Encapsulation can be used to hide malicious traffic. Drop encapsulated packets unless they are part of know, authorized tunnels.

Concept of Least Privilege

As with all other aspects of network and system operation, apply the *concept of least privilege* to router configurations. In the case of router operations, that means explicitly allowing only required traffic through the router and implicitly denying all other traffic. Access-control lists can be used to regulate traffic.

For more information about security for IPv6 routers, visit http://www.nsa.gov/ia/_files/routers/I33-002R-06.pdf.

IPv6 Troubleshooting

As in IPv4, start troubleshooting at the physical layer. Ensure that connectors are firmly seated, that the correct types of cables are in use, that power is on, and link integrity lights are illuminated.

Also, as in IPv4, two of the most helpful commands are *show ipv6 interface brief* and *show ipv6 route*. Often, by using those two commands, you can identify where the problem lies. At the very least, they can help you determine where to start the troubleshooting process.

Soundthinking Point: IPv6 Bypasses All IPv4 Security

At risk of beating this into the ground, nothing you configure in IPv4 will affect IPv6. IPv6 traffic will bypass all IPv4 filters. As part of your IPv6 implementation, review your documentation for IPv4 security so you can re-implement your IPv4 security configurations in IPv6.

Show IPv6 Interface Brief

This command displays a brief summary of the interface configuration on a router.

```
router02(config-if)#do show ipv6 interface brief
Embedded-Service-Engine0/0 [administratively down/down]
    unassigned
GigabitEthernet0/0          [up/up]
    FE80::7281:5FF:FE70:8500
    2001:3::201
GigabitEthernet0/1          [up/up]
    FE80::7281:5FF:FE70:8501
    2001:2::201
Tunnel0                     [up/up]
    FE80::7281:5FF:FE70:8500
    unnumbered (GigabitEthernet0/1)
router02(config-if)#
```

Figure 289:
The "show ipv6 interface brief" command

Show IPv6 Route

This command tells you what routes the router already knows. If you're trying to reach a remote network and there is not an explicit path to it, nor a default route, the router will have no way of directing the packets to the remote network.

In the screen capture below, you can see the static default route, several directly connected networks, and several EIGRP-discovered networks.

```
router02(config-if)#do show ipv6 route
IPv6 Routing Table - default - 8 entries
Codes: C - Connected, L - Local, S - Static, U - Per-user Static route
       B - BGP, R - RIP, I1 - ISIS L1, I2 - ISIS L2
       IA - ISIS interarea, IS - ISIS summary, D - EIGRP, EX - EIGRP external
       ND - Neighbor Discovery, l - LISP
       O - OSPF Intra, OI - OSPF Inter, OE1 - OSPF ext 1, OE2 - OSPF ext 2
       ON1 - OSPF NSSA ext 1, ON2 - OSPF NSSA ext 2
S    ::/0 [2/0]
     via FE80::222:55FF:FEE2:300, GigabitEthernet0/0
D    2001:DB8:1::/64 [90/30720]
     via FE80::21A:E2FF:FE19:AAD, GigabitEthernet0/1
C    2001:DB8:2::/64 [0/0]
     via GigabitEthernet0/1, directly connected
L    2001:DB8:2::201/128 [0/0]
     via GigabitEthernet0/1, receive
C    2001:DB8:3::/64 [0/0]
     via GigabitEthernet0/0, directly connected
L    2001:DB8:3::201/128 [0/0]
     via GigabitEthernet0/0, receive
D    2001:DB8:4::/64 [90/30720]
     via FE80::222:55FF:FEE2:300, GigabitEthernet0/0
L    FF00::/8 [0/0]
     via Null0, receive
router02(config-if)#
```

Figure 290:
The "show ipv6 route" command on a router with EIGRP enabled

Show IPv6 Interface

The command *show ipv6 interface* provides a comprehensive view of the interfaces on a router. Among the things you can see are the IPv6 address, how it was configured, network discovery (ND) information, and multicast group membership.

You can filter the output by specifying a particular interface after the command.

```
router02#show ipv6 interface
GigabitEthernet0/0 is up, line protocol is up
  IPv6 is enabled, link-local address is FE80::7281:5FF:FE70:8500
  No Virtual link-local address(es):
  Stateless address autoconfig enabled
  Global unicast address(es):
    2001:DB8:3::201, subnet is 2001:DB8:3::/64
  Joined group address(es):
    FF02::1
    FF02::2
    FF02::9
    FF02::A
    FF02::D
    FF02::1:FF00:201
    FF02::1:FF70:8500
  MTU is 1500 bytes
  ICMP error messages limited to one every 100 milliseconds
  ICMP redirects are enabled
  ICMP unreachables are sent
  ND DAD is enabled, number of DAD attempts: 1
  ND reachable time is 30000 milliseconds (using 30000)
  ND advertised reachable time is 0 (unspecified)
  ND advertised retransmit interval is 0 (unspecified)
  ND router advertisements are sent every 200 seconds
  ND router advertisements live for 1800 seconds
  ND advertised default router preference is Medium
  Hosts use stateless autoconfig for addresses.
GigabitEthernet0/1 is up, line protocol is up
  IPv6 is enabled, link-local address is FE80::7281:5FF:FE70:8501
  No Virtual link-local address(es):
  Global unicast address(es):
    2001:DB8:2::201, subnet is 2001:DB8:2::/64
  Joined group address(es):
    FF02::1
    FF02::2
    FF02::9
    FF02::A
    FF02::D
    FF02::1:FF00:201
    FF02::1:FF70:8501
  MTU is 1500 bytes
  ICMP error messages limited to one every 100 milliseconds
  ICMP redirects are enabled
  ICMP unreachables are sent
  ND DAD is enabled, number of DAD attempts: 1
  ND reachable time is 30000 milliseconds (using 30000)
  ND advertised reachable time is 0 (unspecified)
  ND advertised retransmit interval is 0 (unspecified)
  ND router advertisements are sent every 200 seconds
  ND router advertisements live for 1800 seconds
  ND advertised default router preference is Medium
  Hosts use stateless autoconfig for addresses.
router02#
```

Figure 291:
The "show ipv6 interface" command on a router with two interfaces

Debug IPv6

There are many debug options for IPv6. As with all debugging, use care. Debugging is resource-intensive and should not be used on a production router except as a last resort when troubleshooting catastrophic fault conditions. In a lab environment, however, it is a great learning tool to better understand how the router operates.

```
router02#debug ipv6 ?
  access-list   IPv6 access list debugging
  address       IPv6 addresses debugging
  cef           IPv6 CEF information
  cpc           IPv6 Common Parsing Cache debugging
  dhcp          IPv6 DHCP debugging
  eigrp         Debug IPv6 EIGRP
  icmp          ICMPv6 debugging
  interface     IPv6 interface debugging
  mfib          IP Multicast forwarding information base
  mld           Multicast Listener Discovery
  mrib          Multicast Route DB
  multicast     Debug multicast related information
  nd            IPv6 Neighbor Discovery debugging
  ospf          OSPF information
  packet        IPv6 packet debugging
  pim           Protocol Independent Multicast
  policy        IPv6 policy-based routing debugging
  pool          IPv6 prefix pool debugging
  rip           RIP Routing Protocol debugging
  routing       IPv6 routing table debugging
  rpf           IPv6 reverse path forwarding debugging

router02#debug ipv6
```

Figure 292:
Options for debugging IPv6

IPv6 Online Resources

This is a ridiculously short list when you consider the many IPv6 resources available on the Internet. Still, it provides a starting point for learning more about IPv6.

http://www.worldipv6launch.org/

http://www.ipv6forum.com/

http://www.google.com/intl/en/ipv6/

http://test-ipv6.com/

http://www.cisco.com/web/solutions/trends/ipv6/index.html

http://technet.microsoft.com/en-us/network/bb530961.aspx

http://www.internetsociety.org/ipv6

http://www.iana.org/

http://www.icann.org/

Perhaps the most valuable resources of all are the many RFCs pertaining to IPv6. My favorite site for reading RFCs is www.rfc-editor.org. Some of the more important RFCs include 2460, 3849, 4193, 4291, 4862, 5871, and 5942. There are, of course, many others. Again, this is meant as a starting point for your research.

Summary

Should you implement IPv6? I can't answer that question for your network. Only you can answer it. I can, however, provide these thinking points for you:

- IPv6 is going to be the main protocol of the global Internet in the not-too-distant future

- It will probably become the dominant transport protocol in private networks in the not-too-distant future

- It offers significant benefits over IPv4 in the areas of security, speed, and end-to-end connectivity

I do recommend that you build a test network and start learning IPv6 right away, if you haven't already. Like I said at the beginning of the chapter, the sooner you get familiar with IPv6, the sooner you'll be ready when it comes knocking on your door.

CHAPTER 15:
Cisco Router Security Fundamentals

Chapter Introduction

As with every other aspect of network and system administration, security with Cisco routers is an always evolving, ever growing part of the job. I've heard people compare network security to the carnival game called "Whack-a-Mole." If you're not familiar with it, it's a game in which little toy moles pop their heads up at random intervals. The objective is to use a mallet to hit as many as possible before they pop back down. That's what network and system security is like. Threats and vulnerabilities pop up at random intervals and in random locations. Our job is to plug as many obvious security holes as we can while, at the same time, plugging all the new ones that keep popping up. Good luck!

This chapter is not meant to be the ultimate guide to securing Cisco routers. That would be an impossible document to write due to the dynamic nature of security threats. Instead, it's written like the rest of this book: A starting point for you to build secure router configs. What follows are some of the basics of security for you to consider as you learn about Cisco routers.

Chapter Objectives

- Understand security at a basic level

- Learn tools and techniques to implement router security

Online Companion Resources

Videos: Watch the companion videos for this chapter. They're available at
www.soundtraining.net/videos/cisco-router-training-videos

Web Page: There is a supporting web page with live links and other resources for this book
at www.soundtraining.net/cisco-router-book

Facebook: www.soundtraining.net/facebook

Twitter: www.soundtraining.net/twitter

Blog: www.soundtraining.net/blog

Physical Security

As with every other aspect of network and system security, securing your router starts at the physical layer of the OSI model. Anyone who has physical access to a router can perform password recovery procedures (Recall how easy it was in chapter 13?) and take control of the router.

Routers should be kept in a locked room or, at the very least, a locking equipment rack. They should never be kept behind the cash register at the bar in the restaurant. Yes, I really did see that at a restaurant in Portland, Oregon!

Make sure to provide cooling and reliable electrical service.

Use Secure Passwords

Create difficult-to-guess passwords for line console 0, for line aux 0, for each of the vty lines, for http and https access, and for privileged mode. An example of a complex password is N3v3rE@t50ggyW@ffle5. The longer, the better. (In case you haven't figured it out on your own, it's "NeverEatSoggyWaffles.")

Remember that only the enable secret is encrypted by default. Use the global configuration mode command *service password-encryption* to apply encryption to line and aux passwords.

Create an Effective Login Banner

Okay, I'll certainly agree with anyone who says a login banner won't deter a bad guy intent on breaking in to a router. It might, however, deter a looky-loo who's just curious and knows enough to be dangerous. Talk to your legal department for the exact wording, but consider something like this:

"WARNING. This is a restricted system. Do not attempt unauthorized access. Unauthorized login attempts are logged and may be monitored. Persons attempting unauthorized logins are subject to possible disciplinary actions including civil and/or criminal penalties."

Like I said, check with your legal folks for the exact wording. I'm certainly not an attorney and not qualified to give legal advice.

Enable Logging

I talked about logging earlier. Although you can send logging information to an internal buffer on the router, best practice is to offload logging to a logging server. Two widely-used logging servers for Windows computers are TFTPD32 (or 64) (http://tftpd32.jounin.net/) or Kiwi Syslog (http://www.kiwisyslog.com/). Of course, most Linux and Unix systems include syslogd which also allows for centralized logging.

Logging Considerations

Set the Logging Level

Logging messages from Cisco IOS devices are assigned a logging level ranging from 0 (Emergency) to 7 (Debugging). You should avoid logging level 7 unless you have a specific reason to use it. It places a heavy load on CPU resources. Consider setting logging at 6 to get maximum information without overloading your router's processor.

  – Router(config)#*logging trap 6*

Set the Logging Source Interface

If you have multiple devices sending logging information to a logging server, use the command *logging source-interface [interface name]* to ensure that all logging messages from a device show the same IP address. For example, you might consider creating a loopback interface for this purpose. (Be sure to assign it an IP address.)

  – Router(config)#*logging source-interface loopback 0*

Enable Logging Timestamps

The use of logging timestamps ensures that you know when events occurred and simplifies the comparison of log entries across multiple devices. Use the commands *clock timezone PST -8* and *service timestamps log datetime msec show-timezone*.

The *clock timezone PST -8* command changes the timestamps for UTC to Pacific time. Obviously, you can modify the configuration for your timezone.

The *service timestamps log datetime msec show-timezone* command enables timestamping of log events, *msec* adds milliseconds to the timestamp, and *show-timezone* does what the name implies.

Consider a Network Management System (NMS)

Another logging tool to consider is to install a network management system (NMS) on a workstation to monitor your routers and other network devices. Both commercial and open-source NMSs are available including:

PRTG—http://www.paessler.com/prtg

Nagios—http://www.nagios.org/

Solar Winds Orion—http://www.solarwinds.com/network-performance-monitor.asp

Whatsup Gold—http://www.whatsupgold.com/

OpenNMS—http://www.opennms.org/

As of this writing, there are free VMWare OpenNMS and Nagios appliances available for download at from the VMWare Virtual Appliance Marketplace (go to www.vmware.com and click on Virtual Appliances).

If you choose to install an NMS, a minimal configuration on your router requires only two lines in global configuration mode. The first command points your router to the NMS. w.x.y.z represents the IP address of the NMS host. {community string} must match on both the NMS and the router.

   – Router(config)# *snmp-server host w.x.y.z {community string}*

The second command tells the router to send notification of configuration changes to the NMS.

   Router(config)# *snmp-server enable traps config*

Consider configuring your router to log configuration changes via SNMP. Use the global configuration mode command *snmp-server enable traps config* to enable configuration change logging via SNMP. For more information about SNMP traps and how to configure them, go to www.cisco.com and search on the term *SNMP Traps Supported*.

If you use SNMP, use SNMPv3 and enable encryption.

Set the Correct Date and Time

Use the network time protocol (NTP) to synchronize your router's clock with an NTP server. That way, your logs have accurate time and date stamps. Without going into a lot of detail about NTP, suffice to say it's a protocol that allows your router to synchronize its time and date with an NTP server connected to an atomic clock. You can use a local time server if you have one or you can use one of the NTP Pool Time Servers at http://support.ntp.org/bin/view/Servers/NTPPoolServers. Since I'm based in North America, I chose north-america.pool.ntp.org. (Obviously, you must have name resolution enabled in order to use names instead of IP addresses. If name resolution is not enabled, you can use an IP address.)

Use the global configuration mode command *ntp server [server name or address]* to create an NTP server association.

```
router02#conf t
Enter configuration commands, one per line.  End with CNTL/Z.
router02(config)#ntp server north-america.pool.ntp.org
Translating "north-america.pool.ntp.org"...domain server (192.168.1.1) [OK]
```

Figure 293: Configuring the router to synchronize with an NTP server

Use the privileged mode command *show ntp status* to verify your configuration.

```
router02(config)#do show ntp status
Clock is synchronized, stratum 3, reference is 198.245.60.153
nominal freq is 250.0000 Hz, actual freq is 250.0000 Hz, precision is 2**24
reference time is D3E13540.78234211 (23:03:28.469 UTC Thu Aug 23 2012)
clock offset is -1.1619 msec, root delay is 150.58 msec
root dispersion is 479.95 msec, peer dispersion is 65.47 msec
loopfilter state is 'CTRL' (Normal Controlled Loop), drift is -0.000000004 s/s
system poll interval is 64, last update was 165 sec ago.
router02(config)#
```

Figure 294: Displaying NTP status on a router

Be patient! My router showed *Clock is unsynchronized* for several minutes after I configured it to sync with the NTP server before it finally showed that it was synchronized.

You can view the NTP associations (which NTP server is providing the time/date synchronization) with the command *show ntp associations*.

```
router02(config)#do show ntp associations

  address          ref clock       st    when    poll reach  delay  offset    disp
*~198.245.60.153   71.63.173.196    2     49      64   377   100.51  -1.161   3.911
 * sys.peer, # selected, + candidate, - outlyer, x falseticker, ~ configured
router02(config)#
```

Figure 295: Viewing NTP server associations

Check the time and date on your router with the privileged mode command *show clock*.

```
router02(config)#do show clock
23:07:02.064 UTC Thu Aug 23 2012
router02(config)#
```

Figure 296:
Displaying the date and time on the router

Maintain Router Configuration Backups

As we discussed in chapter four, this seems like common sense, yet I frequently hear stories about lost configurations. Use tools like Kiwi Cat Tools (http://www.kiwisyslog.com/products/kiwi-cattools/product-overview) to centrally backup, modify, and otherwise manage your router configurations. If an attacker were to wipe your router configuration or an equipment failure were to cause the loss of a config, it's a simple matter to restore it from a current backup. If you keep the config backups in a central location, there's less risk of a bad guy or an accident causing the loss of the backups.

Use Access-Control Lists Wisely

Evaluate the ACLs on your routers to ensure you understand what they're doing and what they're not doing. What traffic is permitted? What traffic is denied? Are there any *permit any* statements? Are they necessary? Use the concept of least access in designing your ACLs. Remember that order matters in writing ACLs, always go from most specific to most general. Remember the implicit *deny any* at the end of every ACL. Remember that ACLs must be applied to an interface to have any effect. Remember, also, when applying an ACL to an interface to be sure you're configuring it in the proper direction. (In or out is from the perspective of the router.)

Consider using access-control lists to limit remote management traffic to trusted networks. For example, you could create an ACL similar to this:

- Router(config)#*access-list 100 permit tcp <trusted network> <mask> host <management interface IP> eq 22*

- router(config)#*access-list 100 deny tcp any any eq 22*

The above list, when applied to the management interface on a router would block all SSH connection attempts except from the trusted network.

Use Encryption Whenever Possible

Avoid the use of Telnet and other non-secure protocols. Use SSH instead to encrypt your remote management sessions. You can disable Telnet and allow only SSH on the virtual terminal lines with the line configuration command *transport input ssh*. Notice, in the following screen capture, that *line vty 04* was originally configured to accept all types of connections (*transport input all*), but I changed it to accept only SSH connections with the command *transport input ssh*.

```
line vty 0 4
 password p@ss1234
 login
 transport input all
router02(config)#line vty 04
router02(config-line)#transport input ssh
router02(config-line)#
```

Figure 297:
Requiring SSH on virtual terminal lines

Same thing with HTTP vs. HTTPS. If you want to use CCP to manage your router, require it to connect via HTTPS instead of HTTP. That way, your entire session is encrypted against snooping.

Use the Cisco IOS Archiving Feature to Save Configs

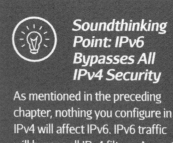

Starting with Cisco IOS version 12.3(7)T, Cisco began offering the Configuration Replace and Configuration Rollback features on routers. Among the benefits, you can configure the router to automatically back up its configuration at regular intervals and save it to the location you specify.

To configure the router to back up its configuration once each day and save a maximum of 14 versions, use the following commands, starting in global configuration mode:

- archive

    - path flash0:archived-config

    - maximum 14

    - time-period 1440

    - write-memory

Soundthinking Point: IPv6 Bypasses All IPv4 Security

As mentioned in the preceding chapter, nothing you configure in IPv4 will affect IPv6. IPv6 traffic will bypass all IPv4 filters. As part of your IPv6 implementation, review your documentation for IPv4 security so you can re-implement your IPv4 security configurations in IPv6.

The last command, *write-memory* archives the configuration each time you save it to memory.

```
router02#conf t
Enter configuration commands, one per line.  End with CNTL/Z.
router02(config)#archive
router02(config-archive)#path flash0:archived-config
router02(config-archive)#maximum 14
router02(config-archive)#time-period 1440
router02(config-archive)#write-memory
router02(config-archive)#^Z
router02#
.Aug 24 01:27:03.980: %SYS-5-CONFIG_I: Configured from console by console
router02#
```

Figure 298: Configuring the Cisco archiving feature

You can view your archived configs with the privileged mode command:

- *show archive.*

```
router02#show archive
The maximum archive configurations allowed is 14.
There are currently 2 archive configurations saved.
The next archive file will be named flash0:archived-config-<timestamp>-2
 Archive #  Name
    1         flash0:archived-config.Aug-24-01-25-58.636-0
    2         flash0:archived-config.Aug-24-01-34-58.287-1 <- Most Recent
    3
    4
    5
    6
    7
    8
    9
   10
   11
   12
   13
   14
router02#
```

Figure 299:
Using the "show archive"
command to display the archive

Secure the Software Image and Configuration File

With IOS version 12.3(8)T, Cisco introduced the Cisco IOS Resilient Configuration feature. When enabled, this feature allows a router to secure a working copy of both the running software image and the configure to prevent an attacker from erasing them from storage.

Resilient Configuration is enabled with two global configuration mode commands: *secure boot-image* and *secure boot-config*. You can use the *show secure bootset* command to display the status of the configuration resilience feature, as well as the primary bootset filename.

In the following screen capture, I first used the *show secure bootset* command to show that the feature was not enabled. I then enabled the feature. After enabling the feature, I used the *show secure bootset* command to confirm that it was indeed enabled.

```
router02(config)#do show secure bootset
%IOS image and configuration resilience is not active

router02(config)#secure boot-image
router02(config)#
.Aug 24 03:57:04.999: %IOS_RESILIENCE-5-IMAGE_RESIL_ACTIVE: Successfully secured running image
router02(config)#secure boot-config
router02(config)#
.Aug 24 03:57:23.019: %IOS_RESILIENCE-5-CONFIG_RESIL_ACTIVE: Successfully secured config archive [flash0:.runcfg-20120824-035722.ar]
router02(config)#do show secure bootset
IOS resilience router id FGL1539207J

IOS image resilience version 15.1 activated at 03:57:04 UTC Fri Aug 24 2012
Secure archive flash0:c1900-universalk9-mz.SPA.151-4.M1.bin type is image (elf) []
  file size is 55364328 bytes, run size is 55529972 bytes
  Runnable image, entry point 0x81000000, run from ram

IOS configuration resilience version 15.1 activated at 03:57:22 UTC Fri Aug 24 2012
Secure archive flash0:.runcfg-20120824-035722.ar type is config
configuration archive size 3945 bytes

router02(config)#
```

Figure 300:
Securing the software image
and configuration file

If you use the command *show flash* to view the contents of the router's flash memory after securing the boot image, you won't see the boot image listed. Reassure yourself that it's safe with the *show secure bootset* command.

Recovery Using the Secure Bootset

Recovering the Software Image

To recover from a tampering incident or an accidental erasure, reload the router. Interrupt the boot process to enter ROM Monitor mode. In ROM Monitor mode, use the *dir [filesystem]* command to view the contents of the filesystem where the secure bootset is stored. (You can determine the filesystem by reviewing the output of the *show secure bootset* command.) Use the command *boot [filesystem] [image filename]* to boot the router with the secured software image.

```
rommon 1 > dir flash0:
program load complete, entry point: 0x80803000, size: 0x1b340
Directory of flash0:

2        55364328    -rw-      c1900-universalk9-mz.SPA.151-4.M1.bin
13519    2903        -rw-      cpconfig-19xx.cfg
13520    2941440     -rw-      cpexpress.tar
14239    1038        -rw-      home.shtml
14240    115712      -rw-      home.tar
14269    1697952     -rw-      securedesktop-ios-3.1.1.45-k9.pkg
14684    415956      -rw-      sslclient-win-1.1.4.176.pkg
14786    3835        -rw-      archived-config.Aug-24-01-25-58.636-0
14787    2559        -rw-      archived-config.Aug-24-01-34-58.287-1
14790    3711        -rw-      archived-configAug-24-18-03-19.783-0
14791    2541        -rw-      archived-configAug-24-18-09-47.547-1
rommon 2 > boot flash0:c1900-universalk9-mz.SPA.151-4.M1.bin
program load complete, entry point: 0x80803000, size: 0x1b340
```

Figure 301: Recovering the boot image

Recovering the Configuration

To recover an erased configuration, perform the preceding procedure to restore the software image, if necessary. Then, in global configuration mode, execute the command *secure boot-config restore [new filename]*. In the following screen capture, I used the *show secure bootset* command to verify that the bootset was still there, but it's not necessary to do that prior to restoring the configuration.

```
router02(config)#do show secure bootset
IOS resilience router id FGL1539207J

IOS image resilience version 15.1 activated at 04:38:47 UTC Fri Aug 24 2012
Secure archive flash0:c1900-universalk9-mz.SPA.151-4.M1.bin type is image (elf)
[]
  file size is 55364328 bytes, run size is 55529972 bytes
  Runnable image, entry point 0x81000000, run from ram

IOS configuration resilience version 15.1 activated at 03:57:22 UTC Fri Aug 24 2
012
Secure archive flash0:.runcfg-20120824-035722.ar type is config
configuration archive size 3945 bytes

router02(config)#secure boot-config restore flash0:restored-config
ios resilience:configuration successfully restored as flash0:restored-config

router02(config)#
```

Figure 302: Recovering the configuration file

After the configuration has been restored to flash memory (or whichever filesystem you chose), you can view the contents of that filesystem to verify the restoration.

```
router02(config)#
router02(config)#do show flash0:
-#- --length-- -----date/time------ path
2         2903 Sep 19 2011 07:18:14 +00:00 cpconfig-19xx.cfg
3      2941440 Sep 19 2011 07:18:30 +00:00 cpexpress.tar
4         1038 Sep 19 2011 07:18:40 +00:00 home.shtml
5       115712 Sep 19 2011 07:18:48 +00:00 home.tar
6      1697952 Sep 19 2011 07:19:02 +00:00 securedesktop-ios-3.1.1.45-k9.pkg
7       415956 Sep 19 2011 07:19:12 +00:00 sslclient-win-1.1.4.176.pkg
8         3835 Aug 24 2012 01:25:58 +00:00 archived-config.Aug-24-01-25-58.636-0
9         2559 Aug 24 2012 01:34:58 +00:00 archived-config.Aug-24-01-34-58.287-1
12        3711 Aug 24 2012 18:03:20 +00:00 archived-configAug-24-18-03-19.783-0
13        2541 Aug 24 2012 18:09:46 +00:00 archived-configAug-24-18-09-47.547-1
14        3696 Aug 24 2012 18:15:06 +00:00 archived-configAug-24-18-15-07.155-0
15        3945 Aug 24 2012 18:30:02 +00:00 restored-config

195899392 bytes available (60588032 bytes used)

router02(config)#
```

Figure 303: Viewing the recovered configuration in flash memory

Copy the restored configuration file into the router's running-config, then copy the running-config to startup-config.

```
router#
router#copy flash0:restored-config running-config
Destination filename [running-config]?
3945 bytes copied in 56.556 secs (70 bytes/sec)

router02#
```

Figure 304:
Copying the recovered configuration into running-config

Disable the secure bootset with the usual Cisco *no* commands:

- *no secure boot-image* and *no secure boot-config*

Secure Routing Protocols

It's beyond the scope of this book, so I didn't cover securing routing updates in the routing protocols section. It is possible, however, to secure and authenticate routing updates from routing protocols such as RIP, EIGRP, and OSPF. If your routers are sending routing updates across a non-secure network such as the global Internet, consider encrypting the updates and requiring authentication.

For more information, visit www.cisco.com and search on *rip authentication, eigrp security,* or *ospf security.*

Implement the Principle of Least Privilege (Cisco Privilege Levels)

The principle of least privilege mandates that no user be given any more privilege than necessary for his or her job. The principle can be applied to router management.

Cisco network devices support 16 privilege levels, of which two are commonly used. When you log in to User EXEC mode, you're logged in at privilege level 1. When you use the *enable* command to elevate your privileges, you're logged in at privilege level 15. You can use the command *show privilege* to display your current privilege level.

```
router02>
router02>show privilege
Current privilege level is 1
router02>enable
Password:
router02#show privilege
Current privilege level is 15
router02#
```

Figure 305:
Displaying current privilege levels

Here's the difference: Privilege level one is read-only (with severe limitations even on what can be read) and privilege level 15 is full control. Suppose that you have an assistant administrator whom you want to be able to view the running-config and startup-config, but you don't want that person to be able to modify configurations. Privilege level one won't allow you to view the startup nor the running-config and privilege level 15 allows you to do anything you want to the router. A possible solution is to associate the commands *show startup-config* and *show running-config* with a slightly elevated privilege level, say level three. Then, you create a user account for the assistant and grant that account access at privilege level three. When the assistant logs in with his/her username, access is granted at privilege level three. Privileges are cumulative. A user logged in at privilege level three has all the rights and permissions granted at privilege levels one and two, in addition to those granted at privilege level three.

To configure usernames and privilege levels, use the following global configuration mode command:

– router(config)#*username [name] secret [password] privilege [1-15]*.

To associate commands with a privilege level, use the following global configuration mode command:

– router(config)#*privilege exec [1-15] [command]*

```
router02(config)#
router02(config)#user don privilege 15 secret p@ss5678
router02(config)#user janet privilege 3 secret p@ss1234
router02(config)#privilege exec level 3 show startup-config
router02(config)#privilege exec level 3 show running-config
router02(config)#
```

Figure 306: Configuring usernames and privilege levels

You must also configure each of the possible login locations to support authentication with the command *login local*. Notice, in the following screen capture, how I configured authentication on both the console and aux ports, as well as each of the virtual terminal lines. If you have also enabled the HTTP and/or HTTPS servers on the router, you must also configure authentication for Web admins.

```
router02(config)#
router02(config)#line console 0
router02(config-line)#login local
router02(config-line)#line vty 0 4
router02(config-line)#login local
router02(config-line)#line aux 0
router02(config-line)#login local
router02(config-line)#
```

Figure 307:
Configuring the router to
require authentication

You can also configure the router to use TACACS+ or RADIUS authentication through a AAA (Authentication, Authorization, and Accounting) server. For more information about that, visit www.cisco.com and search on *router aaa authentication*.

Notice, in the following screen capture, how I logged in with the username of *don* and was granted access at privilege level 15.

```
Username: don
Password:
router02#show privilege
Current privilege level is 15
router02#
```

Figure 308:
Logging in a privilege level 15

When user *janet* logs in, however, she is granted access at privilege level three. Note that she is able to execute the command *show startup-config* because I associated that command with privilege level three logons.

```
User Access Verification

Username: janet
Password:
router02#show privilege
Current privilege level is 3
router02#show startup-config
Using 2541 out of 262136 bytes
!
! Last configuration change at 18:09:17 UTC Fri Aug 24 2012
! NVRAM config last updated at 18:09:45 UTC Fri Aug 24 2012
! NVRAM config last updated at 18:09:45 UTC Fri Aug 24 2012
version 15.1
service timestamps debug datetime msec
service timestamps log datetime msec
no service password-encryption
!
hostname router02
!
boot-start-marker
boot-end-marker
!
!
!
no aaa new-model
no process cpu extended history
no process cpu autoprofile hog
!
ipv6 host router01 2001:DB8:2:0:21A:E2FF:FE19:AAD
ipv6 host router03 2001:DB8:3:0:222:55FF:FEE2:300
ipv6 unicast-routing
  --More--
```

Figure 309:
Logging in at privilege level 3

Summary

The process of hardening a Cisco router (or any other network device) is multi-faceted and ongoing. This chapter is intended to provide you with some fundamental security steps that are often overlooked by people new to Cisco routers. Cisco has a guide to hardening routers available on their website. Search on the term *Cisco Guide to Harden Cisco IOS Devices.* The United States National Security Agency also publishes several guides to hardening Cisco routers. Visit www.nsa.gov and search on the term *cisco router security*.

Remember that today's secure system is compromised by tomorrow's zero-day exploit. System and network security is an ongoing process of monitoring, testing, patching, and continually repeating the process.

APPENDICES

Appendix A:
How to Change IP Settings on a Computer Running Windows 7

Most of the time, computers are configured to receive an IP address from a DHCP (Dynamic Host Configuration Protocol) server. Sometimes, however, it's necessary to configure an IP address manually. Here are the steps to accomplish manual configuration.

Here's what you need to know for a typical static IP address configuration:

- An IP address, such as 192.168.1.101 (This is an example only. Yours will probably be different.)

- A subnet mask, such as 255.255.255.0 (This is an example only. Yours may be different.)

- A default gateway, such as 192.168.1.1 (This is an example only. Yours will probably be different.)

- The address of two DNS servers, such as 208.67.222.222 and 208.67.220.220 (These are the addresses of the OpenDNS servers. If you don't have a DNS server on your network, you can use these.)

On your computer running the Windows 7 operating system, perform the following steps (you must have administrator rights in order to do this):

1. Click on Start, then click on Control Panel

2. In the Control Panel, click on Network and Internet

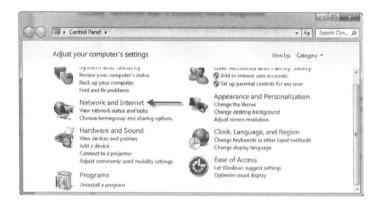

Figure 310:
Finding the network settings in Windows 7's control panel

3. In the Network and Internet window, click on Network and Sharing Center

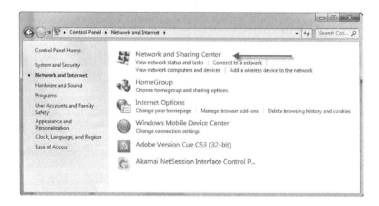

Figure 311:
Finding network and sharing under Windows 7's networking settings.

4. In the Network and Sharing Center, click on Change adapter settings.

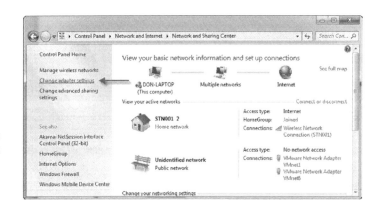

Figure 312:
Finding the link to change adapter settings

5. The Network Connections window will appear displaying one or more network connections. They may have names like Local Area Connection, but they will look similar to what you see in the screen capture. Right-click on the network connection to your router and choose Properties.

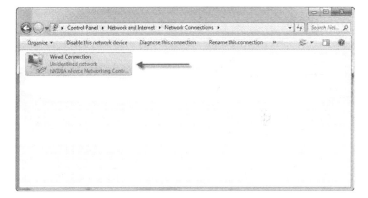

Figure 313: Finding the adapter to modify. On this particular computer, there is only one (the wired connector), but yours might have several. This is the adapter connected to your router

6. In the Local Area Connection properties window, double-click on Internet Protocol Version 4 (TCP/IPv4).

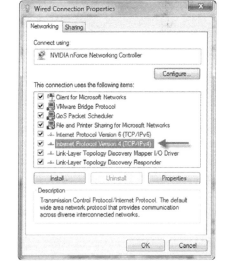

Figure 314:
The item you need is
Internet Protocol Version 4 (TCP/IPv4)

7. In the Internet Protocol Version 4 (TCP/IPv4) Properties window, click the radio button labeled *Use the following IP address* and enter the appropriate values for the following settings (The values indicated are for example only. Your settings will probably be different.):

    – IP address

    – Subnet mask

    – Default gateway

    – Preferred DNS server

    – Alternate DNS server

Figure 315: A sample of network settings. Your settings may be different. The DNS settings are the OpenDNS servers.

8. When you're done, click OK twice to save the settings and exit.

    Note: To configure your computer to obtain an IP address automatically using Dynamic Host Configuration Protocol (DHCP), perform steps one through six above. Instead of step seven, simply select the radio buttons labeled *Obtain an IP address automatically* and *Obtain DNS server address automatically.*

Appendix B:
IP Addressing

Classful IP Addressing

Class of Address	Highest Order Bit Value	First octet	Maximum # of Hosts
A	0	1-126	16,777,214
B	10	128-191	65,534
C	110	192-223	254
D	1110	224-239	N/A
E	11110	240-248	N/A

Subnet Calculator/Binary Converter

	128	64	32	16	8	4	2	1
128	1	0	0	0	0	0	0	0
192	1	1	0	0	0	0	0	0
224	1	1	1	0	0	0	0	0
240	1	1	1	1	0	0	0	0
248	1	1	1	1	1	0	0	0
252	1	1	1	1	1	1	0	0
254	1	1	1	1	1	1	1	0
255	1	1	1	1	1	1	1	1

Private IP Addresses

  – Class A: 10.0.0.0/8

  – Class B: 172.16.0.0/12

  – Class C: 192.168.0.0/16

For more information, see RFC 1918.

Appendix C:
Using Linux or Unix to Configure and Manage a Cisco Device

minicom is included with most Linux distributions and is available for use with Unix systems. minicom is a terminal program similar to HyperTerminal, PuTTY, TeraTerm, or ProComm Plus in Windows.

The steps noted in this document have been tested with Slackware 10 and Red Hat 9. Use with other Linux distros will probably work, but may require slight modifications.

To use minicom, you must configure it for use with a Cisco device. In a terminal, type **minicom -s** to enter minicom setup. Use the arrow keys to select Serial port setup and press Enter. Touch E to modify Bps/Par/Bits to a setting of 9600/8/n/1. (In the Comm Parameters window, when you make a change, the new current settings are displayed at the top of the window.) When you're finished, press Enter several times until you see the [configuration] window. Choose "Save setup as dfl" to save the settings as the default and choose Exit which will exit setup and initialize the modem.

Using minicom to Capture Text (for Linux/UNIX users)

You can display configurations using the usual commands in minicom, then use a mouse to select the displayed configuration text. The key combination of Shift-Control-C can be used to copy the selected text to the clipboard. The clipboard data can then be pasted into text editors such as vim, emacs, or pico and saved as an ASCII text file. The configurations stored in the files can then be sent to the router using cat and redirecting the output to /dev/modem (**cat router.cfg > /dev/modem**). Make sure that the router is in global configuration mode before sending the configuration.

Appendix D:
Resetting a Router to its Factory Default Configuration

Here are the steps to erase any configuration on your router and restore the factory-default settings.

Warning: The following steps will completely erase your router's existing configuration and replace it with a generic, factory-default configuration. Make sure you have a good backup prior to performing these steps.

1. Connect a console cable to your router's console port

2. Open PuTTY and configure it to connect to your router's serial port

3. Power cycle your router

4. When you see the message *program load complete*, enter the break sequence (CTRL+Break on PuTTY) to interrupt the book process.

5. Within two to three seconds, the router should return a rommon prompt:

```
Readonly ROMMON initialized
program load complete, entry point: 0x80803000, size: 0x1b340
program load complete, entry point: 0x80803000, size: 0x1b340


monitor: command "boot" aborted due to user interrupt
rommon 1 >
```

Figure 316: A rommon prompt

6. Modify the configuration register to prevent the router from reading its saved configuration upon booting with the command confreg 0x2142, then issue the command reset to reboot the router.

```
monitor: command "boot" aborted due to user interrupt
rommon 1 > confreg 0x2142


You must reset or power cycle for new config to take effect
rommon 2 > reset
```

Figure 317: Changing the configuration register

7. After the router reboots, it will ask if you want to enter the initial configuration dialog. Answer "no" and press the Enter key.

```
DRAM configuration is 64 bits wide with parity disabled.
255K bytes of non-volatile configuration memory.
250880K bytes of ATA System CompactFlash 0 (Read/Write)


        --- System Configuration Dialog ---

Would you like to enter the initial configuration dialog? [yes/no]: no
```

Figure 318:
Do not enter the initial
configuration dialog

8. You will probably need to press the Enter key to see a prompt. Then, enter the command en (short for enable) to move to privileged mode.

9. Copy the default configuration into non-volatile ram (NVRAM) on the router, so that the default configuration will be read upon the next boot. Here's how: In the router's flash memory is a configuration file containing the router's factory default configuration. It probably has a name similar to cpconfig-19xx.cfg, cpconfig-29xx.cfg, or cpconfig-39xx.cfg, depending on your router model. In the screen capture, I issued the copy command, followed by the location of the file (flash:/) with a question mark (?) to see the contents of flash memory. Once I found the file, I completed the copy command with the file name (cpconfig-19xx.cfg) and the target location (startup-config) for the copy operation. Press the Enter key to start the copy operation.

10. Press the Enter key again to confirm the location (startup-config).

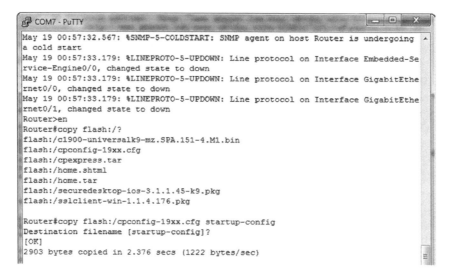

Figure 319: Copying the default configuration into flash with a new name
(startup-config) so it will be read by the router upon booting

11. Reset the configuration value back to the default of 0x2102 so the router will read its saved configuration upon booting with the command config-register 0x2102. You must enter global configuration mode with the command configure terminal in order to enter the config-register command.

12. After you modify the configuration register, you must reload the router for it to load the default configuration and complete the reset of the configuration register. When the router asks if you want to save the modified system configuration, say no. You must confirm that you want to proceed with the reload by pressing the Enter key.

When your router completes the reload, its configuration will be set to the factory-default configuration.

```
Router#configure terminal
Enter configuration commands, one per line.  End with CNTL/Z.
Router(config)#config-register 0x2102
Router(config)#exit
Router#
May 19 23:21:29.631: %SYS-5-CONFIG_I: Configured from console by console
Router#reload

System configuration has been modified. Save? [yes/no]: no
Proceed with reload? [confirm]

May 19 23:22:03.127: %SYS-5-RELOAD: Reload requested by console. Reload Reason:
Reload Command.
```

Figure 320: Changing the configuration register and reloading the router

Appendix E:
Building an Initial Configuration on a Cisco 871 Router Using SDM Express

The Security Device Manager is the previous graphical environment used with Cisco routers. Although now replaced by Cisco Configuration Professional, SDM is still in use in many installations. SDM supports many Cisco IOS Software releases and is available free of charge on Cisco router models ranging from the Cisco 830 Series to the Cisco 7301. SDM Express is preinstalled on all new Cisco 850 Series, Cisco 870 Series, Cisco 1800 Series, Cisco 2800 Series, and Cisco 3800 Series integrated services routers.

Network and security administrators and channel partners can use Cisco SDM to simplify and speed deployment of Cisco routers for services including dynamic routing, WAN access, WLAN, firewall, VPN, SSL VPN, IPS, and QoS.

The following steps should work on other Cisco 850 and 870 series routers.

1. If it's not already connected, connect the RJ45 connector on one end of the yellow Ethernet cable to the router's LAN port FE0 and connect the other end to your computer's Ethernet port.

2. Erase the router's existing configuration by power-cycling the router and pressing the reset button within five seconds after power-on.

   – Use a straightened paper clip to press the reset button on the back of the router

3. Release and renew your management workstation's IP address. (If you're not sure how to do that, notify your instructor.)

4. Wait about two minutes, then open Internet Explorer on your management workstation and navigate to https://10.10.10.1. (Make sure any popup blockers are disabled. To disable the popup blocker in Internet Explorer 7 and 8, click on "Tools", then mouse-over "Pop-up Blocker", and click on "Turn Off Pop-up Blocker." In Firefox, the popup blocker is disabled by clicking on "Tools", then click on "Options." Select the Content section and clear the checkbox labeled "Block pop-up windows.")

5. You'll receive a security warning about the site's security certificate. Select the option to "Continue to this website."

6. In the login window that appears, enter the username **cisco** and the password **cisco**. If other login windows appear, use the same credentials.

7. A new window will open for Cisco SDM Express, followed by an Internet Explorer security warning concerning the Cisco Application Controller. Click "Run."

8. If a Windows firewall alert appears, select the option to not block the program.

9. Cisco SDM Express is a wizard designed to help you quickly configure the router with a base configuration supporting both LAN and Internet or WAN connections. You can use a similar program called Cisco SDM (Security Device Manager) for more complex configurations. Additionally, Cisco in 2008 released a utility called Cisco Configuration Professional, also for graphical management of routers.

10. The Cisco SDM Express overview window will appear. Click "Next" to begin configuring your router.

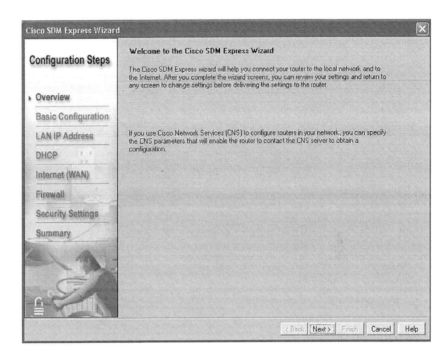

Figure 321:
Starting the Cisco SDM express

11. The Cisco SDM Express Basic Configuration window will appear. Enter the following values:

   – Host Name: (use the name from the label on the front of your router)

   – Domain Name: soundtraining.net

   – Username and Password

      • New username: (use the name "yourfirstname" where XX is your router number, for example student01, student02, student03, etc.)

      • New password: p@ss1234

      • Reenter new password: p@ss1234

   – Enable Secret Password

      • New password: p@ss5678

      • Reenter new password: p@ss5678

   – Click "Next."

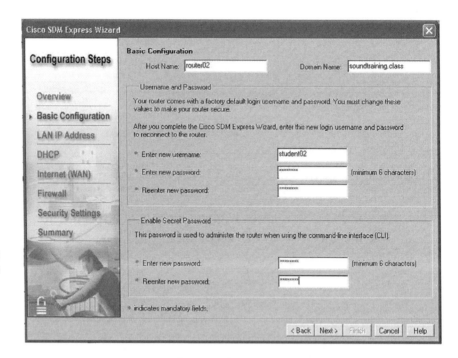

Figure 322:
SDM Express Basic Configuration

12. The Cisco SDM Express Router Provisioning window will appear. Ensure that the default value of SDM Express is selected and click "Next."

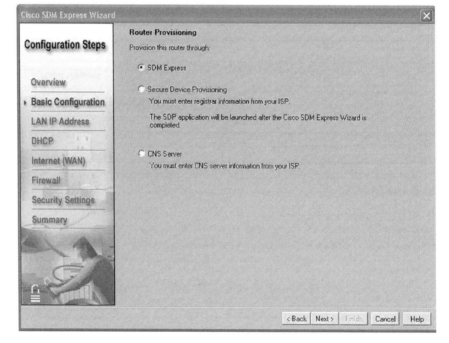

Figure 323:
SDM Express Router Provisioning

13. The Cisco SDM Express LAN Interface Configuration window will appear. Enter the values that correspond with your router, based on the classroom diagram. For example, for router02, you would enter 192.168.102.1 with a subnet mask of 255.255.255.0 (or 24 bits).

14. Click **<Next>**.

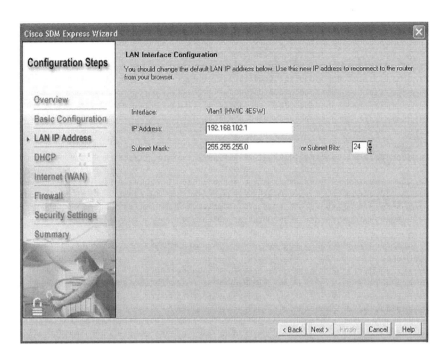

Figure 324:
LAN interface configuration

15. The Cisco SDM Express DHCP Server Configuration window will appear. Ensure that the checkbox labeled "Enable DHCP server on the LAN interface" is checked. The starting and ending IP addresses should be pre-configured with addresses as follows:

    – router01: 192.168.101.1-192.168.101.254

    – router02: 192.168.102.1-192.168.102.254

    – router03: 192.168.103.1-192.168.103.254

    – router04: 192.168.104.1-192.168.104.254

    – router05: 192.168.105.1-192.168.105.254

    – router06: 192.168.106.1-192.168.106.254

    Notify your instructor if your configuration is different from the above values.

16. For primary DNS server, enter 192.168.0.1.

17. Check the box labeled "Use these DNS values for DHCP clients."

18. Click "Next."

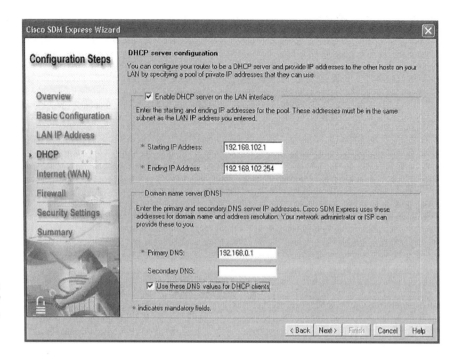

Figure 325:
SDM Express DHCP
configuration

19. The Cisco SDM Express WAN Configuration window appears. Enter the values that correspond with your router, based on the classroom diagram. For example, for router03, you would enter 192.168.0.103 with a subnet mask of 255.255.255.0 (or 24 bits).

20. Click "Next."

Figure 326:
SDM Express WAN configuration

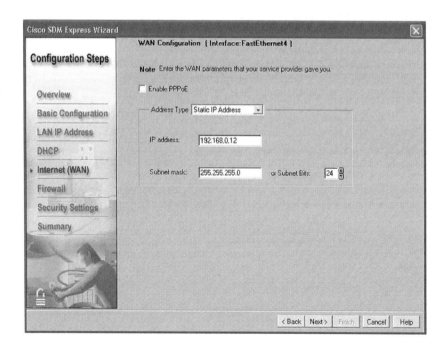

21. The Cisco SDM Express Internet WAN (Advanced Options) window appears. Ensure that the box labeled "Create default route" is checked and the radio button labeled "Use this Interface as Forwarding Interface" is selected. (Both are default values.)

22. Click "Next."

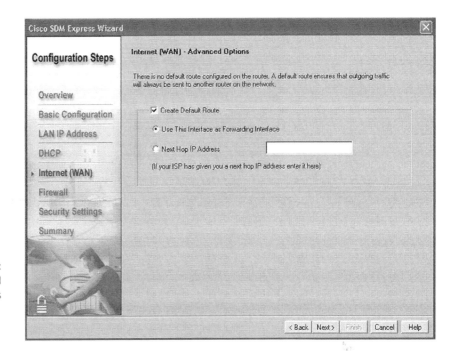

Figure 327:
SDM Express WAN
advanced options

23. The Cisco SDM Express Internet (WAN) Private IP Addresses window appears. Ensure that the box labeled "Enable NAT" is checked. It is not necessary to make any changes on this page.

24. Click "Next."

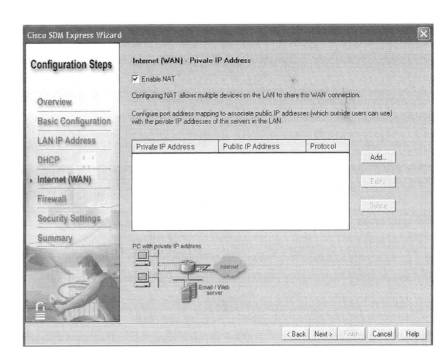

Figure 328:
SDM Express WAN
private IP address

25. The Cisco SDM Express Firewall Configuration window appears. The default setting is to enable a firewall. It is not necessary to make any changes in this window.

26. Click "Next."

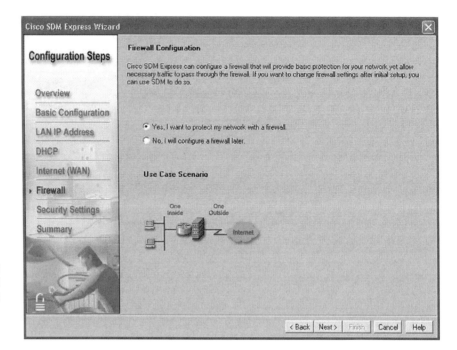

Figure 329:
SDM Express Firewall
Configuration

27. The Cisco SDM Express Security Configuration window appears. The default settings enable common best security practices. Again, it is not necessary to make any changes in this window.

28. Click "Next."

Figure 330:
SDM Express Security
Configuration

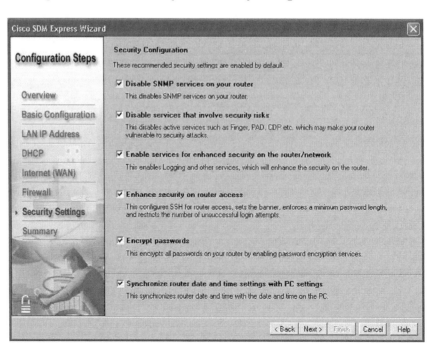

29. The Cisco SDM Express Summary window appears. Review your configuration to ensure that it's what you expect.

30. Click "Finish."

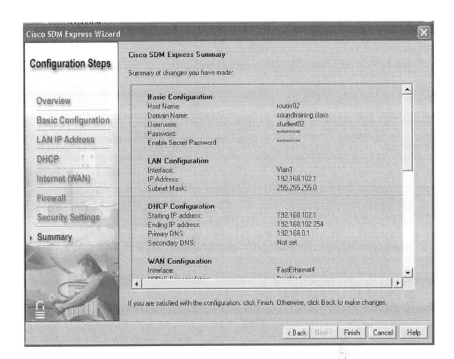

Figure 331:
SDM Express summary page

31. The Cisco SDM Express Reconnection Instructions window appears reminding you that, since you changed the IP address on the router's inside interface, you will lose your connection to the router when you click OK.

32. Click "OK."

33. The Cisco SDM Express Wizard Configuration Delivery window appears confirming that the configuration is being delivered to the router. After several moments, the "OK" button will be activated and you can click it to close Cisco SDM Express.

34. Click "OK."

35. To reconnect, you must ensure that the PC is on the same subnet as the LAN interface by using the following procedures:

    – Configure the PC to obtain an IP address automatically.

    – Open a command window and enter the ipconfig/release command, followed by the ipconfig/renew command.

    – Open a browser, and enter the IP address you assigned to the LAN interface (http(s)://192.168.102.1).

    – Log in with the username and password you entered in the Cisco SDM Express wizard.

Soundthinking Point: When SDM Displays Source Code

When the SDM is running on a computer running Windows XP with Service Pack 2, Internet Explorer may display HTML source code when you try to launch SDM. To resolve this issue, in Internet Explorer, go to Tools >> Internet Options >> Advanced. Then navigate to the Security section (toward the bottom of the list), check *Allow active content to run in files on my computer,* and click Apply. Then restart the SDM.

Appendix F:
Cisco 871 Router Sample Configuration

This is the entire configuration process from a Cisco 871 router. I've included it here, because of the differences in interface configuration compared to the 1941 router and other ISR routers. Notice the use of switch virtual interfaces (VLANs) due to the built-in switch.

```
Router#setup

                    --- System Configuration Dialog ---

Continue with configuration dialog? [yes/no]: yes
At any point you may enter a question mark '?' for help.

Use ctrl-c to abort configuration dialog at any prompt.

Default settings are in square brackets '[]'.
Basic management setup configures only enough connectivity for management of the system, extended setup will
ask you to configure each interface on the system

Would you like to enter basic management setup? [yes/no]: no
First, would you like to see the current interface summary? [yes]: yes
```

Interface	IP-Address	OK?	Method	Status	Protocol
FastEthernet0	unassigned	YES	unset	up	down
FastEthernet1	unassigned	YES	unset	up	down
FastEthernet2	unassigned	YES	unset	up	down
FastEthernet3	unassigned	YES	unset	up	down
Fastethernet4	unassigned	YES	unset	administratively down	down
Vlan1	10.10.10.1	YES	NVRAM	up	down

```
Configuring global parameters:

Enter host name [yourname]: kilgen
The enable secret is a password used to protect access to privileged EXEC and configuration modes. This password,
after entered, becomes encrypted in the configuration.

Enter enable secret: p@ss5678
The enable password is used when you do not specify an enable secret password, with some older software
versions, and some boot images.

Enter enable password: p@ss1234
The virtual terminal password is used to protect access to the router over a network interface.
```

```
Enter virtual terminal password: p@ss1234
Configure SNMP Network Management? [no]: no
Configure IP? [yes]: yes
Configure RIP routing? [yes]: no
Configure bridging? [no]: no
Configuring interface parameters:

Do you want to configure FastEthernet0 interface? [yes]: yes
Configure IP on this interface? [no]: no

Do you want to configure FastEthernet2 interface? [yes]: yes
Configure IP on this interface? [no]: no

Do you want to configure FastEthernet3 interface? [yes]: yes
Configure IP on this interface? [no]: no

Do you want to configure FastEthernet4 interface? [no]: yes
Use the 100 Base-TX (RJ-45) connector? [yes]: yes
Operate in full-duplex mode? [no]: yes
Configure IP on this interface? [no]: yes
IP address for this interface: 192.168.0.102
Subnet mask for this interface [255.255.255.0] : 255.255.255.0
Class C network is 192.168.0.0, 24 subnet bits; mask is /24

Do you want to configure Vlan1 interface? [yes]: yes
Configure IP on this interface? [yes]: yes
IP address for this interface [10.10.10.1]: 192.168.102.1
Subnet mask for this interface [255.255.255.0] : 255.255.255.0
Class C network is 192.168.102.0, 24 subnet bits; mask is /24

Would you like to go through AutoSecure configuration? [yes]: no
AutoSecure dialog can be started later using "auto secure" CLI

The following configuration command script was created:

hostname kilgen

enable secret 5 $1$lDh8$N8gwcNlL5rrl0MbSTLOHA

enable password router

line vty 0 4

password cisco

no snmp-server

!
```

```
ip routing

no bridge 1

!

interface FastEthernet0

no ip address

!

interface FastEthernet1

no ip address

!

interface FastEthernet2

no ip address

!

interface FastEthernet3

no ip address

!

interface FastEthernet4

no shutdown

media-type 100BaseX

full-duplex

ip address 192.168.0.102.255.255.255.0

!

interface Vlan1

ip address 192.168.102.1 255.255.255.0

dialer-list 1 protocol ip permit

!

end
```

[0] Go to the IOS command prompt without saving this config.

[1] Return back to the setup without saving this config.

[2] Save this configuration to nvram and exit.

Enter your selection [2]: 2

media-type 100BaseX

^

% Invalid input detected at '^' marker.

Building configuration...

*Mar 1 00:41:15.883: %LINK-3-UPDOWN: Interface FastEthernet4, changed state to up[OK]

*Mar 1 00:41:17.287: %LINEPROTO-5-UPDOWN: Line protocol on Interface FastEthernet4, changed state to up

Use the enabled mode 'configure' command to modify this configuration.

Router02#

Appendix G:
Backing Up and Restoring Configurations Using HyperTerminal

1. Make sure that your router is in Privileged EXEC mode

2. In HyperTerminal, choose the Transfer pull-down menu and select Capture Text ...

3. Specify c:\classfiles\[router name].txt for the location and filename in the Capture Text dialog box and click on the Start button

4. Now, from the Privileged EXEC prompt, type the "show run" command to display your router's running configuration. You will probably have to touch the space bar at least once to display the entire configuration

5. When the entire running configuration file has been displayed, choose the Transfer pull-down menu again from HyperTerminal's menu bar, select Capture Text ... and choose Stop

6. Find the file you created in step three and open it in Notepad or Wordpad. You'll need to edit the file to remove the --More-- statements and other extraneous statements. Delete all statements before the "version" statement at the top of the file. Leave the "end" statement at the end of the file. Once you're satisfied that the file is clean, save it and exit the text editor.

7. Put your router in global configuration mode and change its hostname to "seahawks." Notice that the prompt changes to reflect the changed hostname:

    –   Router#**conf t <Enter>**

    –   Router(config)#**hostname seahawks <Enter>**

    –   seahawks(config)#

8. Again, choose the Transfer pull-down menu in HyperTerminal, but this time choose Send Text File ... and find the file that you save earlier. Select it and click on Open. You'll now see each of the commands in the saved text file entered and executed in the router console. You'll also notice that your router's prompt changes back to the previous hostname, reflecting the change in the router's running-config. (This procedure can also be used with partial config files such as Access Control Lists or host files.)

BOOKS
For I.T. Professionals
from author Don R. Crawley

Tweeting Linux: 140 Linux Configuration Commands Explained in 140 Characters or Less

In it's first edition, this guidebook is a straight-forward approach to learning Linux commands. Each command is explained in 140 characters or less, then examples of usage are shown in screen captures, and details are given when necessary to explain command usage. You'll see the most commonly-used commands plus a few gems you might not know about!

ISBN: 978-0-98366-071-2
(Available in paperback and Kindle editions through Amazon and other channels)

The Accidental Administrator®:
Cisco ASA Step-by-Step Configuration Guide

Packed with 56 easy-to-follow hands-on exercises to help you build a working firewall configuration from scratch, it's the most straight-forward approach to learning how to configure the Cisco ASA Security Appliance. The chapters cover the essentials on installing, backups and restores, remote administration, VPNs, DMZs, usernames, transparent mode, static NAT, port address translation, access lists, DHCP, password recovery, logon banners, AAA (authentication, authorization, and accounting), filtering content, and more.

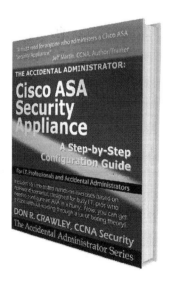

ISBN: 978-1-44959-662-0

The Accidental Administrator®:
Linux Server Step-by-Step Configuration Guide

With easy-to-follow hands-on exercises plus numerous command examples and screen captures, this book will help you build a working Linux server configuration from scratch. Based on version 5.4 and 5.5, it's filled with practical tips and secrets on how to configure a CentOS/Red Hat/Fedora Linux server. There is no time wasted on boring theory—everything is outlined from years of teaching, consulting, and administering Linux servers. The essentials are covered in chapters on installing, administering, user management, file systems and directory management, networking, package management, automated task scheduling, network services, Samba, NFS, disk quotas, mail servers, Web and FTP servers, and more.

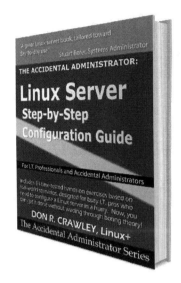

ISBN: 978-1-45368-992-9
(Available in paperback and Kindle editions through Amazon and other channels)

The Compassionate Geek:
Mastering Customer Service for I.T. Professionals

Co-authored with Paul R. Senness, now in its second edition, is a customer service book written especially for today's overworked I.T. staff! Filled with practical tips, best practices, and real-world techniques, *The Compassionate Geek* is a quick read with equally fast results. Learn how to speak to the different generations at work, how to use emotional intelligence to manage your own emotions and influence the emotions of others, how to say "no" without alienating the end-user, what to do when the customer (user) is wrong, how to cope with the stress of the job, and more! All of the information is presented in a straightforward style that you can understand and use right away. There's nothing "foo-foo", just down-to-earth tips and best practices learned from years of working with I.T. pros and end-users.

ISBN: 978-0-98366-070-5
(Available in paperback and Kindle editions through Amazon and other channels)

Index

Onsite Training Makes Sense!

One- and two-day seminars
and workshops for I.T. professionals

Learning solutions that come right to your door!

 soundtraining.net
accelerated i.t. training

Call (206) 988-5858 • soundtraining.net/onsite • Email: onsite@soundtraining.net

Don R. Crawley

Author, Speaker, Trainer for the I.T. Industry

Author of **The Compassionate Geek** and other books for I.T. professionals

- Keynote speaking ...
- Breakout sessions ...
- Half- and full-day workshops ...

Made in the USA
Lexington, KY
26 August 2016